W9-CGY-893

DAYS OF
HONEY,
DAYS OF
ONION

DAYS OF HONEY,

DAYS OF ONION

The Story of a Palestinian Family in Israel

MICHAEL GORKIN

UNIVERSITY OF CALIFORNIA PRESS
BERKELEY·LOS ANGELES·LONDON

University of California Press
Berkeley and Los Angeles, California
University of California Press, Ltd.
London, England

First Paperback Printing 1993

Published by arrangement with Beacon Press.
First published in 1991 by Beacon Press, Boston.

8 7 6 5 4 3 2 1

Text design by Karen Savary
Map by Judith Aronson

Library of Congress Cataloging-in-Publication Data
Gorkin, Michael.
  Days of honey, days of onion : the story of a Palestinian family
in Israel /
Michael Gorkin.
    p.   cm.
  Originally published: Boston : Beacon Press, c1991.
  Includes bibliographical references.
  ISBN 0-520-08186-2
    1. Palestinian Arabs—Israel—Social conditions—Case studies.
2. Israel—Ethnic relations—Case studies.   I. Title.
[DS113.7.G65   1993]
956.94'0049274—dc20   92-30444
                                                 CIP

The paper used in this publication meets the minimum requirements of
American National Standard for Information Sciences—Permanence of
Paper for Printed Library Materials, ANSI Z39.48–1984. ⊗

For Dafna and Maya

CONTENTS

DAYS OF
HONEY,
DAYS OF
ONION

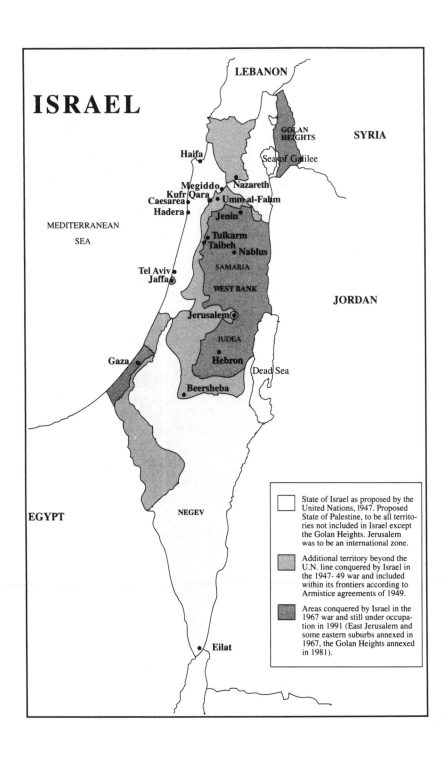

INTRODUCTION

THIS BOOK IS ABOUT an important segment of Israeli society, and a basic element of the Israeli-Palestinian conflict, that is not widely known or understood—not in America, and not even in Israel. As the title suggests, this is a book about Palestinians living *in* Israel. Today there are some 700,000 Palestinian Arabs living in Israel, 16 percent of the total population.[1] Unlike the Palestinians in the occupied territories, they are not, with rare exceptions, actively involved in the *intifada*, or uprising; nor are they, again with rare exceptions, members of the Palestine Liberation Organization (PLO). As a result, they are not the focus of media attention, and little is said or written about them. To use a phrase from Ralph Ellison, they are the "invisible men" of Israel and the Middle East conflict. And yet their story is an interesting and important one, both in and of itself and also for the light it throws on the nature and origin of the present struggle.

---

[1]The population statistics provided here are extrapolated from data provided by Israel's Central Bureau of Statistics for 1989. According to the bureau, there are an estimated 842,000 Arabs in Israel; however, included in this figure are those living in East Jerusalem and the Golan Heights. Inasmuch as the annexation of these areas is not internationally recognized, I have not included them in my estimate of the Arab population of Israel. (Of the entire Arab population—that is, of the 842,000—87 percent are Muslim and 13 percent are Christian.)

With these thoughts in mind, I have attempted to tell *something* of their story. I emphasize *something* since this book is not a general political or social account of Palestinians in Israel. It is, rather, the story of one multi-generational family that lives in a village in Israel: the Family Abu Ahmad from the village of Kufr Qara.[2] My hope and intention is that through a focus on the lives of these individuals, we can understand something of the collective life of Palestinians living in Israel.

How do Palestinians in Israel today regard the possibilities of peace? What is life like for them as Arabs *in Israel*? And specifically, what is life like today in an Arab village in Israel? How has their situation changed these past forty years—education, religion, the role of women? How have they reacted to the message of Muslim fundamentalism now sweeping the area? What has been the impact of the *intifada* on them? These are some of the many issues and areas that this story attempts to address.

Before introducing the family, it is best, I think, to have some picture of their village—Kufr Qara, or, translated into English, Pumpkin Village. Today Kufr Qara is one of approximately 110 all-Arab villages and towns in Israel; about 71 percent of Israel's Arab citizens live in such places. The remaining 29 percent of the Arab population live in about a dozen cities, either mixed Arab-Jewish cities (such as Haifa, Tel-Aviv/Jaffa), or all-Arab cities (such as Nazareth, Umm al-Fahm).[3] As one can see on the map, Kufr Qara is located in the center of Israel, just north of the pre-1967 border with Jordan. The steep, rocky hills of Samaria give way in this

---

[2]The name of the village has been retained, though the family members' names have been changed in order to provide some privacy for them. No other details about their lives have been altered.

[3]According to 1989 data obtained from Israel's Central Bureau of Statistics regarding the Arab population of Israel (excluding East Jerusalem and the Golan Heights), approximately 11 percent live in settlements of up to 2,000 people; 40 percent live in settlements of 2,000–10,000; 20 percent live in settlements of 10,000–20,000; and 29 percent live in settlements (cities) of 20,000 or more.

area to a narrow valley known as Wadi Ara, and then to some hillocks and an extended plain that comprises some of the finest farmland in Israel. Fifteen kilometers away, due west, the plain ends as it approaches the sandy coast of the Mediterranean Sea. On a clear day one can see the Mediterranean from one of the village's hillocks, and Kufr Qara's residents on occasion will wistfully tell a visitor that their lands used to extend "all the way from the village center to the seventh wave of the sea."

But that was back when the village was founded two hundred and fifty years ago, back in the time of the Ottoman Empire. Since then there has been a whittling away of Kufr Qara's lands (see Chapter 1), with the most recent and painful losses taking place forty years ago at the hands of the new Jewish state (see Chapter 9). Moreover, not only the size of Kufr Qara has changed. So, too, has its way of life. Today, like so many villages throughout the world, Kufr Qara is caught up in a clash between tradition and modernity, a clash made all the more poignant because it has been brought about, in large measure, by the very people who took over so much of the land—and the country

In 1947, just before the new Jewish state was established, Kufr Qara was still a secluded place of some fifteen hundred souls. Almost all were *fellaheen*, peasant farmers and their families, who worked their lands in much the same way as their ancestors had done two hundred years before. There were as yet no paved roads within or leading out of the village, no electricity or water in the homes, no tractors, no banks, and no doctors. There was only a solitary one-room schoolhouse (for boys up to fourth grade), a single car (a 1942 Ford), and one battery-run radio, which belonged to the *mukhtar*, or headman. Extended families lived huddled together in the dusty center of the village, in similar one-room houses of stone and mud. Every day they traveled out to their fields on carts drawn by horses or donkeys. Like their ancestors, they marked their time by the sun and the seasons. And, as they were all Muslims, they lived according to the strictures of the Koran: the mosque in the center of the village was the spiritual center of their lives, and nearly every man went there for Friday noon prayers.

Today, Kufr Qara is a vastly different place—physically and spiritually. Like most Arab villages in Israel, it has not progressed at the same rate as Jewish villages and towns, but the changes are nonetheless remarkable. The population of the village is now nine thousand, or *six* times its size in 1947. Due to this enormous growth, as well as the huge land confiscations that took place in the early 1950s, only 10 percent of the villagers make their living from farming;[4] the rest work in other occupations, either in the village or outside. The center of the village is still crowded, as the one-room houses have become two-story buildings made of concrete blocks and cement. Also in the dusty main square, or just off it, are two banks and about twenty shops—grocery stores, fruit and vegetable stores, two butchers, a clothing store, an appliance store, a pharmacy, a beauty parlor, two cafes, and even a videocassette shop. Two additional mosques have been built, including one belonging to the Muslim fundamentalists, the construction of which began in 1986. And scattered throughout the village are a handful of cottage industries—sewing shops, a pickling plant, and three cement-block factories.

Almost all of the hard-dirt lanes that crisscross the undulating terrain of the village have been paved over, and cars, trucks, and tractors ply back and forth; there are now one thousand registered vehicles in Kufr Qara, with only a half dozen or so horse-drawn carts remaining. The fields, which used to begin just outside the village center, have been encroached upon by a housing boom, as married sons no longer stay in their fathers' homes. Ranch-style houses, each with its own particular mélange of arched windows, columns, terraces, and red-tiled or cement roofs—reflecting both Arab and Western design—have sprouted up in all directions. All now have electricity and indoor plumbing. Rectangular tracts of vegetables and olive groves still dominate the landscape on the northern and western peripheries of the village, but they too, in part, have been slated for de-

---

[4]An additional 10 to 15 percent earn their living as farm laborers in outside (Jewish) settlements.

velopment by the village planner (yes, there is a village council with a planner).

Just as striking as these physical changes in the village's appearance have been the psychological and spiritual shifts in the people themselves—above all, in the generation that has come of age since the establishment of Israel. In 1947 there was hardly an adult in Kufr Qara who had more than four years of education, and almost every woman was illiterate. Today there are five schools in the village, including a high school. Among the younger generation, there is almost 100 percent literacy, with the majority literate in Hebrew as well. (Signs above some village shops, and even some graffiti on walls, are written in Hebrew.) About one third of the high school graduates (about twice as many men as women) go to college or university, and Kufr Qara now has its own physicians (6), dentists (3), and schoolteachers (approximately 175).[5]

In short, in Kufr Qara, as in all Arab villages in Israel, there has been an educational boom in the last forty years. And as could be expected, this boom has ultimately fostered a challenge to the very bases of their traditional society— their religion, their clan-based politics, and the structure of relationships between men and women. Where all this is going is still unclear. But the tensions and reverberations are everywhere to be seen as Kufr Qara's people go about their daily lives as individuals and members of the society.

Within the extended family of Abu Ahmad there is ample opportunity to observe these tensions and changes. And indeed, that is one of the reasons I chose to focus on them. But apart from that, I also chose them for the same reason that most anthropologists or other professional observers, I suspect, choose their subjects—simply put, I liked them and found myself interested in them. I wanted to tell their story.

[5]The numbers provided here refer to those who work *in* Kufr Qara. An additional fifteen physicians, two dentists, and about a hundred teachers *from* Kufr Qara work in areas outside the village.

The family of Abu Ahmad comprises three generations: Abu Ahmad and his wife, Umm Ahmad; their nine living children; and their twenty-six grandchildren. (Four other children died in childbirth or infancy, and a fifth died in 1988 in an automobile accident.)

Both Abu Ahmad (70)[6] and Umm Ahmad (63) are descendants of the original clan that founded Kufr Qara in the 1730s; in fact, they are distant cousins. They both have spent all their lives in Kufr Qara, and except for an eleven-month period during the war (1948/49), when they were forced to flee, they have seldom been outside the village. They are *fellaheen*. He has been retired since 1973, and she is still working in the fields with their youngest son, Hassan. In a word, they are a rather typical peasant couple, whose perspective and values are distinctly traditional, although they have been influenced by their children as well as by the turbulent era in which they have lived.

All of their children (and, of course, their grandchildren) have grown up in the period since the establishment of Israel. There are six daughters: Fatma (45), Nihal (41), Rafiqa (39), Jamileh (31), Rana (27), Maysa (24). And there are three sons: Ahmad (35), Ghanem (33), Hassan (29). As is traditional, until Ahmad was born his parents were known by their own names, Ali and Fadwa; thereafter, they became known as *Abu* and *Umm Ahmad*, that is, Father and Mother of Ahmad, their oldest son.

Among the children, there is a wide variety of educational and occupational experience. The three oldest daughters—Fatma, Nihal, and Rafiqa—went through Kufr Qara's school system as far as it went in their time, that is, through the eighth grade; all are housewives. Of the three youngest daughters, Maysa graduated university and is a social worker, Rana went to a vocational high school and is a housewife, and Jamileh graduated a two-year teachers college and works in the primary school. Except for Maysa, all are married, with children. Of the sons, Ahmad finished

---

[6]Ages represented here are as of December 1988, when I first met the family.

three years at university and is a businessman, Ghanem is a university graduate and junior-high-school teacher, and Hassan is a high-school graduate and farmer. The two older brothers are married, with children; Hassan, in December 1988, was as yet unmarried.

All members of the extended family live in Kufr Qara, with the exception of Rana, who lives in Umm al-Fahm, a city ten kilometers to the east. In December of 1988, Maysa and Hassan were the only children still living at home. As is typical of Arab patrilineal families, the married daughters have tended to become part of their husbands' extended families, whereas the sons and their families remain firmly within the orbit of their father's home. As a practical consequence of this structuring of family life, the married daughters visit the home of Abu Ahmad and Umm Ahmad far less frequently than the sons and their families, who, in fact, are daily visitors. Also, the sons, unlike the daughters, are in daily contact with each other and collaborate with Abu Ahmad in making family decisions.

Beyond the circle of the extended family is the wider circle of Abu Ahmad's *hamula*, or clan, which, in its own way, defines and influences them. The clan—all descendants of a common great-great-grandfather—is still an important unit in Arab family life, especially in the villages, although its influence is shifting. A generation or two ago, for example, members of the same clan used to help each other with harvests and in constructing each other's houses. Today such mutual assistance is no longer expected, but clan relations are still important politically, with members of the same clan expected or pressured to vote for common candidates (especially on the local level); and socially, there is still considerable pressure on children to marry within the clan or, at least, someone from an allied clan. In the story of the Family Abu Ahmad, this thread of clan loyalty—or disloyalty—can be traced in many of their interactions, not least of all because Abu Ahmad has been an important figure within his clan of seven hundred people. And, traditional patriarch that he is, Abu Ahmad has done all he could to instill in his children, in his sons especially, a sense of clan loyalty.

To follow the narrative of the Family Abu Ahmad it is helpful to have in mind a broad outline of the history of Palestine/Israel. It is important to stress, however, that any rendering of Palestinian/Israeli history is unlikely to please both Arabs and Jews alike. My account is no exception. I do not believe that the members of the Family Abu Ahmad would agree with all points or emphases in my synopsis. But they will tell their story shortly. Here, I relate what seem to me the relevant highlights.

In my view, the conflict in Palestine/Israel can best be summarized as a prolonged struggle between two peoples for rulership over the same land. In the first one hundred years of this struggle, the Jews have had much the upper hand. With their national aspirations initially better defined and organized, the Jews have proved more successful in defending the Zionist ideal of a Jewish state than have their counterparts, the Arabs of Palestine, in staking their own national claim. In the last decade or two, however, the tide has begun to turn, and the Palestinians have become increasingly well organized and politically assertive. At present, the outcome seems anything but certain.

I think it accurate to say that the seeds of this struggle were first sown in the 1880s, when Jews from Europe—particularly Russia—began trickling into Palestine to found the initial Zionist settlements. The Ottoman Empire was crumbling. The initial trickle of Jewish settlers attracted little notice and only sporadic local resentment. It was not until the time of the First World War and its aftermath that conflicting Jewish and Arab national claims began to take on a prominent and entrenched character.

During World War I, in part to curry favor with world Jewry and thereby bolster Britain's war effort, the British made a promise to the Jews that soon led to an escalation of tensions in the area. On November 2, 1917, the British foreign secretary, Lord Balfour, sent a letter—subsequently known as the Balfour Declaration—to Lord Rothschild which stated that the British government "viewed with favor the establishment in Palestine of a national home for the

Jewish people," and further added that it should be "clearly understood that nothing shall be done which may prejudice the civil and religious rights of existing non-Jewish communities in Palestine." During 1917 and 1918, the British succeeded in occupying Palestine, in no small measure as a result of the Arab Revolt against the Turks, commanded by the British officer, T. E. Lawrence ("Lawrence of Arabia"). Four years later, the new League of Nations gave the British a mandate to rule Palestine. Incorporated in the terms of this mandate was the promise of a home for the Jews. At the time, there were in Palestine 84,000 Jews, 486,000 Muslims, and 71,000 Christians.[7] Understandably, the Jews were overjoyed; just as understandably, the Arabs felt mistreated and even betrayed.

Throughout the period of the British mandate—which ended after twenty-six years on May 15, 1948—the Jews and Arabs waged an internecine struggle, with each side attempting to assert its claim to the land. The Jews sought to strengthen their claim by attracting immigrants, purchasing land, and establishing settlements. The Arabs attempted to cut off immigration, to prevent Jewish land purchases, and to get rid of the British and establish their own national entity. All this led to a series of uprisings (nobody used the word *intifada* then) on the Arab side: in 1920/21, 1929, 1933, and, most prominently, from 1936 to 1939.

The final uprising, known locally as the Arab Rebellion of 1936–39, was a widescale revolt which raged over the whole of Palestine and was fought between the Arabs on one side, and the British and Jews on the other. In response to the rebellion, the British set up a royal commission, the Peel Commission; for the first time, in 1937, it was recommended that Palestine be partioned into two states, Jewish and Arab. The Jews accepted the idea of partition, though not the particulars of the Peel Commission's plan; the Arabs rejected it outright. The plan then was scrapped.

World War II resulted in an intensification of the strug-

---

[7]These population statistics are taken from the Report to the General Assembly of the United Nations Special Committee on Palestine (September 3, 1947).

gle and ultimately led to the British exodus from Palestine. From the Jewish perspective, the Nazi atrocities in Europe made it more imperative than ever to establish a Jewish state. Whereas from the Arab standpoint, the continuing influx of Jewish immigrants made it clear that the position of Arabs as a majority, and their hopes to rule in Palestine, were in ever-increasing jeopardy. The two communities were at desperate odds, and with the British no longer willing or able to control the situation, the United Nations was given the task of coming up with a solution. Once again partition was recommended. This time the Jews were in favor, while the Arabs again rejected the idea. On November 29, 1947, the United Nations voted to accept partition. The result was war.

The war, known to the Jews as the War of Liberation and to the Arabs as the Disaster (il Nakba), was to set the future contours of the conflict. It was the longest, and in many ways the most costly, of the six Arab-Israeli wars fought since 1947.[8] From the time of the partition decision until the exodus of the British and the declaration of Jewish statehood on May 14/15, 1948, the battle was a civil war between Palestinian Arabs and Jews. Thereafter, until armistice agreements were signed in 1949, it was an all-out war between the new state of Israel and five Arab countries—Lebanon, Syria, Iraq, Transjordan,[9] and Egypt. During the fighting, the territory that was to have become the Palestinian state, according to the partition plan, was conquered in the west by Israel and in the east by King Abdullah of Transjordan. As for the Jewish state, it grew through conquest from about 5,400 square miles (as per the partition plan), to about 8,000 square miles. Moreover, instead of a population that was almost one-half Arab, Israel in 1949 had only 160,000 Arabs within its borders (compared to 1 million

[8]The six wars have been: the War of Liberation/Independence War (1947–49), the Sinai War (1956), the Six-Day War/June War (1967), the War of Attrition (1969–70), the Yom Kippur War/October War (1973), the Lebanon War (1982).

[9]In 1948, King Abdullah renamed the Emirate of Transjordan as the Hashemite Kingdom of Jordan. The new name—more commonly shortened to Jordan—became current in 1948–49.

Jews). Some 600,000 to 760,000 Palestinian Arabs fled or were driven out of their homes by advancing Jewish forces, and they became refugees—for the most part in Gaza (conquered by Egypt) or eastern Palestine.[10] And thus began the Palestinian refugee problem.

With the end of the war, the Palestinians in Israel became citizens of the new state, but—in their own minds—second-class citizens. For the next seventeen years, until 1966, the predominant areas of Arab population in Israel were under the rule of a military government. This period is outlined in some detail in this book (Chapter 9), but it is relevant to mention here that one of the results of this rule was that some 870,000 *dunams*[11] of land were confiscated from Palestinians still living in Israel. What this meant was that tens of thousands of Palestinian *felaheen* partially or totally lost their livelihoods. Thus, though they, and even more their children, came to benefit from the enormous economic growth that occurred in the country, Palestinians in Israel continued to feel resentment toward the Jewish state. In 1967, when Israel again found itself in a war for survival with its neighbors, many, if not most, Palestinians in Israel were praying (under their breath) for an Arab victory.

But such a victory did not come. On the contrary, the armies of Egypt, Syria, and Jordan were once again beaten, and this time in an overwhelming and humiliating fashion—in six days. The Jews savored their triumph. They had managed to capture in that brief week vast territories from Egypt (Gaza and the Sinai Desert), Syria (the Golan Heights), and Jordan (the West Bank, or eastern Palestine). At the very

[10]The statistics on Palestinian refugees are taken from a recent and well documented account of the Palestinian refugee problem, *The Birth of the Palestinian Refugee Problem, 1947–1949*, by Benny Morris (Cambridge: Cambridge University Press, 1987). The author also provides a summary listing how and when each of the 369 Arab settlements was evacuated.

[11]A *dunam* equals one fourth of an acre. This statistic on confiscated land is taken from *Palestinian Arabs in Israel: Two Case Studies*, by Hasan Amun, et al. (London: Ithaca Press, 1977), p. 39. The authors estimate the number of confiscated dunams to be 872,000. Another writer puts the estimate at more than 1 million dunams. See Sabri Jiryis, *The Arabs in Israel* (New York: Monthly Review Press,

moment of this ultimate victory, however, with all of Palestine of the mandate now in its hands, Israel had unwittingly created a situation that would give an enormous boost to Palestinian nationalism. Israel could not absorb these new occupied territories, with their 1 million Palestinians, as readily as it had absorbed a mere 160,000 Palestinians in 1949. Rather, it was saddled with the role of conqueror and occupier over a large, aggrieved population. And all the time that it continued—and continues—to play this role, it has solidified Palestinian nationalism, especially within the occupied territories of Gaza and the West Bank, but also within Israel itself. The Palestine Liberation Organization (PLO), created in 1964, now stands before the world widely recognized as the representative of Palestinians in the occupied territories and the "diaspora." And since December of 1987, the population in the territories has waged an ongoing *intifada* against the Israeli army.

Where is all this heading? Israel, despite its enormous military power and despite its peace with Egypt since 1979, seems strangely and sadly uncertain. Should it negotiate with the Palestinian people, and if so with whom? Should it agree again to some form of partition of the land, and if so how much land should it cede? Such are the questions that obsess the Israeli public today—and not least of all the 700,000 Palestinians living in Israel. At the moment, it is difficult to guess what is going to happen next in the area. But it does seem likely that the current situation will change, and that the ultimate shape of Palestine/Israel has yet to be determined.

Before turning to the story of the Family Abu Ahmad, I would like to add a few personal notes about why and how this story was written. The initial wish to do such a book began twenty years ago, when I was a young freelance jour-

---

1976), pp. 81, 131. Jiryis states that these confiscations (his estimate) represent about 65 percent of the land owned or cultivated by Arabs in Israel prior to 1948.

nalist specializing in Israel. In 1970 I spent half a year on a kibbutz (Jewish collective farm) near the Jordanian border in order to gather data for a book, *Border Kibbutz*. When the book was completed, I had the idea to write a kind of companion volume about an Arab village in Israel. The plan got sidetracked, however. In part, this happened because I returned to university in the United States in order to study clinical psychology. But, to be frank, the plan also fell through because of a certain reluctance on my part, as a Jew and a Zionist, to write anything that might reflect unfavorably on my people. I decided that the book was a worthwhile project, but not for me.

In 1982, with my training in clinical psychology behind me, I returned to live in Israel. I found work at the student counseling services of the Hebrew University. As fate would have it, working there at the same time was a Palestinian psychologist, Dr. Shafiq Masalha. The two of us became friends, and out of this friendship emerged the idea to co-lead a seminar on the psychotherapy of Arab patients—a seminar attended by a half dozen or so therapists, Jewish and Arab, who were treating Arab patients at the counseling services and at other clinics in Jerusalem. It was while "teaching" this seminar that I became more aware than ever of the profound lack of comprehension on the part of the Jews (myself included) of the Arabs we were treating and, by extension, of Palestinian Arab society in general. As one who was supposedly leading a seminar, I felt the professional need to broaden my understanding of Palestinian society in Israel. Moreover, on a personal level, I came to believe that this ignorance and ignoring of the Palestinian people, with whom we share the land of Israel/Palestine, is both morally *and* politically untenable: if there is to be a chance for peace, it can only come through seeing and knowing Palestinians as they truly are. With all this in mind, then, the old thought of writing a book about an Arab village was rekindled. I went to my colleague and requested his assistance in finding such a village in Israel. He directed me to Kufr Qara, where he had some family ties, and it was there that I met, among others, the Family Abu Ahmad.

Influenced by my psychological perspective, I soon decided that for purposes of the book I would focus not on the village as a whole but on one family. As I indicated earlier, the choice of the Family Abu Ahmad was largely an intuitive one: I took a liking to them, particularly to the patriarch, Abu Ahmad; I found myself curious about him and his family. He was responsive, and much to my surprise he did not seem especially suspicious about my intention to write about them. One might wonder why this was so, in light of my being a Jew and one who had come to live in Israel. The most obvious and salient reason for his cooperation, no doubt, was that my colleague was someone he knew and trusted. But beyond that, I am convinced, he and his family and others whom I have included in this book are people who feel that their story—the story of Palestinians in Israel—has not received sufficient exposure, and they are willing, even eager, to have it told. Indeed, with only one or two exceptions, they put no restrictions on the content of what is revealed here. They even were willing to have their real names used, though I made the choice not to do so.

I first met with the family in December of 1988, and my involvement with them continued until September 1990. During this time I visited almost every week for periods of one to three days. In order to better know them, I chose to work with Hassan, the family farmer. Typically, I would spend the mornings working in the fields and the afternoons conversing with or formally interviewing one or another of the family or their friends. For the most part our conversations were in Hebrew. Most of the young people, as well as Abu Ahmad, are fluent in Hebrew, as am I, and it was easiest to speak in this language. With some of the older people, such as Umm Ahmad, I spoke Arabic—which I studied for three years, though I am not fluent. I carried a small notebook with me at all times and recorded events and conversations as they happened. If a particular conversation was not altogether clear to me, I reviewed it afterwards with one of the participants. It is my belief that the material gathered in this way is an accurate record of what took place and what was said.

In the book I present all this material in the form of vignettes from daily life or recollections and historical flashbacks told by one or another of the family members or their friends. Included, for example, are chapters that portray the daily life of the farmer (Chapter 3), the celebration of the holy month of Ramadan (Chapter 4), an engagement (Chapter 15), a wedding (Chapter 10), the management of a family illness (Chapter 18), and a day at the local high school (Chapter 16). Historical flashbacks capture something of the village's origin (Chapter 1), the family's experience in the 1947–49 war (Chapter 8), and their life under the military government (Chapter 9). In addition, there are chapters that focus on the impact of such current phenomena or events as the *intifada* (Chapter 7) and Land Day (Chapter 14). And then there is the odd tale or two that manages, precisely because of its unusual nature, to highlight family and village attitudes—the story of the brother-in-law who became a *fedayee*, a guerrilla (Chapter 20), and that of the neighbor who is married to a Jew (Chapter 17).

While something of my psychological orientation has undoubtedly entered into the choice and presentation of this material, I have not attempted a formal or academic analysis, nor have I, as the narrator, assumed a prominent role in the unfolding of the story. My preference, rather, has been to allow the events and anecdotes and recollections to speak for themselves. I hope that they will be for the reader, as they were for me, sufficiently evocative to provide a richer understanding of this family, their village, and their people.

1

KUFR QARA:
THE BEGINNINGS

WHEN HE WAS ONLY NINE YEARS OLD, Abu Ahmad—known then by his first name, Ali—was granted an unusual privilege by his aging father. He was allowed to join the company of men who sat every evening in the *diwan* (men's sitting room) and to listen to their conversation. He was seldom allowed to speak, at least not at first. His job was to keep the coals in the clay brazier burning, to serve newly arriving guests the customary cup of thick, unsweetened coffee, and, if needed, to move a cushion or two for the men seated cross-legged in a circle on the floor. But just being there in the *diwan* was an honor, an unspoken accolade from his father. And besides, it was a chance for him to hear and learn things of which other boys his age were completely unaware.

It was there, during those lingering evenings, in the half-light of a paraffin lamp, that he first heard about the history of Kufr Qara, Pumpkin Village. Of all the topics that the men rambled over—and most often the conversation was on matters of the moment, on crops, prices, taxes, local politics, marriages—nothing was more fascinating, he thought, than the talk about political intrigues of the past, the battles proud and shameful, of his forefathers. This history was not something taught at his one-room school house. This history was not written down anywhere. It was "written only in the minds of men," and passed on from grandfather to father to son—and at last to him.

"I had a sense even then that what I was hearing was important," he recalls now, sixty-one years later. It is a rainy winter afternoon, shortly after we met, and we sit unaccompanied, sipping cups of unsweetened coffee in Abu Ahmad's *diwan*. "I knew I was being let in on something of great value," he continues. "The men gave me to understand this. When finally I began asking questions, they would answer seriously. And often later, when I was alone with my uncle, who was *mukhtar* [headman] of the village, I would ask for additional details. He knew more about our history than anyone else. He wanted me to know and to pass it on. And so I have. To my sons and others. But the truth is, many young people in Kufr Qara today do not know these things. They are interested in Palestinian history, and that is good. But the history of *our* village, *our* forefathers, still does not find a place in their heads, as it did in mine."

He pauses, refills the small enameled coffee cups. Then, smiling softly, he turns to me and adds that indeed it would be worthwhile if some of this history were written down. Yes, he could talk and I could write; and if the details were not clear, I could ask him. And so we begin. . . .

"The village of Kufr Qara has been in existence for seven hundred years, although we have lived in this area where we are today only the last two hundred fifty years. What happened was this. You have heard of the great Saladin, surely? He was the Muslim leader who chased the Crusaders out of the heart of Palestine back in the twelfth century. Well, after his great victories, the interior of Palestine was almost empty. So, in order to people this land with Muslims, he sent forth messengers to the south, to Saudi Arabia and Egypt. He let it be known that respectable families could come here to Palestine where there was fertile land and where they could live under his protection. My ancestors lived at the time in Medina, in Saudi Arabia. We do not know what they did there. Maybe farmers or shepherds, only God knows. What we do know is that they answered Saladin's call and came north and settled in a place twenty miles southeast of here, a place which is today in the West Bank. To this place they gave the name Kufr Qara.

"My ancestors lived there for almost five hundred years. They lived there in peace, and their lives were good, and probably our village would still be there if they had not been forced to leave. What happened is that a stronger clan living just to the south had for years coveted their good lands. So one day, two hundred fifty years ago, this stronger clan attacked with sticks, stones, and God knows what else. Many were killed and wounded. Those that survived and were able to flee, fled—some to the east, some to the north. The group that went north, perhaps thirty souls in all, traveled for several days until they came to the fertile lands of Wadi Ara, where we are today. They saw that this was a good place to settle. There was just one problem. A very small clan, the Seeas clan, who originated in Egypt, were already living here. But just as my ancestors had been the weaker clan and thus were chased out of their lands, so now they were the stronger and they chased off the Seeas people. With sticks and stones they threw them out. Was it right? Well, who's to say? That's just the way things were done. The part of our clan that went east resettled over there. And my great-great-great-grandfather and his people rebuilt their lives here. Not wanting to give up the name of their original village, they called this new place by the old name, Kufr Qara.

"They lived here as they had lived before—as farmers. They grew wheat, barley, maize, sesame, and some vegetables. Also, they raised sheep and goats, and had cows and horses to pull the wooden plows. There was always enough water around because we are in a valley and there were adequate wells. And there was much land. From here to the sea, fifteen kilometers away, it was all ours. No man owned the land then in his own name. The land belonged to all, to the village, and each was free to take whatever parcels he wished, as long as nobody else was farming them. Thus, no man became rich, but no man was poor either. God provided for all.

"In time, after twenty or thirty years, when others could see how good our lands were, they too wanted to come and settle here. My people let them. As long as these others came in peace, *ahlan wa sahlan*, welcome. There was after all so much land, and our clan was small. In having more people come to Kufr Qara there was greater security and less chance that what had happened before would happen again. So other clans, mostly from the region to the south, came to live here—five or six clans in all. This happened gradually, over a generation or two. And finally, in the 1830s, they were followed by a group from Egypt, who were accepted here at first only as laborers on the lands of others. These people, called Musarwas [those from Egypt], were soldiers who had fought with the Egyptian, Muhammad Ali, against the Turks in his drive on Palestine. Defeated, these soldiers chose not to return to Egypt, but sought to stay here. They were without anything, even bread, when they came to Kufr Qara, and we took them in, although, as is the way of things, they were exploited in the beginning. To this day, there is a feeling of resentment in the village between the many descendants of the Musarwas and members of other, more established clans, the ones who came before them—"

Abu Ahmad stopped suddenly as the rain began falling heavily and the wind buffeted the shade tree next to the *diwan*. He warmed his hands over the charcoals in the brass brazier before him, then pulled a pack of Marlboros out of his long tunic, lit one on the coals, and motioned for me to write on.

"By the 1830s, according to the Turkish census, which was the first one ever taken here, Kufr Qara had grown to four hundred thirty souls. We were a good-sized village, secure and well established. But then, as fate would have it, we one day found ourselves under threat. It happened like this. Living near our village at the time—this was about 1840—there was a fairly large tribe of Bedouins. These were not the kind of Bedouins who went on raids. They were peaceful and in good relations with us. We called them, in fact, 'Kufr Qara's Bedouins.' However, as you know, Bedouins have large herds, and one day a Bedouin shepherd brought his goats and sheep to graze in the wheat fields of my grandfather. My grandfather told the Bedouin to get his herds out immediately. The Bedouin cursed my grandfather up and down. Infuriated, my grandfather grabbed his long clay pipe and thumped the Bedouin across the head. The man died on the spot. Now, even though this man had no right to be in my grandfather's fields, still my grandfather should not have killed him. Our village was in great danger then of a revenge attack from the Bedouins—that is, unless compensation was paid, either a life for a life or an agreed sum of money. A *sulha* [peace meeting] was arranged, and the Bedouins demanded an enormous sum of money. Kufr Qara's elders agreed, even though the only way they could raise this money was to sell off land. They found a buyer, a certain wealthy *effendi* from Haifa or Beirut. With this money they paid off the blood debt to the Bedouins. Nobody in Kufr Qara had to pay with his life. But the village lost ten thousand dunams—all the land from the sea to the present-day Pardess Hanna road.

"This, unfortunately, was only the beginning of our village's loss of its lands. I'm not referring here to what the Jews took from us. That's another story. I'm talking about how people in Kufr Qara, not too long after this first incident, once again found themselves having to sell land to pay a blood debt. This time it was the result of a shooting incident. Three villagers from the Jenin area, to the east of us, came to Kufr Qara and broke into one of the houses. They were looking to steal. The owner of the house caught them in the act, pulled out his loaded rifle—it must have been of the type used by Napoleon's army in Egypt—and fired a bullet into the head of one of the thieves. The other two escaped back to their village. Once again, in order to avoid retaliation, the village elders arranged a *sulha* and agreed to pay off the blood debt. This time it cost five thousand dunams, all the land from the Pardess Hanna road to where Kibbutz Mishmarot sits today.

"The most serious killing in our village, though, did not involve the killing of outsiders. It involved a murder within

the village, two men from our clan killing a man from the
Zahalka clan. This murder changed the village, and resent-
ments from that time still are with us. It happened exactly
ninety-three years ago. I don't want to go into all the details
except to say that it involved a matter of family honor, a
sexual matter. A young fellow from the Zahalka clan had
seriously offended a family in our clan. What should have
happened is that the offended family should have consulted
first with the entire clan before taking matters into its own
hands. But they were hotheaded, they did not consult. Instead, two men from the family went after the Zahalka fellow and with their own hands murdered him. They expected
the rest of our clan, which was the largest in the village, to
support their action. But the others said, 'No, you have done
this without consulting us, without our agreement, and we
will not support you.' This led to the breakup of our large
clan, the clan that had originally settled in Kufr Qara. Three
factions emerged from this split, and that is the way we
remain today. All three factions are again large—and are
now separate clans—but we are not united and powerful, as
we once were. As for the killers, they were arrested by the
Turkish police and sentenced to fifteen years in jail, though
the Turks let them out after twelve years, in 1908. No *sulha*
was ever arranged. To this day, even though there have been
some marriages between them, the Zahalkas and this other
clan still do not like each other and often talk bitterly of
each other. Unfortunate, really . . ."

Abu Ahmad hesitated and began coughing deeply, a
smoker's cough. He appeared slightly agitated. He drank a
glass of water and coughed again. Then, poking into his
mouth the most trusted remedy, another Marlboro, he continued:

"You might think from all these battles that life here
was very unsettled. But this is not so. Life was usually not
so eventful and actually went on more or less the same, year
after year. The Turks preferred it that way. They were not
great believers in change, these Turks. And you will remember, they ruled here for four hundred years, from the 1500s
to World War I. It wasn't until the 1850s that they pushed
their noses into Kufr Qara. They were looking to raise more

tax money from their provinces, so what they did was pass a law that all land in the area had to be registered individually, not communally. Each man could claim whatever parcels he wanted, but in doing so he was obligated to pay taxes on them. This way, they figured, they could collect even more money. These taxes were collected by a local official who was in charge of ten or twenty villages, and they were sent to Beirut. The Turks used these monies for their own pleasures, not for our benefit. Yet as long as you paid these taxes, they left you alone.

"At least until World War I they did. By then, they were a dying empire. The British and French had them on the run. So they turned to their provinces not just for money, but men. Every able-bodied man from eighteen to sixty was conscripted if he could not somehow bribe his way out. Nobody from Kufr Qara could, so the village was emptied of its men. My father, in his late forties, was taken to Libya. He was away for four years. Several men from the village got killed in the war, including an uncle who died in Syria. Several more were wounded and many were taken prisoner. Some of these fellows who were captured by the British later fought with T. E. Lawrence in the Arab Revolt, though I can't say I ever heard talk about this, since these men did not sit in my father's *diwan*.

"What I do know about that period, as far as my father was concerned, is that the war itself didn't seem to bother him. Sometimes, in fact, he talked about it as a kind of adventure. The thing that bothered him was the political situation that came out of it. As you know, when the war ended the British took over Palestine and brought with them the Balfour Declaration, their promise to turn our land into a home for the Jews. This was in November 1917. The men, my father included, always talked about this as a black date for our people—the beginning of our end. I listened to them and tried to understand. But I was too young at the time. I was born, after all, in 1918—less than a year after the Balfour Declaration. Only later, much later, did I begin to understand what my father and his friends were so worried about."

2

ABU AHMAD: RECOLLECTIONS FROM HIS YOUTH

JUST OFF THE DUSTY MAIN SQUARE of the village, where the pot-holed road curved north, Abu Ahmad lived in December of 1988 with his wife, Umm Ahmad, and his youngest son and daughter, Hassan and Maysa, who were still unmarried. Their house was a single-story building of whitewashed concrete, three rooms in all, or four if you counted the large unattached veranda-*diwan* in front. The family had lived in this house since 1954, and all ten children had been raised there. Abu Ahmad loved the place. In recent years, as the family made some money, he could have moved out to the uncrowded western reaches of the village, where the fields were and where his two oldest sons had built their own large houses; but he would have no part of such a scheme. He preferred his own unpretentious space, with its veranda-*diwan* facing out toward the main square, and with the steady stream of cars, tractors, and strollers passing by, sometimes making enough noise and commotion that you could barely hear yourself talk. The noise did not disturb him, and besides, he liked all this activity, this being at the center of things. Indeed, had he taken up the suggestion to move to a new house out by the fields—in Kufr Qara's suburbs so to speak—he would have felt a loss and, as much as such a feeling was possible in the village, even a loneliness.

For Abu Ahmad was, above all else, a passionately social man. He needed others around him. And the central location of his house and *diwan* assured him of a flow of visitors—family and, of course, friends. At seventy, sitting around the *diwan* and swapping news and stories with men was still as invigorating to him as it had been when he was a boy. In fact, since he had stopped working as a farmer fifteen years ago, he had spent most of the day sitting in his *diwan*—or, more accurately, sprawling there, his short, burly body lying sidewise on a thin mattress on the floor. He still wore the same clothing he had always worn while working in the fields: a shirt tucked into, or a long tunic slipped over, his pajama-like bloomers that sagged in the crotch. He rarely wore shoes around the house, even in winter. And while he had the time now to shave in the mornings, he usually did not bother. He knew that his casual appearance did not offend his guests, since they were men like himself, retired farmers, and except on ceremonial occasions they too preferred a little scruffy informality.

Abu Ahmad had known the dozen or so men who came regularly to his *diwan* all his life. Like him, they were born around the time of the Balfour Declaration, and so they too had been witness to the enormous changes that had swept across their village, their land, in the last seventy years. The Kufr Qara they were born into had been a drowsy place of not more than seven or eight hundred people. In their early years there had been no cars or tractors, no electricity, no running water in the houses, no doctors for miles around, no banks or offices, and alas, almost no Jews. Some of the changes they had witnessed—who could deny it?—had been for the good. But many things, they felt, were better as they had been before. And, as if signifying their loyalty to this remembered past, these men, with one or two exceptions, had not shifted to the Western clothing of their sons, but had gone on wearing their *gallabiyeh*s (long tunics) and *keffiyeh*s (head coverings fixed with a black cord), just as their fathers had before them.

On occasion the men would reminisce about this past, but their reminiscences were seldom sustained enough or exact enough for an outsider to get a clear picture of what life had been like. And so it was that I decided one week to corner Abu Ahmad alone and ask him to recall these years. He was eager, as ever. The early afternoons, he said, were the best time, after his nap and the afternoon prayer, before the flow of family and friends began. Once again, he could talk and I could write; as many afternoons as it took, *ahlan wa sahlan*. And thus we continued. . . .

"I was born here in Kufr Qara on July 11, 1918," he began. "I am the second oldest of four sons, three of whom lived long enough to marry. There were also four daughters, two of whom died before marriage. My father was fifty-one years old when I was born, my mother was forty. Like everyone in the village, they were *fellaheen*, who worked every day of their lives except for feast days.

"My father was a very religious man. Only religious people could like him or were liked by him. Sometimes I would wake in the middle of the night and there he would be, praying. He prayed all the time, each prayer at its time, and also went to the mosque a great deal. The mosque was about two hundred meters from our house. As a boy I often would go with him, hand in hand. My father didn't see well, and he walked with a cane—just like the one I sometimes use today. I was close to him, he trusted and believed in me, so he liked me to accompany him to the mosque. I did until he died, which was when I was seventeen years old, just before the Arab Rebellion of 1936–39.

"The house we lived in when I was a boy was up on the hill, over there." Abu Ahmad sat up and pointed his ever-present Marlboro to the south, in the direction of the old mosque, Kufr Qara's only mosque until 1968. "Our house, like every house in the village, was only one large room, eight meters by eight meters, with two doors and no windows. It was built with large grey stones and with mud for mortar. The roof was made of tree trunks and large branches. The one large room of the house was divided in two, with a meter or so drop to that part of the room where the sheep and goats were stabled. Shortly after I was born, our family made a separate room for the animals, but this was not common. People and animals usually lived together. As for my father's *diwan*, that was located outside the main living quarters, separate from everything and everyone.

"The houses were built close to each other and all were located in the area which is today the center of Kufr Qara. Outside this area the fields began. There were no paved roads in those days, not inside the village or anywhere around in the Wadi Ara area. The first paved road in the village wasn't built until 1958. Until then, all roads were just hardened dirt. Men went out to their fields by foot or by horse and donkey. Until 1930, when I was twelve years old, there weren't even any carts here in Kufr Qara.

"Our nearest well—a very good well—was about a kilometer outside the main area of the village. The women would go there two or three times a day to bring back water, either in jars which they carried on their heads or in goatskins which they strapped onto the donkeys. The women also would go out there to gather wood for cooking. It's hard to imagine today, maybe, but back then there were forests of *baloot* trees around Kufr Qara. In World War I, the Turks had made us cut down a lot of *baloot* to fuel their trains. But these trees grew back quickly, and when I was a boy, all around Kufr Qara there were again areas of thick forest.

"In these forests, and further off in the hills and in caves, there were all kinds of wild animals—foxes, wolves, bobcats, wild boars, jackals, and even some leopards. At night you could hear them howling. Yes, howling like mad in the distance, believe me—" Abu Ahmad turned to me and to his two grandsons, Ussama and Abed, who had just stopped by on their way home from junior high school. The boys, sons of Nihal, were fond of Abu Ahmad and enjoyed hearing him reminisce. They usually stopped by the *diwan* once a day, and if Abu Ahmad allowed them, they would sit down unobtrusively and lap up whatever was being discussed.

"Today, of course, none of these animals are left," Abu Ahmad continued. "And no forests either. But, believe me, when I was a boy I didn't dare go out of the main village area at night. It was too dangerous. Sometimes it happened that a boy or girl was grazing the sheep or goats in the daytime, and one of the animals would stray off into the forest. If they couldn't find it before night, they would have to leave it there, and the next day or so when they found it, all that would be left was the carcass.

"However, I don't want you to have the impression that life in the village was frightening and unpleasant. It wasn't. As a boy, I had lots of fun here. In the wadi there was a stream, and in the spring and summer I would go swimming there with my friends. That's where I learned to swim. We also had our own games—ball games that we'd play with a stick and a rock or, when someone had one, a *tabi* [small ball]. And we'd go on trips now and then. Until I was sixteen years old, I never went to the big towns, Jaffa or Haifa. But as a boy I went a lot to Caesarea, where my older sister lived with her family. Caesarea, as you know, is over on the coast about fifteen kilometers from here. To get there we'd ride on donkeys for maybe four or five hours, passing Arab villages and even some Jewish villages along the way. It wasn't dangerous, nobody bothered you.

"In Caesarea we had lots of fun. We'd go swimming and fishing all the time. My sister's husband's brother was a fisherman. He would fish with huge nets, and you could see the fish in the water because it was so clear in those days. Sometimes he also used dynamite to catch the fish. Always, he caught a lot—grey mullet, sea bream, sardines. He'd sell them to people, and we also ate a lot. Broiled over charcoals they were especially delicious. To this day, I can still taste them."

Abu Ahmad looked over at Ussama and Abed, who were hanging on every word now. Sensing that their grandfather had given them an opening, they began to chide him lightly for never taking them fishing. They had never been fishing in their lives, they insisted. Abu Ahmad shrugged his shoulders and made a comment or two to the effect that today's kids were indeed deprived. The boys sat there as if sulking. Abu Ahmad was about to continue his narrative, but the telephone rang and he was called away. When he returned some guests appeared, and we had to stop.

It was not until a week or so later that I again found Abu Ahmad alone in his *diwan*. He was just winding up the afternoon prayer when I arrived, and I sat down across from him. My presence during his prayers, or anyone else's presence for that matter, did not faze him at all. Upon finishing, he sat back on the mattress, sighed deeply, and returned to this world. He poured us each a small cup of coffee from the copper *finjan* (kettle) that Umm Ahmad had just brought him. We chatted briefly. Then, accomplished storyteller that he was, Abu Ahmad picked up where he had left off the previous time.

"Where the children today are more fortunate than we were," he said, "is in the excellent schools they have. They have it all now in Kufr Qara, kindergarten through high school. What did we have? Just a one-room school that was set up here by the British. Our teacher was a man from Jaffa who lived here with his family. Altogether, there were about forty of us in the school, all boys except for the teacher's two daughters. There were four grades and all of us were in the same room with our one teacher. We learned Arabic grammar, math, geography, Muslim history, and Koran. The teacher was a good one and I loved the school. I went from age seven to eleven. And the truth is that already at age seven I was the best student, even better than the older boys. The teacher was proud of me and so was my father. When I finished this school, I wanted to go on and learn more. But where? If you were wealthy, you might be sent to Beirut to learn in the high school there. Of my generation, very few from this entire area went, only a few sons of rich landowners. The other possibility was to go study for free at the Muslim religious school, al-Azhar, in Cairo. There you could study to become a religious scholar, a *sheikh*. I wanted to go, I wanted to be any place where I could learn more. My father liked the idea that one of his sons would become a *sheikh*. However, the teacher from Jaffa discouraged him. The teacher told him it was too dangerous to send off a boy of twelve to Cairo alone. There were thieves, kidnappers, all kinds of evil people there, and who knows, I just might disappear. So my father didn't send me. I stayed here in Kufr Qara.

"I realized then that the only way I could learn was to read on my own. So that's what I did. When I wasn't working in the fields or sitting in my father's *diwan*, I was busy reading. I read everything I could get my hands on—my uncle's newspaper, *al-Carmaliye*, from Haifa, books on history and geography, and novels. I'd read by the paraffin lamp, sometimes hundreds of pages a night. This is how I got my education.

"It's also how I came to learn more about the Jews. The men in the *diwan* had much to say about the Jews, and on trips outside the village I saw them working in their *moshavim* and kibbutzim [cooperative and collective farms]. I was curious about them. I began reading about their history in Europe—the persecutions, the Dreyfus case. It was all new to me. When I was thirteen years old, I had someone buy me a Hebrew grammar book in Haifa. I studied this book for three or four years, and occasionally, when Jews came to the village to buy and sell, I would talk to them. In that way, I became the first one in our village who could speak Hebrew. Little did I know that one day this knowledge of Hebrew would become so useful, would even save my life."

Abu Ahmad nodded sadly, but said he preferred to save that story for another time. It was too complicated, and he didn't want to get off the track. He wanted me to have a better idea about what his life had been like as a youth, when he was not so busy with or worried about the Jews. His main concerns at that time had been with the work to be done, and as a *fellah*'s son that meant the daily work in the fields.

"I didn't really begin working hard," he said, "until I was twelve years old and left school. Before then I had it easy—only an hour or two here and there. My father was no longer working then, he was sixty-three years old and almost blind. My older brother, who was twenty-four years old, was in charge, and my sister and mother worked with us. My mother was very strong and an excellent worker. In fact, she continued working in the fields until she was about seventy-five years old. My older brother was very kind to me. He broke me in slowly—easy jobs first, like sowing and weeding, and then little by little the harder work, like harvesting with the scythe and plowing behind the horse with the wooden plow.

"We worked long hours, from sunrise to sunset, and in the winter we began even before sunrise. We had seventy-five dunams in those days. Like almost everyone else, our lands were made up of small parcels, ten dunams here, five there, and so on. Many of our plots were a distance from our house, maybe two or three kilometers. So we spent the entire day out there. We took our food with us. We took pitot—long discs which the women would bake in clay ovens and which were rich and delicious, unlike the stuff they sell today. We'd also take olives, eggs, butter, and *labneh* made from our own sheep, and whatever else happened to be left over from the night before. We ate well. We had to, because the work took a lot out of you.

"The work we did depended upon what the season was. Each season had its own particular task. In general, the year was made up of four work periods. There was the fall plowing and sowing, and the winter plowing and sowing, and then the spring harvesting and summer harvesting. As you know, we have rain in this country only from late October until April, and the rest of the year not a drop. So our work went like this. At the end of October we began plowing those plots we owned down by the wadi, where the soil was always soft, and once the rains began we plowed the rest of the plots we intended to sow. We plowed three times and then sowed—wheat, barley, lentils, and *kursana* [a legume] for the animals. All this took until the end of January. Then we immediately began the next round of plowing and sowing—this time corn, watermelons, and vegetables such as tomatoes, cucumbers, peppers, and beans. The last sowing ended in April, and we usually had a couple of weeks rest after that. From May to the beginning of October, we harvested all the time, each crop in its time. After that, we had a short rest again, and then we started plowing and sowing all over.

"The hardest work was the harvesting of the grains, where you had to bend from the waist all day long. I can't say I liked this work at all. We worked with simple hand scythes—the men doing most of the cutting, and the women gathering the grain stalks into bundles. The work required many hands and had to be done at the right time, when the grain was ripe and before it shattered. If it shattered, only the birds had a good harvest! Once the grain stalks were gathered, they were brought to a threshing area, and a threshing sledge pulled by a horse or cow would be dragged over them. Afterwards, with a wooden fork, the grain would be separated from the chaff. You don't see this way of working anymore in Israel, but if you go over to the West Bank you can still see it. It's good to watch, but I don't recommend doing it.

"We worked in this manner until about 1937. By then, my older brother was married, and he had me take over the work. I didn't mind, I liked the responsibility. Shortly after I took over, I met a fellow who showed us how we could use irrigation. Until then, we relied only on the rains. The fellow showed us how to use the water from the stream in the wadi." Abu Ahmad took my pen and began diagramming the irrigation system. Essentially, the system involved damming up the stream for an hour or so and then, by a series of diagonal trenches, allowing the water at this elevated level to flow between the rows of crops. It was so simple, he said, that he could not believe they hadn't figured it out before.

"Naturally, this gave us much higher yields," he continued, "and we began to make enough money so that we could go to town and buy new clothes, and we could afford to eat meat much more often. We became known as 'the meat eating family.' We had more vegetables not only to sell but for our own use too. Altogether our standard of living became higher. The biggest reason for this, though, is that the irrigation system allowed us to plant tobacco. You need to grow tobacco in the summer months, for about one hundred and twenty days. With our irrigation system, we were able to water during those months and thus grow wonderful tobacco. As for selling it, the British law required that you bring the tobacco to licensed cigarette manufacturers, where you were paid a low price. We did this—in part. But where we really made out well was selling our tobacco for twice the price on the black market. We sold to Arabs from Gaza and Jaffa, and Yemenite Jews who lived nearby and liked smoking the *narghile* [water pipe]. These people would come at night and pack huge bundles of tobacco, which they transported by donkey, horse, or sometimes by bus. If caught, there would have been a stiff fine, but thanks to God we were never caught. As a result, we began to make big money."

Abu Ahmad chuckled, his luminous grey eyes radiating a mischievous pleasure. It had been good making the money, he said, but it was also enjoyable putting one over on the British authorities, who by then were thoroughly disliked by everyone. Abu Ahmad began to describe this anti-British sentiment and the Arab Rebellion of 1936–39, but then stopped abruptly. He looked across at Ussama and Abed, who were again sitting with us, and then excused himself. Ussama and Abed looked at each other, exasperated. Afterwards, they explained to me that Abu Ahmad was unwilling to discuss in their presence anything related to his war experiences. They knew that he had fought against the British in the Arab Rebellion of 1936–39 and against the Jews in 1948, but he wouldn't tell them about it. Why, they didn't know. And they never dared to ask him.

A few days later, when we were again alone and about to resume our talk, I decided to ask Abu Ahmad if his grandsons' impression was correct, if he really did avoid discussing these things with them. He looked at me, surprised, and answered, "Well, yes, this is true. Or mostly true. I told them a little about those events once, after their teacher at school gave them an assignment to ask their grandparents what happened here in Kufr Qara. But really, I prefer not to talk much about these things with them. War is a bitter thing, and the British are no longer enemies, and we live our lives among the Jews. Why take a chance of filling their young hearts with sadness and anger?

"But *you* need to write these things," he said, motioning for me to be sure to take notes, "so let me tell you a little about the British and our rebellion against them in 1936–39. I was only seventeen years old when the rebellion broke out. Many men from Kufr Qara and other villages around here began taking part. They fought as irregulars. They'd get together for a particular battle or sabotage action, and then they'd return to the villages, or hide out elsewhere. The targets of these actions were the Jews and the British— mostly the British. The aim was to establish our own independent country, Palestine.

"I was all for the rebellion. I wanted us to have our own country and I wanted the British out. I didn't mind having the Jews here, though. Unlike most Arabs, I was not worried about them—not then. I saw them as a kind of unfortunate people, a persecuted people, and if some of them wanted to seek refuge here in Palestine, *ahlan wa sahlan*. Maybe we could also learn some things from them, I thought. The ones I knew were intelligent, and they could help us improve some things, like medicine. As long as they were willing to live in peace with us, as a minority in *our* country, then *ahlan wa sahlan*. It was our British rulers who had to go. It was against them, not the Jews, that I personally took up arms.

"My older brother was against my joining the irregulars. He needed me to run the farm, and he was afraid something would happen to me. I listened to him for a while. But finally I could listen no longer, and one night, in 1938, I sneaked away and joined. An uncle on my mother's side was conducting operations out of Tulkarm, about twenty kilometers from here. He had a thousand men under him. I went immediately to him and joined up. There was no real training. Just a little target practice with a rifle, and that was it— you were ready. In the first month I got to participate in a couple of actions. Once a group of us, thirty or forty men, ambushed a British convoy of thirty trucks. We killed one soldier, wounded a few others, and then got away. Another time, a band of us cut the telephone line between Tulkarm and Nablus. I was the one who did the cutting since I was light then and could climb quickly. Again we got away.

"However, the day after this sabotage action, an unfortunate thing happened to me. It was just before dinner, and a friend and I were sitting on the floor relaxing. My friend heard that I had a good pistol and he asked to see it. I gave it to him. He was examining it and by accident it fired. A bullet passed right through my ankle. I was sent immediately to Damascus, where we had a hospital that treated Palestinians wounded in the rebellion. For seven weeks I was laid up there, until the wound healed—more or less." Abu Ahmad pulled up his baggy bloomers, revealing the scars on both sides of his right ankle. He still had pain from time to time, he said, and now walked with a cane. But really, he had gotten away lucky; it could have been worse.

"After I recuperated and was able to walk again, our organization in Damascus found work for me there. They had me act as a liaison between the wounded soldiers and the hospital staff, in the same hospital where I had been treated. It was light work, nothing much really, and by ten o'clock in the morning I was finished. That was good. I had never spent any time in a big town, so this was my chance. I liked Damascus and enjoyed sitting in the cafes playing cards and backgammon. There were women around too, and many fellows took advantage of the opportunity, but not me. I believed then, and still do, that a man should have sex only with his wife—if he went with other women, God would find a way to punish him. So this I avoided. But I enjoyed myself there all the same—for thirteen months. My brother knew I was all right because I had written him, explaining that I'd come back as soon as I could.

"Getting back home turned out to be more difficult than I expected. This was because the Syrian authorities decided to crack down on our organization. Remember, the Syrians were then under the French, and the French and British were allies. This was in 1939, and World War II had just broken out. Me and my friends, as rebels against the British, wound up in jail. I sat there for a few weeks until a lawyer got us out on the basis that we were political refugees. We were set free and told we had to get out of Damascus, though we couldn't go back to Palestine. So I went to Beirut. I stayed there a month in horrible conditions—hardly any food or water, blackouts all the time, and nothing to do. I couldn't stand it. The only thing to do, I realized, was to try to sneak back into Palestine. It wasn't easy, but I came up with a plan. I took the train back to Damascus and, once there, switched into the clothing of a gentleman—silk suit, white shirt, and red *tarboosh*. I boarded another train for Deraa, on the Jordanian border. The Syrian officials gave me no problem. I had learned to speak with the local accent, and I was a 'gentleman' after all. Once in Deraa, I shifted out of the suit and into the clothing of a *fellah*. I rented a donkey from a farmer, and at night rode back to Kufr Qara.

"My brother and family were weeping with joy to see me again. They thought I would never return. We had a *hafla* [party], of course, and that was it. I was back, thanks to God. The British came around once and asked a lot of questions. But there was no problem. I had no weapons and, as far as they knew, no blood on my hands. World War II was under way, and they were glad to let the rebellion and the past be forgotten. I too was eager to get on with my life in the village, and was happy to return to farming. I had had enough adventures. I wanted only to get back to work, get married, and raise a family, and, God willing, have sons who would help me and someday take over from me. And also, with God's help, to live in peace."

3

HASSAN:
THE FAMILY FARMER

A S IF HE WERE A BRIGADE COMMANDER inspecting the troops, Hassan stood with his hands on his hips, looking sternly out over the edge of the fields. He peered to his right, where there were, quite literally, a bunch of cabbage heads; straight ahead, where dill, parsley, and carrots stood in orderly rows; and to the left, where green squash plants, one after the other, held their silent ground. Glancing overhead at the darkening sky with its high clouds, puffs of steel wool, Hassan knew that soon it would rain, and probably rain hard. That was good; it would save him the expense of watering. But most important that morning, he could see that the frost which had been predicted the night before had not arrived. He had been spared. *Il hamdu lillah*, he said softly to himself, God be praised.

As he walked over to his new house, just being built at the edge of the fields about a hundred meters from those of his brothers, Hassan smiled in relief. His mother, Umm Ahmad, who had ridden out on the tractor to work with him, was also beaming.

"*Il hamdu lillah*," she said, clasping her hands in front of her. Like Hassan, she was dark and thin, with high cheekbones and an easy smile.

"Yes, thanks to God." Hassan fingered his thin moustache. "Just another degree or so and we would've lost out again. *Il hamdu lillah.*"

The two of them began moving out to the fields, where, rain or not, they intended to pick the green squash that were just ripening. They walked briskly, savoring their good luck as they went. They each remembered all too well how last February much of the squash crop, and the pepper and tomato seedlings too, had succumbed to a frost. The leaves had been scorched black, as if a fire had swept through the fields, and thousands of shekels had been lost. Moreover, though neither of them commented on it that morning, they each had in the back of their minds what had happened years ago, when Hassan was a schoolboy. Five dunams of tomatoes and cucumbers that stood almost ready to be picked, and which would have paid much of the family's expenses for that season, were suddenly ruined in an April hailstorm. Who could forget it? Hassan had come rushing to the fields after school that day, only to find his mother and father sitting there like statues, gazing silently out at the vegetables that lay under a blanket of huge white hailstones. For a full week after that his mother had lain in bed mourning, though his father was back in the fields the next day.

Such were the dangers and risks of farming: frost in the winter and hail in the spring, and then all those bacteria, viruses, and fungi which attacked the vegetables (they no longer grew wheat and barley) throughout the year. But even with these problems, Hassan did not regret that he had made the decision to become the family farmer. He loved this land, all twenty-nine dunams of it. He knew every tree and rock on it, and its gentle slope was pleasing to his eye. Besides, he had played and worked here all his life, and it seemed to him that no place could ever be so familiar or so much *his*. And probably no work could be more satisfying to him than farming.

The actual decision to be a *fellah* had been taken back in 1978, when Hassan graduated from high school. A number of his friends had decided to go off to university, but he was not ready for that. Furthermore, he knew that if he left, the family would no longer farm its own land. His oldest brother, Ahmad, then twenty-five, was a teacher and insurance salesman, and had made it clear that the life of a *fellah* was not for him. And Hassan's middle brother, Ghanem, after four years of running the farm, was himself, at twenty-two, finally headed for Tel Aviv University. So where did this leave the family?

A decision had to be made, and so it was not surprising that one afternoon shortly after his graduation Hassan found himself sitting together with his brothers in Abu Ahmad's *diwan*. They often sat there in the afternoons or evenings, talking with their father. But this occasion was slightly different, for Abu Ahmad had indicated by his tone that a serious matter needed to be discussed.

"We all know," Abu Ahmad had begun, looking closely at each of his sons, "that soon Ghanem is going off to Tel Aviv University. He has worked hard on the farm, and education is important. It is good that he is going. And you, Ahmad, well, you're busy with your work, your business matters. . . . So where does that leave us?"

Abu Ahmad did not mention, since they all knew, that he could not be counted on to do physical work. His leg and back hurt him, and he could no longer lift heavy equipment or boxes. For the past few years his role had been restricted to managing the farm's finances.

"Well, as I've said before," offered Ghanem, "I intend to come back every weekend, and during the summer I'm available full time."

"Yes, that's good," said Abu Ahmad. "But you'll have much studying to do, and you cannot neglect that."

"No, of course."

Abu Ahmad glanced at his oldest son, who was conspicuously silent, and then over at Hassan. "There's always the possibility of renting the land . . ."

"No, absolutely not," Hassan found himself blurting out. "I am ready—"

"Wait a moment," Abu Ahmad demanded. "Hear me out. We could rent the land or find someone who would work it for a percentage—say, thirty or forty percent. This is always possible. And we could keep a small piece for our own use."

"No, absolutely not," Hassan insisted. "I want to do it. I want the responsibility. I can manage it."

Abu Ahmad smiled warmly. He had probably expected Hassan's response, but still the matter had to be left open, with Hassan free to refuse.

"And I'll work on the weekends," reaffirmed Ghanem. "Harvests, too."

Abu Ahmad nodded in agreement. "All right, as you wish. And Mother, she'll work with you Hassan, as always, may God bless her. And I'll keep managing the finances. That part will be mine for now." Abu Ahmad looked at Hassan carefully, sensing perhaps that his son wanted to manage the money too, since he knew how much Hassan liked having cash in his pockets. But Hassan said nothing.

"So, that's how we'll do it," Abu Ahmad concluded. "Let's see how it works. For now it is decided, and that is good."

Thus, Hassan became the family farmer. And perhaps for the first time in his life, he felt, the family began to look upon him as truly responsible. There was honor in going off to the university, of course, but in a family of *fellaheen* there was also a special feeling reserved for those who stayed on the land. His brothers might earn more money and have better educations, but he would hold together the one enterprise that bound them all, and in this there was also honor.

As he thought about his decision eleven years later, Hassan still had few regrets. Besides, he could see more clearly that there had been a certain inevitability to his becoming a farmer; in a way, it had been his fate. "My brothers had taken high school seriously," he explained one afternoon as we worked together removing some oversized rocks from the fields. "They were looking to get out of the village for awhile. But not me. I never wanted to get out. I always took one day at a time and didn't look ahead. That's just the way I am—or was."

Hassan sat down at the edge of the fields, beneath a fig tree planted the year he took over the farm. He lit up a Time cigarette, the popular Israeli brand, and continued, "I had not been a good student in high school and was in no way ready to study hard at university. 'Lazy' is what the teachers said. 'Smart' and 'lazy.' For years, ever since junior high, that's the way they described me on my report cards. And they were right. I just preferred having fun with my friends.

"Even when it came to working in the fields after school or on vacations, the truth is I wasn't much of a worker. Not when I was in junior high, anyway. Ghanem and even Ahmad were the ones who did the heavy work—plowing, spraying, things like that. Me, I got the easy jobs—turning on the water spigot to the irrigation pipes, carrying the buckets with vegetables, or steering the plow horse so he'd stay between the rows. I really didn't like any work back then, when I was twelve or fourteen years old, and I was always looking for ways to go off with my friends. My father wouldn't listen to my excuses, so I'd go to my mother and she'd talk to him. She'd tell him that I wasn't feeling well or that I had homework to do. Then I'd be free to go with my friends.

"*Ya habibi*, what a time we had! We'd head off to the far fields, someplace where nobody could see us, and we'd smoke cigarettes. That was a big thing. At first what we'd do is take dried eggplant leaves and then, just as we'd seen my father do with his tobacco, we'd roll them into cigarettes. Really, they made my head spin, but it was fun anyway. Later, we began with the real thing. Some big guys in junior high school managed to get them, and we'd all go off smoking. I'd stink afterwards from cigarette smoke, so at dinner I'd sit away from my mother and next to my father. He always had cigarette smell on him, so he didn't notice mine. Except once he caught me. I was about fifteen years old at the time. To my surprise, he didn't punish me. He just said, 'Look, you want to smoke, it's your business.' From that time on I smoked, though not in his presence.

"Another thing we did for fun in those days is that we'd go to the banana fields of the Jewish settlements nearby. We'd haul off a big bunch, and enjoy ourselves singing and telling jokes. Once we got caught by an Arab guard, but he turned out to be related to my cousin, and he let us go. Another time, we got caught by the kibbutzniks themselves. They caught us with a huge bunch, sitting there and eating away. We told them that we had been looking for a sheep that got lost. 'So why the bananas?' they asked. 'Well,' we said, 'we just found them on the ground.' They didn't believe us, I'm sure, but they let us go. We got out of there as fast as we could and were laughing all the way back to the village.

"But really the best fun of all," Hassan continued, "both in junior high and high school, had to do with girls. Girls! *That*, more than anything else, is what made me a rotten student. You see, I had girls on my mind all the time. I don't mean that I went out with girls, like they do in the cities here, or in America. That's forbidden in the village, absolutely forbidden. No girl would go with you. She'd be beaten by her father or brothers. But nobody could stop you if at school you exchanged stares, or if you carefully passed notes back and forth. I was good at this, really sly. So my friends used to get me to help them out, passing notes for them too. *Ya Allah*, the close calls I had!

"This one time, *Ya Allah*—" Hassan broke off a twig from the fig tree and began gnawing on it with his cigarette-stained teeth. "This once, I almost got myself in real trouble in my role as messenger. It was in my senior year in high school. A friend of mine liked this girl, and since I was close to her family, he asked me to see if she liked him too. I managed to see her and dropped the word about my friend. But she answered sharply that she wasn't interested at all. I didn't want to see my friend hurt, so I told him the situation wasn't clear. He would have to send her a letter and I'd deliver it. The next day I got this letter from him. He'd spent the whole night writing it. I read it, and my God, he was crazy in love with her. I saw I couldn't get out of it then, so what I did was write a letter back as if I were her, in what I figured would be her style. It worked. My friend was overjoyed. And so, for the next several months letters went back and forth between him and 'her.' Then one day, convinced that she loved him, he said that surely she wouldn't mind giving him a lock of her hair if I asked her. What could I do? I thought it out, and then went to my cousin who worked in the village beauty parlor. I requested a lock of hair, just the right length and color. She came up with it, and I packaged the hair in a letter. Again my friend was happy. Fortunately, my friend was too shy to ever talk to this girl, and when we graduated high school, he got a scholarship to study physics in West Germany. I breathed a sigh of relief. What happened in the end? The girl got engaged shortly after he went off, and that was that. He eventually came back to the village, a doctor in physics, and got engaged himself. One evening I decided to tell him what had happened. He listened, and then laughed and laughed. Although if he had found out back then, I'm sure he would have wrung my neck!"

Hassan laughed too. It was escapades like this, he said, that had made high school such fun, and yes, had taken him away from his studying. He had done so poorly in his senior year, in fact, that he was not at all prepared for the Bagrut[1] examination. To his embarrassment, he failed it. He could have studied hard and taken it again, but he just wasn't ready. Moreover, he could see that with Ghanem off at university, his role was on the farm. There, at least, he had begun to show some seriousness during his last year in high school. He had worked hard, especially during vacations, and everyone knew it. True, he still had a lot to prove, to himself and to others, but as a farmer he felt he could do it.

And indeed, to the surprise of almost everyone, in those early years after he took over the main responsibility the farm did very well. Hassan found himself possessed of a new steadiness and a sustained enthusiasm for work that hitherto had eluded him. He found it easier rising at dawn (how he had hated to do that in high school!) and, after a quick cup of tea and a sandwich, heading off to the fields. He worked long hours, six or seven days a week, just as his parents had always done. He also kept abreast of some of

---

[1]The Bagrut is the national matriculation examination given to Israeli high school seniors and must be passed in order to enter university.

the new developments—in seed varieties, pest control—that were taking place in Israeli agriculture.

As it happened, it was Hassan's good fortune that just about the time he took over the farm the family had acquired that most cherished piece of farm equipment—a tractor. Prior to that, plowing had been done by horse-drawn plow, and spraying was managed by carrying a heavy canister on one's back. These were gruelling tasks, even if one had a powerful back and shoulders; and Hassan, thin as he was, did not. But with the Fiat 450 tractor, all this was rendered easy. Also making his work easier was a new system of irrigation and fertilization which he learned from the Jews and which he installed right after taking over the farm. The new "drip" system was a set of plastic hoses that were placed for the season between the rows of vegetables and through which water and liquid fertilizer dripped from spaced holes to the individual plants. It was very economical, and besides, it saved him the effort of fertilizing by hand and lugging the aluminum irrigation pipes back and forth between the rows every day.

Still, even with all these technical improvements, Hassan could never have managed alone. He needed the help of others. And in this too he was fortunate. True to his word, Ghanem showed up on weekends and vacations and whenever else Hassan suddenly needed him. During harvests, some of his older sisters also pitched in, and so did a cousin or two. Yet, above all, it was his mother whom he counted on day after day. Umm Ahmad, bless her soul, had a capacity for work unequalled by any of the men in the family. She thrived on it, and without her Hassan could not have managed. For her part, Umm Ahmad was as determined as Hassan that he succeed, not because he was her favorite (that role was reserved for her oldest son, Ahmad) but because she knew how important it was to him and to the family.

And succeed he did. There were good prices on the market for vegetables in those years, the late 1970s and early 1980s; it seemed like every season Hassan "caught a price" on some vegetable, and he made big money. Always good in math, he turned out to have a sound business sense, and affable as he was, he built solid contacts with a number of wholesalers and merchants, Arabs and Jews. In recognition of all this, Abu Ahmad turned the farm's finances over to him in 1982.

"That was a big thing for me," Hassan recalled. "It meant that my father and the family trusted me. It also meant—I'd be a liar if I didn't admit it—that I had some money in my pockets, which I liked. I didn't waste it, hardly ever. But at the time none of my friends had much money. In the evenings, sometimes we'd go over to a cafe on the coast, in Caesarea or Netanya. I'd always pick up the tab. I'd buy the food, the cigarettes, and the gas for the car. This gave me a good feeling, a kind of status. Everyone saw me as a rich guy.

"But the truth was, I wasn't really a rich guy at all. Much of the money which I made on the farm then, I turned over to my father. He never told me to do this, but I knew that it was expected of me. His needs weren't all that great. He had already paid for the weddings of all my sisters except Nabila and Maysa. And he had helped Ahmad and Ghanem build their houses. But still, with only seven hundred shekels a month coming in from Bituach Leumi, he needed the money.[2] I wasn't worried. I figured that when I was ready to get married there'd be enough money to build my house, too. Money from the farm, and maybe Ahmad too, who had made some money in his business ventures. Unfortunately, three years later when I wanted to build my house, vegetable prices began to slide, and Ahmad was in trouble with the income tax people. Suddenly there was not much money in the family. I could see I was in trouble. Without a house, you can't get married. You can get engaged, but until you've got a place to live in you stay in your father's house as a single man. It didn't look good. I was twenty-six, and I could see that the way things were going then it would take me a

---

[2]Bituach Leumi is the Israeli social security system, and the money Abu Ahmad received was his pension. At the 1989–90 exchange rate of approximately 2 shekels for 1 dollar, Abu Ahmad's 700-shekel pension was worth approximately $350. (The same exchange rate applies to all sums given in shekels throughout the book.)

good five years to put up my house. What could I do? Wait—
just wait, that's all. There was no other way. Not without
some kind of miracle."

As it turned out, "some kind of miracle" did occur. And
it occurred in an ironic way: as a gift from the Jews, so to
speak. All Arab farmers in Israel knew that 1986/87 would
be a good year for them. It was the year of *shemitta*, the year
that orthodox Jews bought fruits and vegetables almost exclusively from Arab farmers, thus driving up prices.[3] Few in
Kufr Qara understood exactly why the Jews did this, but
they knew that every seventh year they could count on merchants in yarmulkes and sidecurls coming to the village and
paying high prices for the crops. So during *shemitta*, at least,
they knew they would do well.

Exactly how well Hassan had done that year I discovered one morning as we sat drinking coffee on the unfinished
porch of his new house. Hassan's close friend, Samir, also a
farmer, had dropped by on his way out to his own fields.
Samir, who was always teasing and joking, began to humor
Hassan on his new house, his "villa."

"Tell me, Hassan," Samir began, his broad face at full
grin, "what's my chance of getting a guided tour of the villa?
I haven't been inside for a few weeks."

"Of course, *ahlan wa sahlan*," answered Hassan. "But
try not to dirty my clean floors!" He directed us inside, where
the cement floor of the living room was scattered with tiles
and masonry tools. There was still a good deal of interior
work to be done, but one could see that Hassan wasn't too
far from moving in. One could also see that much thought
and expense had gone into the house. It was not only huge,
with two bedrooms upstairs, two more in the basement, and
a spacious living room and kitchen on the main floor; it was

---

[3]According to the Old Testament, every seventh year—the year of *shemitta*—
the farmer must allow his lands to remain fallow and thereby rest them. The
majority of Jews in Israel today ignore this Old Testament decree. But the orthodox
Jews (15 to 20 percent of the Jewish population) observe the current rabbinical
ruling that produce grown during the year of *shemitta* can be eaten only if that
land is owned by non-Jews, on whom the Old Testament prohibition is not binding.

also tastefully done, with lots of woodwork—built-in cabinets and shelves—that was somewhat unusual in Kufr Qara.

"Tell me the truth," Samir prodded. "What did all this
cost you?"

"About a hundred and forty thousand shekels, not counting the carpentry. A hundred sixty thousand, say, altogether."

"*Ya Allah!* The Jews were really good to you during
shemitta! Tell me, you're still in touch with the *dos* from
Netanya? I want his telephone number for the next *shemitta.*"

"Sure I'm still in touch. But, sorry about the telephone
number. It's unlisted."

They both laughed. Then, as we headed back out to the
porch, Hassan began telling me about his Netanya connection, the *dos*.⁴ "I met this guy just at the beginning of *shemitta.* It was absolute luck on my part. I didn't know at the
time that he was the main vegetable wholesaler for Netanya's orthodox Jewish community. All I knew is that one day
here is this *dos* out next to my fields in his small truck, and
he wants to buy three boxes of red peppers. 'You have any?'
he asks me. I say, 'Sure.' 'I'll give you twenty-five shekels
for a twelve-kilo box,' he says. I can't believe it. I'm expecting to get only twelve shekels in the regular wholesale market. I figure he's made a mistake, so I say, 'Twenty shekels
is good enough.' He says he'll write me a check, he doesn't
have cash. I tell him, never mind, he can give me the cash
when he comes back. He's happy, I'm happy. The next thing
I know, this guy is visiting me regularly. He not only wants
to buy from me, but he wants me to help him buy from
other farmers—"

"Like me," interrupted Samir. "Suddenly, I've got Hassan coming to my fields in his new truck—"

"The *dos* let me use his truck every day," Hassan clari-
fied.

"And Hassan, my fellow farmer, is buying up all my

⁴*Dos* is Hebrew slang for an orthodox Jew.

vegetables—squash, eggplants, tomatoes, everything I've got."

"Tell me, you didn't have a good year, Samir?"

"Sure, but not like you. You were a damned saw, cutting in both directions, no? Tell the truth. The Netanya *dos* was giving you a commission on every box, right? And from us you were getting a big cut, too. You'd take my squash for ten shekels a box, sell to him for fifteen shekels, and pick up another shekel or two as a commission from him, no?"

Hassan smiled weakly. He seemed, for the first time, slightly uncomfortable. Samir, sensing that he had made his friend uneasy, quickly backtracked. "I don't blame you," he said reassuringly. "You needed the money to build the house, so why not? I would have done it too. And, well, at least you played it honest, not like that thief, Abdullah."

Hassan chuckled. "And Qasim, he was doing the same crap." Then turning to me, he added, "These Kufr Qara guys were middle-men too, my competitors. And what were they doing? They were buying not just from Kufr Qara farmers, but going out at night and buying vegetables from Jewish farmers at low prices and then bringing them back to their own fields and selling them for high prices to *dos* wholesalers, as if they had grown them themselves or had bought them from another Kufr Qara farmer."

Samir added, "What did these *dos* wholesalers from Bnei Brak in Tel Aviv know? Qasim and Abdullah sell them vegetables and tell them they're grown by Arabs in Kufr Qara. So how do they know?"

"They're not so stupid," Hassan said. "They came out to the fields a lot and inspected."

"Inspected? What the hell did they know? Abdullah sold two thousand sacks of carrots to this *dos* wholesaler from Bnei Brak who was coming out to his fields every day to be *sure* he knew where the vegetables were coming from. Abdullah told the *dos* that all the carrots were from his own fields, and the guy believed him. Two thousand sacks from fields that couldn't have had more than three hundred! All the rest he bought cheap from Jewish farmers and brought to his fields. What did the *dos* guy know? His Torah, and that's it."

"But remember," said Hassan, "Qasim got caught on the pumpkins, right?"

Samir hesitated a moment, as if looking for a retort. "Well, Qasim was an idiot. Maybe he figured the *dos* would think that because the name of our village is Pumpkin Village, we grow a lot of pumpkins here. They were bound to see that all those pumpkins couldn't be coming from just one little pumpkin field. And besides, Qasim let the *dos* actually catch him transporting the pumpkins from the outside."

"A real fool," Hassan added. "Qasim ruined his contacts. They know he's a thief now. Come next *shemitta*, he won't make a shekel from them."

"Come next *shemitta*, I'm going to take his place!" Samir wagged his finger at Hassan in mock threat. "I'm not an old man like you, Hassan. I'm only twenty-six, but God knows, it's getting time for me to have my house, too. Maybe not a villa, but something. Come next *shemitta*, Hassan, be ready. I'm going into competition with you!"

Samir slapped Hassan roughly on the thigh. Then, stretching his long arms and legs, he rose and walked off jauntily to his tractor. When he left, Hassan filled me in on a few more details of his *shemitta* year. All his friends, he said, were envious of him. He had made a fortune—enough to trade in his Fiat 450 tractor for a newer and larger Fiat 640 and to buy such accessories as a plow, a sprayer, and an earth-moving attachment. Even more important, he had earned enough money to build his house, and to build it faster and better than he ever dreamed. And what all this meant was that finally he had the wherewithal to get married. He had it made.

"It was too good to be true," Hassan said, sighing. "It all came too quick, and it really turned my head. My friends, like Samir, accused me of thinking too much of myself. As I look back on it they were right. All that money coming in suddenly from nowhere made me feel better than others. The whole year of *shemitta* I had driven around the village in the Jewish guy's truck, feeling I was smarter than everyone else. I had no time for anyone, only time to make money. People told me that I was getting carried away, that I ought to be careful. Some said that I was inviting the evil eye. No good could come from all this money. It was money from the Jews, and it could bring no blessing. I heard this, but I paid no attention."

Hassan shook his head slowly, knowingly. "Now I know what they were talking about," he concluded. "I have thought about it a great deal, and now I know what the evil eye is all about. You think you can avoid it, but you can't. When you behave like I did, you invite it. Suddenly, instead of riding high above others you are brought down to earth like a falling stone. You who are rich in money are suddenly a poor soul!"

4

RAMADAN

EVER SINCE MUHAMMAD BROUGHT THE MESSAGE of the Koran
to his people in the seventh century, Muslims have observed the month of Ramadan as a period of fasting. The
choice of Ramadan as a holy month is based on the fact that
it was during this month, the ninth in the Muslim calendar,
that Muhammad had his initial revelation—the first in a
chain of revelations that later were transcribed as the Koran
and which are considered by Muslims to be the word of God.
In observance of Ramadan, believers do not eat, drink,
smoke, or have sex, from dawn to dusk for the entire month.

Of the five pillars of Islam,[1] the fast or *sawm* is the most
rigorous and demanding. This is particularly so when Ramadan falls during the long, hot days of summer,[2] and one is
obliged to work outdoors under the sun; not to swallow a

---

[1]The five fundamental, ritual obligations, or pillars, of Islam, are: (1)
attestation of faith, (2) prayer, (3) almsgiving, (4) fasting during Ramadan, (5) pilgrimage to Mecca. For an excellent discussion of the fourth pillar, the *sawm*,
see G. E. Grunebaum's *Muhammadan Festivals* (London: Curzon Press, 1951),
pp. 51–65.

[2]The Muslim calendar is a lunar calendar, and each year has only 354 days.
Therefore, the twelve Muslim months are not fixed in any specific seasons; they
move forward about ten days each year in terms of our solar calendar. In addition,
any given month, depending on the moon's position, may be either twenty-nine or
thirty days long.

drop of water then is truly a challenge. Yet despite such rigors—or perhaps because of them—it turns out that many Muslims who are slack in performing daily prayers nonetheless observe the *sawm*, considering it the most important expression of their faith.

In Kufr Qara, an all-Muslim village, there used to be almost complete observance of the *sawm*. As Abu Ahmad recalls, when he was a boy "every adult fasted, except for four or five people who were considered strange." After 1948, however, with the establishment of the Jewish state and the implementation of universal secular education, many of the younger generation turned away from religion; they did not observe the *sawm* or, for that matter, any other pillar of Islam. Once again the pendulum has begun to swing back. Since the mid-1980s, in part due to the influence of the burgeoning Muslim fundamentalist movement, religion is again taking hold among many of the young. Ramadan is more widely observed now, it is said, than at any time in the last three decades. As many as three fourths of Kufr Qara's adults currently fast during Ramadan, according to Abu Ahmad's guess (and other estimates which I heard). In his own family, everyone observes the fast except for Hassan and Ahmad.

"I do not force anyone in my family to observe the fast," Abu Ahmad explained. "It is my right to do so, according to the Koran, but I do not believe in using force. I try to explain and convince, yet each is free to go his own way. My daughters all keep the fast. Ghanem too, he's the purest and cleanest of my sons. Hassan fasts a few days, then gets tired of it. And Ahmad, what can I say about him? He's my first, though long ago he took another path. May God watch over him.

"When I was a boy I felt it to be an honor to join in the fast. As soon as I was able, I did. You are not expected to fast until you are an adolescent, though I started early, like a lot of other boys at that time. Actually, when I was seven I began fasting—for seven days. And the next year, too, I fasted part of the month. At nine, I was already fasting like an adult. I would sit in the *diwan* at night with my father and his friends. During Ramadan, more than at other times of the year, they would discuss the Koran and tales of the

Prophet, and other religious matters. Until midnight, or
sometimes even two o'clock in the morning, they'd talk. I'd
stay with them as long as I could keep my eyes open. At two
o'clock or two-thirty we'd eat breakfast, and that would be
the last food and drink until the next evening. In the winter
this was not too hard. But when Ramadan fell at harvest
time, say, and you were working twelve or fourteen hours
with no water, this was difficult. A true test!

"That, of course, is part of the reason one is supposed
to fast—to feel the pain of what it is to be without food and
water. That way one can feel close to the poor of the world.
Also, the hardship of the fast prepares you for life and all
other hardships you have to face. Me, I am sure that the fast
is a good thing. How many years now have I done it? Sixty
or sixty-one, I think. Occasionally I have had to miss a day
or so because I was ill or traveling. Yet, as is written in the
Koran, I made these days up later. Even when we were
refugees in the war, in 1948, my wife and I kept the fast. It
is good to do so. It is a way of being close to God and close
to all other Muslims who are also observing the fast. The
Jews have their Yom Kippur fast—one day, twenty-four
hours straight. But we have the whole month. It is harder,
much harder, and if you ask me, a truer test of one's faith."

It was an hour or so past dawn on the fourth day of Ramadan, and a haze still hovered over the village. The eastern
sun, trying to breach the bruised sky, threw occasional shafts
of light across the village center as the first tractors rumbled
slowly through the streets and out to the fields. Hassan,
barefoot and in his underwear, fumbled through the dark-
ness for his work pants and sandals. Abu Ahmad, having
risen to say the dawn prayers, was now sleeping again, while
Umm Ahmad, also having prayed, was fetching her son and
me a light breakfast, although she herself was fasting.

"*Ya Allah*, I can't wake up this morning," said Hassan.
"I just went to sleep a couple of hours ago. *Ya Allah*, have
mercy on me." He wiped his eyes slowly and then poured
us both a cup of tea. Also there on the silver tray was a
small dish of fried eggs, some homemade strawberry jam,

and, of all things, a pile of matzoh, the unleavened flat-bread eaten by Jews during Passover. I was aware that Passover was just a few days off—this year it happened to fall during Ramadan—but matzoh was not something I expected to see in Kufr Qara.

"How come matzoh?" I asked Hassan.

"Why not?" he answered and then said half-jokingly, "We Arabs like matzoh even more than the Jews. At least I do."

"During Ramadan?" I persisted.

"Look, if you're not going to keep the fast, what difference does it make what you eat?"

Hassan poked a matzoh spread with jam into his mouth and slurped some tea. "It's a funny thing. This year it wasn't so easy to get matzoh. We had to go all the way to Hadera to get some. Actually, Ahmad went and got it. He likes it too. It used to be that during Passover season, every store in the village carried it. Then, since the start of the *intifada*— I don't know why—suddenly stores stopped carrying it. Last year only one or two stores had it, and this year not a single place in Kufr Qara. So, for us matzoh lovers . . . well, either you go to Hadera to get it, or you go without. Eat up. It's good for you!"

By the time we reached the fields, Hassan and Umm Ahmad and I, the sun had broken through the cloud cover and it was already hot. Quickly glancing at the fields, one could see that all the winter vegetables—cabbage, onions, and green squash—had been harvested, and the rich soil was now plowed into neat furrows for the next planting. That morning we were putting in tomato, eggplant, and pepper seedlings, which Hassan had just bought at Kufr Qara's new nursery. "I hate the color of brown," he said as we unloaded the seedlings. "I look out at the fields and I want to cover them with green as fast as I can. Brown means there's no money coming in."

Grabbing a handful of twenty or thirty seedlings, we each moved off to the rows and began planting. Hassan and Umm Ahmad worked rapidly, tucking each plant into the soil with a quick play of the fingers. Umm Ahmad, in her ankle-length dress and kerchief, moved along effortlessly.

Bending from her waist and with her legs completely straight, she worked with unusual grace. Hassan, less graceful but just as quick, worked beside her, chatting playfully with her as they went. I, alas, was unable to keep up with them and soon wound up with the task of bringing them seedlings. They could—and would—plant the whole lot, all fourteen hundred seedlings, in the span of two hours. And while Hassan stopped a couple of times for a cigarette break, Umm Ahmad glided on, pausing only to mop her brow with a sleeve of her dress. She was unwilling to take a real break until the work was fully completed.

At about ten o'clock, with the sun bearing down, we all headed over to Ahmad's backyard to sit in the shade of an olive tree. Just as we were sitting down, a tractor pulled up at Hassan's new house, and, spotting us, Samir came walking over. He too had been planting seedlings all morning, but without any help. "Hello, *effendi*," he teasingly said to Hassan. "I wish I had a work crew like you." He sat down.

"You want something to drink, eat?" Hassan asked.

"No, don't bother."

"No bother. I just asked Nufissa to bring some stuff out."

"Actually, I'm fasting."

"Come on, really?" Hassan seemed genuinely surprised.

Samir turned to me. "All my brothers and sisters keep the fast, so this year I'm trying."

"Good for you!" Umm Ahmad jumped in. "Talk to Hassan. Convince him. Good for you, Samir!"

Hassan patted Samir on the shoulder and said, "Not for me. I can't do it. In this heat, I've got to eat and drink something if I'm working. Maybe at the end of Ramadan I'll take a few days off and keep the fast."

Nufissa, Ahmad's wife, came walking toward us with a platter of food and a pitcher of ice water. Ahmad was walking just behind her. They seemed an odd contrast at first glance: she, chubby and plain-looking, with a frock over her baggy pajamas, and he, lean and handsome in a sports jacket and tie. Ahmad poured a glass of ice water and handed it to Samir.

"No thanks," Samir said almost apologetically.

"Samir's fasting this year," explained Hassan.

Ahmad burst into a harsh, sardonic laugh. "What? You? Who are you kidding Samir? Here, have some water."

Samir seemed embarrassed. "Seriously, this year I'm trying."

"Why? What's your problem?"

Umm Ahmad looked at Ahmad sharply and said, "Good for Samir. May he succeed and influence all of you."

"Right," agreed Nufissa.

Ahmad waved his hand in disgust and stood up to leave, saying he was due in Jerusalem in a couple of hours. Then, drinking the cold water he had meant for Samir, he said, "Tomorrow you'll stop, my friend. It's not for you, Samir." And he walked off with a grin on his face.

"Don't listen to him," said Umm Ahmad. "You are doing the right thing."

"Really, you are," seconded Nufissa.

"I know," said Samir, self-consciously. "But can I keep it up in this heat?" He looked over at Hassan, who was eating voraciously. "Maybe yes, maybe no. *Inshallah.*"

The most gruelling time of the day for those fasting was the mid-afternoon, especially in the hot weather. And this Ramadan, so far, had been unusually hot, with a *hamsin* (hot desert wind) blowing up from the south and baking the country. A stillness settled over the village as people sought refuge in their cool houses, where they dozed away the last hours before dusk or watched television or, more ambitiously, immersed themselves in the Koran. The village seemed closed down except for a few shops in the center square that remained open even during these mid-afternoon hours—in particular, two butcher shops, which did a brisk business all through Ramadan, and a videocassette store that likewise thrived during the holy month.

On one of these afternoons, about two weeks into Ramadan, I arrived at Abu Ahmad's house with Hassan, having spent the morning working with him. In the salon were a group of young people seated on floor mattresses, watching television along with Umm Ahmad. And in the other room, the main bedroom, Abu Ahmad was lying on a floor mattress next to the window, his mouth moving rapidly as he read the Koran to himself. He did not see me at first, and I was about to join the others when he called me over.

"*Itfadal*—please, sit down," he insisted. "I was just getting ready to stop for the day." He took off his reading glasses, yawned, and massaged his pale, unshaven face. "The most important book in the world," he declared. "Every time I read it I am again in awe." And he began telling me how ever since he was a boy he had spent time during Ramadan reading the Koran. Now that he was older and retired, he had even more time to pore over it. In the course of the month, he estimated, he would read the three-hundred-page Koran six or seven times. "Some of it I know by heart, of course. Particularly a *sura* [chapter] or two that I memorized when I was a boy to please my father. He used to have me recite in front of his friends in the *diwan*. At the time, I did it just to please him. Only later did I come to value it myself." Abu Ahmad sighed and pointed in the direction of the salon. "Maybe I was lucky, I didn't have television and videocassettes to distract me when I was a boy. What can you do? My children and grandchildren prefer television. Another world, no?"

Indeed it was, and even more so than I would have expected. Just on the other side of the wall, four of his teenage grandchildren, along with Hassan and Maysa, had just put on an R-rated movie of American vintage. Umm Ahmad was dozing now, her head resting on Maysa's lap. Hassan had rented the videocassette the evening before, and some of them were watching it for the second time. The movie, *No Way Out*, starred Gene Hackman, Kevin Costner, and some attractive actress who was romantically involved with both of them. A number of scenes were explicitly sexual, and it just happened that during one of them Umm Ahmad awoke. She peered at the video—a few bar girls were dancing bare-breasted—and then at her grandchildren, and said, aghast, "My God, they're naked!" The grandchildren laughed nervously, and Maysa got up and pushed the fast-forward button, skipping the film ahead. Umm Ahmad continued sitting there for the next few minutes, watching intently. She did, that is, until Gene Hackman began bedding the actress. "This is not for me," she erupted, leaping off the floor. "I want no part of this." And she stalked off to join Abu Ahmad in the next room as the grandchildren snickered. (Later I asked Hassan if his mother would tell Abu Ahmad about the movie. "No point in that," he answered flatly. "Why upset him, since he wouldn't do anything about it? She wants to keep the peace, so I'm sure she didn't say a thing.")

An hour or so later, as if nothing had happened, Umm Ahmad was merrily setting out dinner on a white plastic tablecloth placed on the straw mat in the middle of the salon. Maysa—short, wiry, and quick-footed like her mother—was helping her. The blue floor mattresses were drawn around in a square, and a plate and spoon were set out for each of us. This meal, the one that would break the day-long fast, was the most elaborate and plentiful, a kind of banquet. There were two meat dishes, roast chicken and meatballs in tehina sauce, stuffed grape leaves and squash, a variety of salads, pickles and olives, rice, pita bread, and a bowl of roasted-wheat soup for each. We all took our places, filled our plates, and then sat waiting until the muezzin's loudspeaker call from the mosque announced that the day's fast was over. At 6:12 P.M. exactly, "*Allahu akbar*, God is greater," came blaring out, and we all dug into the food.

Abu Ahmad and Umm Ahmad ate only a quick biteful at first, enough to break their hunger. They then went off in turns to pray briefly in the adjacent room. Maysa, who was also keeping the fast, did not join them. Unlike her parents, she did not pray five times a day, but only on occasion, when the spirit moved her. She continued eating with the rest of us, Hassan and the grandchildren and me. Hardly anyone spoke while eating, and all ate with great speed, fingers with pita bread dipping into the dishes. Within fifteen minutes the mounds of food had disappeared, and Abu Ahmad, belching contentedly, leaned back and had his just dessert—a long-awaited Marlboro.

While the women were busy carting off the dishes, there was a sudden knock at the door, and two white-cloaked fellows poked in their bearded faces. They were Muslim fundamentalists, young men in their twenties, and they were looking to sell some movement literature. Nobody seemed enthusiastic to buy, though after an awkward moment Khaled, the oldest grandson, gave them a shekel or two and took the pamphlet, which he later flipped into the corner. "Even in Kufr Qara we've got them now," Abu Ahmad said dismissively. "But thank goodness, they have no strength. Not here, anyway."

Abu Ahmad's remark immediately triggered an outpouring of opinion on the fundamentalists, who earlier in the year had scored impressive successes in the municipal elections in some of the nearby Arab communities, although in Kufr Qara they had come up empty-handed.

"There's only about two hundred of them now in the village," explained Hassan. "But they're beginning to grow. Some guys I used to go to high school with—guys who became alcoholics or drug users—now they've done a turnabout and are with the fundamentalists."

"I'm no supporter of the fundamentalists," added Maysa, "but in Umm al-Fahm, where I work, they *have* done some good things. They've built some roads and clinics and nurseries. So they've got a lot of people behind them."

"Baaaach!" exclaimed Abu Ahmad. "Half of their supporters were voting for the Communists only five years ago. So now they've crossed over to the fundamentalists. It won't last."

"I hope not," said Hassan, grinning. "With God's help, it won't."

"Believe me, it won't last," repeated Abu Ahmad, ignoring Hassan's joke. "The Israeli government won't let them get too strong." Then, turning to me, he stated, "Religion, yes. I'm all for religion. But we don't need fanaticism. Let each man find God in his own time and in his own way. Without the fundamentalists!" And so saying, he rose slowly, asking Khaled to drive him to a neighbor's house. An old friend who was a judge on the religious court in Jerusalem ("a *real* Muslim and true man of God," Abu Ahmad affirmed) was visiting there, and Abu Ahmad was looking forward to discussing the Koran with him.

After Abu Ahmad and Khaled had gone, Umm Ahmad brought out a tray of *kunafeh* (a sweet cheese concoction) and some fruit. Everyone munched away quietly. The brief exchange on the fundamentalists had left something of a pall over the room, and nobody seemed eager to continue it. Hassan finally went over to the TV and, as if the thought had just struck him, said to his mother, "You know what, let's watch a video." Everyone giggled uneasily. "Seriously, I've got another one here. A real good one."

Umm Ahmad flashed him a look of disapproval and said, "I've seen enough videos today."

"No, Mother, this one you'll like." He winked at Maysa, whose doll-like face was at full smile. "It's clean family entertainment."

"Like the last one?"

"No, much better. Come, you'll see." He plunked a video in place as Umm Ahmad scooted off toward the kitchen. "A little wild dancing, but all clean. Come back here."

"No thanks."

And then the video was on: a party scene with Arabic music and with Hassan and an attractive young woman in a bridal-type white dress dancing in the center of a circle, Umm Ahmad and her daughters dancing all around them.

"Come back here, Mother," bellowed Hassan, as the others laughed aloud. "Don't you want to see yourself? It's the video of my engagement party. Really, come back here and have a look!"

When the hot, dry *hamsin* breaks, it often gives way to cool damp weather and, in the springtime, a shower. Hassan, gazing at the gray clouds overhead, cursed the heavens and cursed his fate as a farmer. "All it has to do now is rain and I'm in trouble," he said. "The new seedlings will be full of fungus afterwards. Son of a whore!" He kicked a clump of weeds and spat into the air. "I can't afford another bad season," he said. "This summer I've got to make real money. I've just got to!"

He sat down at the edge of the fields and lit up a cigarette, trying to calm himself. He was worried, he said, because in three months he was getting married, and once again he was in debt. He hadn't expected that. After *shemitta* and all the money he had made from the Jews, he thought everything would be all right. However, since then he hadn't "caught a price" on one vegetable. He wasn't alone in that. Almost all Arab farmers, small operators like himself, were having trouble these days. They didn't have the good marketing arrangements which most Jewish farmers, organized in cooperatives, had worked out for themselves. And even though the yields were good, by the time one finished paying all the expenses—fertilizer, pest control, and water—one often wound up with no profit, or even with losses. Last season, in fact, Hassan had barely broken even.

"It seems like ever since *shemitta*," he mused, "a lot of things have just gone bad. A run of bad luck. Or, really—at least I believe it—the curse of the evil eye. People warned me while I was making all the money during *shemitta* that something bad might happen. Money from the Jews would bring no blessing, they said. Well, you know what happened? Right after the end of *shemitta*, I ran over a kid in the Jewish guy's truck and killed him. Dead. Finished. . . ." Hassan's face tightened, and he sat there in silence. He looked up at the sky and then, shaking his head, resumed. "I don't suppose anyone's told you yet. It was a kid from my clan. A distant cousin. He and two of his friends were in the road up by the school, and I was driving by too fast. Like a maniac, I was going. I saw them too late, tried to swerve, and caught the boy. He didn't die on the spot— only a couple of days later in the hospital. There's going to be a trial in a few months or so. I'm being charged with manslaughter, or something like that. I'm not too worried at the moment, my record up to then was clean. But the thing itself is still with me. Every time I go past the schoolyard I can still see the boy lying there with that terrible gash on the back of his head. . . ."

Hassan stood up and began pacing about. Noticing that Ghanem's wife, Latifa, was hanging wash in the backyard, he called over to her and requested that she bring us some coffee. Sitting down again, his head cupped in his hands, he continued. "And that wasn't all that happened. Right after *shemitta* there was another tragedy for me and my family. My sister, Nabila. That you heard about, no?" I nodded that

I was aware. "Only a few months after I ran over the boy, she was dead too. In an automobile accident on the Wadi Ara road. Head-on collision, and everyone walked away except her. That about finished me. Me and the rest of the family too. And do you know where she died? Not on the spot where she was hit, but a couple of days later in Beilinson hospital in Petah Tikva—the same hospital where the boy I hit had died.

"I really began to feel I was cursed," Hassan said. "I hadn't really believed in the evil eye before then. Now I do. Some thought I should go to a *sheikh* and try to remove the curse. My mother, she's one of these Koran readers. She knows how to read the Koran and get rid of a curse. But me, I don't believe so much in all this Koran reading or in going to *sheikhs*. The curse was from God, I believe, because of all my arrogance and thinking I was better than others. Nobody can read it away. Only God, if He decides, can rid you of the evil eye. That's what I believe, anyway."

Hassan rose to take the tray from Latifa, who was coming in our direction. She had prepared not only coffee but also some cake and fruit. Declining to eat anything herself since she was fasting, she stayed only a moment and then went back to hanging wash. "Ghanem's lucky," said Hassan, nodding toward Latifa. "She's not just beautiful, she's a fine person, too. A little shy, that's all. Sort of like my fiancee, Zaynab. You haven't met her yet, have you? In a few days, during Id al-Fitr, she'll be coming over."

Hassan sipped at his coffee, lit up another cigarette and began talking about Zaynab. He had met her, he said, just before Nabila's death. Actually, Nabila and another sister, Jamileh, had set up the introductions. After he had made all the money during *shemitta* and could build his house, he wanted to get married. But he had nobody in mind, no prospects. An earlier girlfriend, someone he had wanted to marry at one time, was no longer available; anyway, his father would have opposed her because she came from a clan he didn't like. So he had asked his sisters to search for him, and they had come up with Zaynab. His brother, Ghanem, also supported this choice, because she had been his student in junior high school, and he thought well of her.

"I only knew her vaguely," said Hassan. "I had seen her on occasion, when I visited her brothers. They have a transport business and I send a lot of vegetables with them. Zaynab had served us coffee a few times, but I paid no notice. She was pretty and shy, that's all I knew. But I figured, why not have a better look? She had hinted through her sister that she was willing to meet me, so why not? Well, we met and hit it off real well. I liked her a lot. She was smart, even though she was just finishing high school. And she was really pretty, even more than I had thought. She liked me, too, I could see. But then there were some snags. It's a long story, but what it came down to was that her father was against our getting married. He wouldn't give his consent. Why? Because a couple of years before, he was trying to marry off his younger twin brothers, and he had tried to get my father to give him Maysa and Nabila. My father turned him down. So he was still holding a grudge. In the end, though, he gave in because all his sons liked me, his daughters too—and of course Zaynab. Once we had his consent, we immediately got engaged. Just last summer, we had the big party, the one you saw on the video. We didn't know whether to have such a large party, since it was only a half year after Nabila's death. In the end, though, we decided yes. Personally, I was glad. With all that bad luck, that curse which had followed *shemitta*, finally something good was happening. And this was something to celebrate. So we really did."

Everyone was waiting for the crescent of the new moon, which would mean that Ramadan was over and the three-day feast of Id al-Fitr, Festival of the Fast Breaking, would be under way. Yet nobody—no observant Muslim, that is— was about to say whether it would occur that night, the twenty-ninth of the month, or not until the following night, the thirtieth. According to the newspapers, which based their reports on modern astronomy, the new moon would not arrive until the next day. Abu Ahmad and his friends, however, did not believe the newspapers, saying instead that "such things are in the hands of God." That evening, right up until midnight, they kept stepping outside the house to look at the heavens, or turning on the radio, hoping to hear that Ramadan was over. All five butcher shops in Kufr Qara and several men who sold sheep also stayed ready and available. For if the new moon were seen, there would be a sudden rush for fresh meat, as people would begin celebrating immediately.

But, at least this time, the newspapers had it right. There was no new moon that night, the twenty-ninth of Ramadan, and fasters had to put in one more day. By mid-afternoon of the following day, however, certain that the new moon was coming at last, villagers were all going about their preparations. Umm Ahmad, her daughters-in-law, and Maysa had begun working in the late morning. Helped by the four granddaughters—Latifa's two little girls and Nufissa's two older ones—they were cleaning the house and *diwan* from floor to ceiling, and had already begun preparations for the elaborate meal which would break the fast that evening. Umm Ahmad, uncharacteristically, was in a sour mood. She seemed to feel that the men of the family were dawdling in their task of fetching and slaughtering the sheep. Yet she was not about to criticize Abu Ahmad openly, not in front of the others, and except for a hint or two about "how much time it takes to prepare the meat," she had to wait until Abu Ahmad rounded up his sons and grandson (Ahmad's son) and went to buy the sheep.

The fetching and slaughtering of the sheep was something of a ritual, a man's task which Abu Ahmad enjoyed doing with all his sons. Just as his father and older brother had taught him, so he had taught his sons how to choose the meatiest sheep and then how to slaughter and butcher them. On holidays such as Id al-Fitr he refused to buy already-butchered meat. He had to do it himself. And so, waiting until all his sons were ready to join him (Hassan worked in the fields until mid-afternoon), it was only at four o'clock, a couple of hours or so before the evening meal, that he set out to buy the sheep.

There was a line when we got to his neighbor's sheep pen. Abu Ahmad, walking with his cane, went right into the pen and began feeling the haunches of several male sheep.

"The males have more red meat and less fat than the fe-
males," he explained, and then he shouted to Ghanem,
"*Khud hadol!* Grab those two!" Ghanem, stocky and mus-
cular, leaped into the corner and grabbed one and then the
other, passing them to his brothers who hoisted them onto
the scale. Ali, the nine-year-old grandson, fought to hold
them in place. Each weighed about forty-five kilos and sold
for three hundred shekels. Within minutes they were tossed
into the trunk of Ahmad's 1968 Mercedes, and we were on
the way back to the house.

Ahmad, the oldest, drew the job—it was considered an
honor—of slaughtering the sheep. With everyone watching,
including the five grandchildren, he mumbled the customary prayer before slaughter: "God has granted us the permission to sacrifice you in the name of Allah, the Compassionate, the Merciful." Then he slit their throats. Afterwards,
as Abu Ahmad stood by choreographing the proceedings, the
sheep were hung on a thick branch of the shade tree, and
Ghanem and Hassan swiftly butchered them. With huge
silver platters, the women hauled off the large hunks of
meat. Not a morsel went to waste. Over the next three days
all of it would be eaten—including the liver, spleen, testicles,
and entrails—at dinner, lunch, and even breakfast.

That evening, though, for the festive meal of the fast
breaking, the menu was lamb chops and *shishlik*. Umm Ahmad and the other women worked in a frenzy, trying to get
it prepared and cooked in time before the muezzin's call.
They just about made it. At 6:20, with the meat just finishing
on the grill but the rest of the banquet spread out on the
floor mat, the loudspeaker call from the mosque announced
that Ramadan was over. And all fourteen diners, fasters and
non-fasters alike, dove into the food with the gluttony of
those who had waited an entire month for this very moment.

Later that evening, moving with some difficulty, the
various family members went their own ways to make informal visits. Hassan went to see Zaynab; Ghanem and Latifa went to see friends; Ahmad and Nufissa went to see her
family. Apparently many villagers had a similar thought,
because at nine o'clock there was a traffic jam in the village
square such as one saw in Tel Aviv only at rush hour. Horns

tooted good-naturedly as pedestrians in their bright holiday clothes walked nonchalantly between the cars. All shops were open and doing a lively business, especially the butchers, a toy store, and a place that sold ice cream. And adding to this unusual carnival atmosphere, and to the congestion, was a procession of one hundred or so Muslim fundamentalists, white-robed and bearded, who just then were passing through the square and chanting, "*Alllllahu akbar.*" Ahmad, stuck in the traffic jam, nodded at them and said, "A lot of nonsense, these guys. Tell me, we don't have enough traffic here without them? May they all go to blazes!"

The next three days were devoted to nonstop family visits, with all the sisters and their families, and most of the aunts and uncles and many neighbors coming by Abu Ahmad's house. For their part, Abu Ahmad and his sons spent the first day visiting all the sisters, who, with one exception, lived within three hundred meters of his house. ("I tried to keep them all near me, in the village," explained Abu Ahmad. "It's better that they married men from here whose families I know.") These visits to the sisters were customary on the first day. And so too was the more solemn visit to the graveyard, where the men, but not the women, went to say prayers shortly after dawn on the first day.

"The family has come back to itself," Hassan whispered to me, at one point. "Last Id al-Fitr nobody was in the mood to celebrate. Nabila was on our minds every minute. Now, it is better. We can laugh again."

And so they did. For three days they carried on, and, of course, not only they. All of Kufr Qara was celebrating too. The pungent smoke of roasting lamb hung over the village the whole time, and each night there was a mini–traffic jam in the main square, though the fundamentalists did not return. When it was all over everyone seemed exhausted, and it was only with great difficulty that people returned to their work. "Id al-Fitr takes more out of you than a week in the fields during *hamsin*," summarized Hassan on the first morning after the holiday. To which Abu Ahmad answered, "Yes, but we had a fine Id, didn't we? This year, God be praised, we really had a good one!"

5

UMM AHMAD: RECOLLECTIONS FROM HER YOUTH

A T SIXTY-FOUR, UMM AHMAD MOVED with the quickness and fluidity of a woman half her age. She had a fine-boned face, with hazel eyes, and she held her head erect, as if ready to carry a water jug or load of kindling. Her spare, hard torso was also held upright, and she walked with her feet pointing slightly outwards and her arms swinging freely at her side. In another time and place, she might have become a dancer. In Kufr Qara, she became the mother of ten and a *fellaha*—twin fates which she not only fulfilled, but enjoyed.

With all of her children raised and her husband no longer working in the fields, Umm Ahmad had earned the right to a little relaxation as matriarch of the family. But she was not ready, she jokingly said, "to go on pension," so nearly every day she rode out with Hassan to the family's fields and put in a long morning's work. There, moving quickly from row to row, she planted or weeded or harvested. She was tireless and did not seem to need the coffee breaks that energized Hassan and his friends. Even in the scorching heat, she seldom drank water. She simply worked on, at one with the plants, her nimble fingers tending to them as if they were her children. Her daughters-in-law, women of the new generation, never joined her in the fields, though occasionally an older woman friend or neighbor would pitch in during the harvests. Then there would be songs and jokes and gossip, with Hassan and whoever else was with him joining in the revelry.

Umm Ahmad would not have said so (maybe not even to herself), but it seemed to me that it was out in the fields that she was most free and content. It was not that she minded being at home, ministering to Abu Ahmad in his requests for coffee, fruit, water, and so on. She did all this willingly when she was there, and if Abu Ahmad were feeling ill she would not leave him even at the height of a harvest. Yet out in the fields she had something to offer that went beyond the call of wifely duty, something she was unexpectedly good at; and self-effacing though she was, she nonetheless enjoyed her reputation as the family's best and most durable farm worker. Perhaps sensing this, Abu Ahmad, unlike most men of his generation, who demanded that their wives remain available at home, encouraged her to work each morning in the fields.

It was while working there with her and Hassan that I first came to know Umm Ahmad. During the initial months of visiting the family, I had spent time mostly with Abu Ahmad, and she had remained in the background, appearing only to serve coffee and fruit. We never talked. Once I began working in the fields, however, she started chatting with me. She worried aloud about such things as Hassan's upcoming wedding and Maysa's reluctance to get married. At one point, when she realized that I was writing a book about *all* of the family—not just her husband—she boldly stated that she too had "an encyclopedia of stories" to tell; and what is more, she wanted to tell them to me. For this, I needed Abu Ahmad's permission, of course. When I approached him about the matter, somewhat to my surprise he balked at first. "I remember the facts of her life better than she does," he volunteered. But soon he agreed that as long as she was willing, he would not stand in the way. And so one afternoon, with Maysa nearby, Umm Ahmad and I sat in the salon of their house, and she related what she called "the first chapter of my life."

"I was born some time in 1925," she began, "though I do not know exactly when because my parents never remembered the date. I was the second child and second daughter. Altogether we were nine—four boys and five girls. My father was from one of the old clans that are related to my husband's clan. My husband and I are distant cousins.

"As a girl, I lived with my family in a house not far from here, in the direction of the fields. We all lived in one room, together with the animals. I can't say I minded that. That's how everybody in the world lives, I thought. Besides, I was close to the animals. I was the one chosen to care for them and feed them. So having them with me in the house was good—I could watch over them all the time.

"I did not go to school as a child. Only one year, when I was seven years old, my parents sent me to the house of an old lady where she taught me and others how to sing and dance and make playthings with our hands. It was all right, nothing special. I didn't feel at the time that I was missing out by not going to real school like the boys. They learned Koran, how to read, and numbers. As a girl, none of that interested me. Only later, as an adult, did I regret not knowing how to read or even tell time. At one point, a few years ago, I got my children to try to teach me these things . . ." Umm Ahmad turned to Maysa, who was at her side, listening intently. She stroked her daughter's hair tenderly. "Remember, you children had to read the time for me, until Ghanem finally taught me. He also tried to teach me to read and write—I think I paid him ten agorot an hour for this—but by then it was too late. Today's children, especially the girls, are much luckier than we were in that way.

"In other ways, too, the children are luckier today. They eat better and are never hungry, as we sometimes were. And they have much better health. When I was a girl, there were terrible diseases all around, smallpox and malaria, and also rabies that came from foxes that used to live just outside the village. We had no doctor in the village, and the nearest one was a Jewish doctor over in Karkur [a Jewish settlement five kilometers away]. Many people died from these diseases, especially children. There was nothing you could do. That's just the way it was.

"In one way, though, I think we *were* definitely better off than today's children. We were freer. Our parents were busy working all the time, so they couldn't keep an eye on us. We were more able to do as we liked and get away with things. Like, for example, the trick we'd play to get sweets. What we'd do is steal some wheat or barley or eggs, and when the traveling merchant came around we'd exchange these things for lots of candies and cookies, which we'd then hide away. Mostly, my older sister did the dirty work of stealing the wheat and barley. It was stored in the wood ceiling of the house in a huge container that had a mud cork on bottom and a small opening on top that was hard to get at. My mother kept her eye on the cork, but my sister would manage to climb up to the top and scoop out handfuls of grain. My sister was very tricky and selfish and would have kept it all for herself, I'm sure, but she had to include me and my younger sister so we wouldn't squeal on her. We did this for years, and even though we were caught and punished once in a while, it never stopped us.

"We also had fun by making our own toys or inventing games. We didn't have store dolls like today's children do. But we'd make our own. We'd make them out of mud, the same mud that was used to build houses. We'd make figures using sticks for arms and legs, bottle tops for heads, and spare pieces of cloth for the *keffiyeh*s, *gallabiyeh*s, scarves, and long dresses. We'd take an eyeliner and draw in the faces. Then we'd make up a story and play it out with the dolls. Almost always it was a story about a bride and groom. We really enjoyed that.

"We also played a bride and groom game without dolls. We ourselves got dressed up as brides and grooms. Nothing too fancy, just a shawl or *keffiyeh*, that's all. It was a little risky to play in this way because many mothers didn't like their daughters dressing up as brides. They were worried that it might fill their daughters' heads with the wrong ideas. How old were we? Seven or eight. But no matter. The parents believed that something sexual might happen this way. Even though no boys were involved in this game—we were never allowed to play with boys—they still thought that something might go wrong, or that their daughters would grow up with no morals and bring *aeb* [shame] to the family. That was always, always on their minds."

Umm Ahmad chuckled a bit self-consciously, but it was difficult to tell what she was thinking. Maysa laughed, too, though in a disdainful way, making it more clear where she stood. Neither said anything. There was a slightly awkward silence, during which Umm Ahmad shucked almonds for all of us. She then resumed—on another subject.

"Most of the time we were not so free to play games or fool around. We all had work to do in the house or in the fields, helping either my father or mother. In the house there were always chores like cleaning or washing clothes or cooking. I never did any real cooking—not until I got married—but I'd help my mother by chopping vegetables or preparing the dough for pitot. I'd also help by taking care of the younger children. As the second oldest, I had all these younger sisters and brothers who had to be watched over. Especially Ali, the first boy in the family. We had waited for him for a long time—there were four of us girls before he came. My mother wanted him to get special care. She herself gave him the best food and best clothes and the best of everything. When I watched over him, I spoiled him, too. I used to let him steer me around like a goat when he was small, maybe two years old. He'd take hold of my long braids—I kept my hair long then, just like today—and he'd drive me around the house, yelling 'Ha, Ha, *Yallah!*'. . ."

Umm Ahmad hesitated, as Maysa was shaking her head disapprovingly. She put her hand on her daughter's shoulder and, as if answering her, said, "That's the way it is with boys, especially the first one. You have to spoil them a little. Besides, it was just a game, and we all enjoyed it. There was no harm in it, none at all." Maysa said nothing, and Umm Ahmad made no further effort to appease her.

"Apart from helping my mother in these ways," she continued, "I used to go almost every day to the well to get water. We were a large family and needed lots of water for

ourselves and the animals. The well was a pretty good distance and we'd usually make two trips in the morning and
another in the late afternoon. We'd usually take the donkey
so we could bring back a lot. Until I was maybe ten years
old, I was afraid to take water from the well. It was a large
pit, the size of a room, and very deep. If you fell into it and
didn't know how to swim, you'd drown for sure. I didn't
know how to swim, so I was afraid. But I liked going down
to the well anyway. There was always lots of talk and joking
down there between the women. Sometimes, a few men
would come by to water their horses. They might try to
catch the eye of a particular woman, but this was very
dangerous. If a woman started talking with the man, or even
if she just exchanged glances—glances which other people
saw and began talking about—then she could be in great
trouble. Her father or brothers would beat her or might even
kill her. At least, that's what she feared, though I don't
remember anyone being killed that way.

"What I do remember is the talk, the gossip, down by
the well. Women would talk with each other about who was
getting engaged or married—things like that. I remember
this one time when a woman had been engaged to marry
this man. Her parents had made the arrangement without
her consent. That's how it was often done in those days.
Well, this girl was very sad, so each morning she'd come to
the well and start singing sadly. She'd sing about some
woman, not herself exactly, whose parents had engaged her
to a very ugly man, and how sad this girl was, and how
rotten the man was, and how if only her parents knew maybe
they wouldn't have done it, and so on. What she was hoping
for was that the word would get back to her parents and
they'd call off the engagement. I don't know if the word got
back or not, but the engagement was not called off and she
had to marry that man.

"In another case an even sadder thing happened. Again,
it was where this girl was forced into an engagement by her
parents. There was lots of talk about this down at the well,
too. The story was that she was really in love with another
man, but she couldn't marry him because her parents were
against him. Maybe he wasn't from the right clan, or some-

thing like that. I don't remember. Anyway, what happened is that this girl was so disappointed that she jumped into the well and drowned herself. We all found her there one morning in the well, floating. Some men came along with a rope and hook—"

Umm Ahmad paused as the door leading into the salon opened and Abu Ahmad appeared. He stood there for a moment, eyeing over the situation. She quickly concluded, "And with the hook they dragged her swollen body out of the well. And that was that." Umm Ahmad rose to go to her husband, who apparently had grasped the gist of the conversation and wanted to know if she were talking about "that Musarwa girl." She nodded. And he, swatting the air as if an infestation of flies had just entered the room, insisted we take a break. A guest had arrived, he said, and he wanted Umm Ahmad to fix something for them to eat. She immediately went off to the kitchen, and Maysa joined her. I was invited by Abu Ahmad to join him, but instead I returned to work with Hassan, who needed some help packing the tomatoes we had picked that morning.

It was not until a week or so later that I caught up again with Umm Ahmad. In the meantime I had talked a few times with Abu Ahmad, and in passing, as it were, he again volunteered to tell me his wife's story. I avoided the heavy hint, determined to hear Umm Ahmad's story in her own words. She too seemed eager to continue. And so once again, while Abu Ahmad slept away the hot early afternoon in his *diwan*, Umm Ahmad and Maysa and I sat in the salon, and she resumed her story.

"I think I've told you about the work with my mother," she said. "But I've not talked about working with my father, have I? You see, with him too I worked a lot. I got along well with my father. I wasn't his favorite—he had no favorite among the girls. But he was good to me, and he liked to have me work with him. And there was lots of work to do. We had a big farm in those days—one hundred dunams. We grew tobacco, sesame, wheat, barley, melons, and some vegetables just for our own use. The land was spread out over a large area and we had a few hired workers. My father supervised them. Until I was ten years old, I didn't work in the fields. I had the job of harnessing the horse in the morning and hitching it to our new cart. My father would take the cart out to the fields with the workers. About midday, after I returned from the well, I'd take food my mother prepared out to him and the workers. I'd go by donkey. Sometimes he'd let me sit and eat with him, but usually I'd sit off to the side and eat by myself or with my sisters who came with me. I'd cut fodder when I was out there, and then load it onto the donkey and bring it back to the house for the animals.

"I was very glad when my father finally allowed me to stay out in the fields and work with him. It was an honor. My brothers were all small, so only me and my sisters were available to help. To tell the truth, my sisters were not much help either. They had no patience for working in the fields. They'd start fooling around, playing games, or they'd just sit down because they were tired. Me, I could go on all day. Only God knows why. At harvest time, when you had to gather and tie up all these bundles of wheat and barley, I wouldn't get tired. I liked the work, and I could do it like a man or a boy. I was very strong even though I was never very big. My father appreciated this about me. He could see that I was serious and that he could trust me. He never really said anything about it, but I knew that of all us sisters he trusted me the most.

"One day I really found out how much he trusted me. It happened in a strange and frightening way. My father needed me to help him fool the police, to try and cover up a murder. How? Well, it had to do with an uncle of mine who had killed his cousin. You see, this uncle had a sister, my aunt. And what happened is that their family engaged her to marry someone from another clan. By doing this, they ignored the wishes of their cousin, who also wanted to marry her. This was considered a big insult, because really the cousin had a right to her. That's how things were done, or supposed to be done. Anyway, the cousin who had been passed over was very angry. One day, he and his friend saw my uncle alone in the fields. My uncle was only a boy of sixteen at the time. These two came up to him and started cursing him and his parents, and threatening him. My uncle, who was a shepherd, carried a sharp knife with him, and he lost his head and stabbed his cousin. Stabbed him dead. With the knife still in his hand he came running to my father's house and told my father what had happened. My father calmed him down, took the knife from him, and sent him home. Then he went out to the well and threw in the knife.

"I guess my father knew that the friend would talk and that there would be a police investigation, because what he did was come to me and tell me to help him. He said that when the police came I was to tell them this story—I should say that I'd been making a pee-pee in the backyard when I found this knife. I didn't want my little brothers to find it and be hurt, so I took it with me to the well and threw it in. I was only twelve years old at the time and I was scared, but I knew my father was counting on me. So I did exactly what he said. When these tall British police came, they asked what happened with the knife. I jumped up and told them my story. I think they believed it. They never came back to question me, and my father was very happy about that. Unfortunately, they arrested my uncle anyway. He confessed and was sentenced to three years in jail—only three years because he was so young. His family had to pay the dead cousin's family one hundred dunams as part of the *sulha*. And the sister went on to marry the man from the other clan. As for my father, he didn't talk to me again about what happened, but from then on I was sure he had great trust in me."

Maysa, who apparently was hearing this story for the first time, patted her mother on the back. Umm Ahmad smiled somewhat uncomfortably and said that, yes, she had been proud at the time to help her father, but that later she realized she had made a big mistake. Maysa looked at her in surprise. Umm Ahmad hesitated, as if not sure she wanted to continue, and then said, "By lying like that about a murder, I was doing something very wrong. I was inviting the evil eye." Maysa looked at her questioningly, but said nothing. And Umm Ahmad added, as if for Maysa's benefit, "I know that some people today, especially young people, don't believe in these things. But I do. And when I was a girl, everyone in the village believed in the evil eye. Our parents too. It was something we all had in our minds, and we tried to be very careful not to invite the evil eye—or Satan himself. But sometimes the evil eye or Satan would show up in strange ways.

"I remember when I was a girl, I heard from friends how they had been playing out in the fields and a devil scared them off. The devil came out from behind a haystack, really two haystacks that were next to each other, and suddenly started chasing them. They were terrified and ran home. And then there was this other time—everyone in the village knows about it—this she-devil was hanging around here. I was about ten or twelve years old at the time, and I heard these things. For example, a man was riding his donkey one night and he was stopped by a woman who wanted a ride. He went over to her and looked at her, and suddenly he saw that she was horrible looking and had these long eyes shaped like dominoes. He was sure she was some kind of devil and was really scared. And do you know what? Shortly after that, another man had a similar thing happen. He had taken his garbage out to the area in the village that we used as a garbage dump. He saw a woman there crying, running her hands through her hair and tearing it out. He asked what had happened. She said her husband had beaten her. So he pitied her, and he took her to his house. But when he got there he realized that she was this same woman with the long domino eyes. He slammed the door shut. However, after that, from time to time this she-devil would reappear at his door and try to call him away.

"I was only a child at the time, but I believe these things really happened." Umm Ahmad looked at Maysa, who was maintaining a respectful, if noncommittal, silence. However, Abu Ahmad, who had just entered the salon to get the fan, could not contain himself. "A lot of nonsense," he said dismissively. "It was all in his imagination. She-devils with domino eyes—just rubbish!" Taking the fan, he began walking back to his *diwan*. Umm Ahmad, not wanting to contradict him openly, waited until he left and then continued.

"It's not rubbish at all," she said. "It's true. I believe this she-devil existed, and still exists. I don't know what these men did that caused her to appear, but it must have been something very bad. That's how it is, you do something wrong and you invite Satan, or the evil eye.

"Once you've been stricken by a devil or the evil eye, though, there are ways to rid yourself of the curse. You usually have to go to some *sheikh* or Koran reader who knows how to remove the spell. When I was a child there were a lot of these *sheikhs* around. Usually they were women—*sheikhas*. My husband's mother was not a *sheikha*, but she was a Koran reader. She knew how to touch a person's head and read a special passage from the Koran over them which would help get rid of the curse. She taught me the art, but I only do it a little now. I can't do what some of these *sheikhas* can do. They are really powerful. There are still some around. They can tell just by touching your hand if you are cursed. Or if the *sheikha* starts yawning while you are there, it's a sign you're cursed and the evil spirit is trying to exit through her mouth. Back when I was a girl, people went quite a lot for all kinds of things—if they were having trouble getting pregnant, or they had a bad marriage, or just any kind of bad luck. And the *sheikha* would help them.

"I remember my aunt went one time. She had had some bad luck. Her cows had been stolen. She wanted to know why this had happened, and also how she could get her cows back. So she went to this famous *sheikha* in Haifa. I don't know what the *sheikha* told my aunt about why it happened, but she told her that the stolen cows were just then under a tree in the wadi. My aunt rushed home and went out to the wadi, but there was nothing there. Not then, and not later either. She was very unhappy, and she thought that maybe the *sheikha* was no good or knew nothing. But do you know what happened? I swear this is true. Twenty years later I was sitting and talking with some people. There was this man there who had just come back from the *hajj* to Mecca, and he was talking freely about some bad things he had done in his life. And what he said was that twenty years ago he had bought some stolen cows. He had heard that some *sheikha* in Haifa told the woman who lost the cows— he didn't know she was my aunt—that her cows were out in the wadi under a tree. Well, the truth was he had bought those stolen cows out there in the wadi under a tree. The *sheikha* had been right after all!

"So you see, I believe in these things," Umm Ahmad concluded. "I could tell you many, many stories like this. But either you believe in these things or you do not. When I was a girl, I first heard about all this. And everything that I've seen since has convinced me it is true. Just as sure as God exists, so too does Satan in all his ways. About this I am sure."

6

AHMAD:
THE OLDEST SON

WHEN HE WAS TWO YEARS OLD, Ahmad almost drowned in the well in his grandfather's backyard. Umm Ahmad, who saved him, remembers the incident this way:

"We were over at my father's house, me and two of the children, Fatma and Ahmad. The men were building a new roof to the house. The work involved many hands, and I was there to do the cooking with the women. Out in the middle of the yard was a well, about six meters deep, where winter rains and water could be stored. The children were playing in the yard. Normally the well was covered by an iron lid, but because construction was going on, they put a straw mat over it so they could easily get to the water when they needed to make the mud mortar.

"What happened is that Ahmad climbed on top of the mat, and it slid into the well with him on it. A girl cousin saw him fall and came yelling, 'Ahmad's in the well! Ahmad fell into the well!' I ran and looked into the well. I saw the mat in the water and Ahmad's feet on the surface. The rest of him was under the water. I jumped in. I didn't have time to think, I just jumped. My fall made him disappear altogether. I stood there with water up to my chin, and since I didn't know how to swim, I began feeling around for him.

He wasn't in the mud where my feet were, but suddenly I felt him near my knees. I yanked him out and put him as high as I could—on my head. He began spitting up water. I shouted for help and then I saw a lot of faces up at the top looking down. They lowered a ladder and someone came down to help me out. Ahmad's eyes were closed. So someone came quickly with one of the two trucks in the village and rushed us to the Jewish army doctor in Karkur. He was the nearest one. When we got there the doctor pulled back Ahmad's eyelids and he awoke. Just like that! The doctor said everything was going to be all right. Then he turned to me and said that I didn't look so good. I almost fainted. I was pregnant in the fifth month with Ghanem, and a rock from the well must have cut my head. Blood was all over me. So the doctor sewed up my head, and soon I was feeling better.

"When it was all over, I took Ahmad in my arms and we went to pay the doctor. He asked me then if I knew how deep the water was when I jumped in the well. 'No' I said. Did I know how to swim? 'No,' I said. 'My good lady,' the doctor said, 'I can't take money from someone like you.' And he didn't. I felt very good. I could see that everything was going to be all right. It was only later, when I began thinking about it—and this I never told my husband, not even until today—I realized what must have caused it all. I understood that this had been God's way of punishing me—and also His way of showing mercy on me. I had been the one who had lied about the murder, lied about the knife in the well. And now God had brought me back to the well, and then spared me and my son."

Ever since he was born, Umm Ahmad had feared that her first son might be in danger of attracting the evil eye. That was the way it was with people or things that you most treasured: they managed to attract the evil eye, to serve as a fateful magnet for God's or man's revenge. And yet how could she not treasure her first son? All mothers in the village were guilty of the same thing: the first son was the jewel, the one who would lead the family someday, the one who gave *her* her deepest value, and the one she and her husband were named after. Of course she treasured Ahmad. And in her case, she adored him even more because he had come after a ten-year wait, after four daughters.

She remembered, as if it were yesterday, that bright, crisp January morning when Ahmad was born. Her husband had been over at a neighbor's house. She was at home, where she gave birth to all her children, and the women of the family and the midwife were there with her. It had been a difficult labor and she was in terrible pain. But when the midwife finally pulled the infant from her and announced, "It's a boy," all pain disappeared. There was a great celebration then—a celebration that would not have taken place if she had given birth to a girl. All the women began singing in joy and rushing out to the street to distribute candies to passersby. Someone immediately went off to bake a cake. And one of the women, the wife of her husband's brother, Ibrahim, had gone to find Abu Ahmad, who until that moment, of course, was still known simply as Ali. When his sister-in-law told him the news, he pulled a lot of money out of his pocket and gave it to her. He was overjoyed too. He, after all, had been waiting all those years, never criticizing, but hoping and praying for this day when his first son would arrive.

Umm Ahmad was the first to admit it, but felt it was only natural that right from the beginning she had "spoiled" her son. And not only she—everyone in the family. He had been given the best of everything: the best clothing, the best toys, the best food. And while she had nursed the other children for no more than a year, Ahmad was given the breast for almost two years, until he was talking and telling her, "Come here Mama, give me the breast," and then she had finally stopped. Umm Ahmad loved all her children, those that came before and after Ahmad, but she knew from the beginning that he was and always would be her favorite. And precisely because of this she worried and prayed for him constantly. The near-disaster in the well had only strengthened her worries and her prayers. She knew there was danger in treasuring Ahmad so much, but she could do nothing about this feeling. All she could do was to go on praying to God, whom she trusted with all her being—praying that her son would be given the blessings of health and happiness, and that some day he would grow to be a man who brought honor to the family.

At thirty-six years of age, Ahmad had the look of success. He was a thin man of average height, but handsome in a darkly elegant way, with piercing brown eyes and a carefully trimmed black moustache and black hair. He wore only the choicest fabrics from Europe, silk shirts, polished cotton slacks, and cashmere-velour sportscoats, and was probably the most dapper man in the village. Although he had built his expansive modern house out by the fields—he was the first to move so far from the village center—he seemed oddly out of place there, like a businessman visiting his relatives in the country.

In fact he was a businessman, and a very good one at that. After a few hesitant starts—as an electrical appliance salesman, an insurance broker, and a building contractor— he had at last found his way as a publisher and distributor of books. Since 1985, he had been working in this business. It was rumored that he had made a small fortune in just four years, and some even jokingly claimed that the battered white Mercedes he drove was merely a subterfuge to throw the income tax people off his trail. Ahmad, in any case, was not talking, and with the possible exception of his wife, Nufissa, nobody in the family, not even his brothers or father, knew about his finances. For their part, his brothers were willing to overlook this particular secretiveness, but Abu Ahmad felt it to be unnecessarily aloof and private and, indeed, just one more example of how his eldest son had strayed from him.

Actually, the two of them, Abu Ahmad and Ahmad, had been locked in a battle for as long as anyone could remember. Both were people with strong opinions, and each in his own way longed to be at the center of things. However, while Abu Ahmad sought power and influence through the use of tact and discretion, Ahmad delighted in display and even provocation. Like all his family, Ahmad was proud of his father's status within the clan and the village, and he himself was as loyal as anyone to the clan. Yet, unlike Ghanem and Hassan, he was determined somehow to step outside the shade of his father's protective umbrella and to seek his own spot in the sun. All his life he had felt that he had something special to offer, something uniquely his own, and long ago he had decided that nothing and nobody, not even his father, was going to get in his way.

"I've always been a rebel and had to do things my own way," Ahmad said to me one Friday afternoon as we sat in lounge chairs next to the rose garden he had planted in his back-yard, facing the fields. He looked relaxed that day, his day off from work, and was sipping a Scotch on the rocks while recalling some of his early years in the family. Ali, his nine-year-old son (named after Abu Ahmad), was playing basket-ball with a friend next to the garage, and Howla (11) and Siham (10) were helping their mother prepare a late lunch in the kitchen. "I suppose I was a tough kid," Ahmad contin-ued. "But I also tried very hard, at least for a few years, to show them—my father especially—that I could do what was expected of me around the farm. Actually, I tried to do the work better than anyone else. The hardest work was plow-ing, leaning on the wooden plow as it cut its way behind the horse. I was good at it though, good enough so that when I was twelve years old the family was even renting out me and the horse to plow our neighbor's fields."

Ahmad chuckled and poured himself another Scotch from the bottle that was hidden, in deference to Nufissa, inside a black plastic bag. "That old horse was a stubborn thing, but I got along with him. We called him Bilu. We *had* to call him Bilu—he wouldn't answer to any other name. It's actually a Jewish name, because he had belonged to a Jew. We bought him from this Jew, and when we tried to give him a new name, an Arab name, he wouldn't answer to it. So we called him Bilu, and for me he was willing to work real well.

"Until I was about fourteen years old, I worked hard and did my share around the farm. But I was getting tired of it, I admit. I could feel that the life of a *fellah* was not for me. I love the land, always have, and I love the village too. Yet I wanted to get out, see something, do something more. Anyway, it all came to a head one day in a strange way. I had been plowing all day with Bilu and I was exhausted. I was about to wind up work when my mother, not my father, called me over to help my brothers and sisters finish picking the string beans. 'I'm tired,' I told her. 'Never mind, we're all tired, you come help us,' she insisted. Well, I exploded. I started cursing her and the farm and the village. 'Go shove it all. I'm getting out of here. I've had it!' And then I said something like, 'You stay if you want, but I'm leaving. I'm getting out of here!' I stalked off. They must have thought I was just going home, but I knew differently. I was running *away* from home. And just like that, in my filthy work clothes, I took off.

"Now this was a wild thing to do right then, because there was a war going on. I haven't mentioned that. But it was about three or four days after the start of the June 1967 war. And there I was running away from home. I knew there was a war going on, but I had my own war with my family and that's all that mattered right then. And where did I go? The first night I made it to Baqa al Gharbiya, about ten kilometers from here, on the old border with Jordan. And the next day I crossed over to the West Bank and just began walking east through the hills. It was really crazy. I could have been killed easily by Israeli soldiers, who were all around. The fighting in the area had stopped, yet you could still smell the war—burnt out Jordanian tanks and over-turned autos, and fields cluttered with rocket and mortar casings. Me, I just kept walking high up in the hills. I suppose I looked like some shepherd boy, so nobody shot at me even though—I learned this later—there were curfews in the area where I was walking. By nightfall, I made it safely to Jenin where an aunt and uncle of mine lived. They fed and washed me. They also set about contacting my parents. This took a day or so because there were no telephones in the houses then. Anyway, three days after I left, my family came in a car and brought me home.

"And then I got the beating of my life! Not from my parents, they were too much in shock. They were furious at me for having left home and risking my life, but they were glad to have me back. My uncle Ibrahim, who's got a temper like nobody else I know, was the one who did the beating. He threw me into the shed behind my parents' house and locked the door. Then, like I was some animal, he bound my hands and feet with rope. With a stick, with his feet and fists, with anything lying there, he beat the shit out of me. I was screaming at the top of my voice. I think he would have killed me, or half-killed me, if it weren't for my mother and sisters, who broke down the wooden door and pulled him off me. My father didn't do a thing. He was just standing off to the side. He never would have beaten me like that himself, but he was glad it was done. He felt I deserved it. And in a way, I suppose I did."

Ahmad took a last swill of Scotch and then lit up a Nelson (British) cigarette. He called for Ali to go bring the lamb chops from the house, so he could put them on the grill. But Ali, engrossed in his game, answered that he would do it in a minute. Ahmad began screaming at him, though Ali did not move until his father rose from his lounge chair to come after him. Ahmad turned to me and muttered in a voice too low for Ali to hear, "Just like me, so help me God. Except even worse!" Then, poking the coals with a vengeance, he resumed his recollections.

"A few months after that episode of running away, I actually had to leave home anyway. There was no high school in Kufr Qara at the time. We didn't get one until 1972. So for boys my age, you either went to work in the fields or in construction, or you had to leave the village to go to high school. I went to Nazareth, about forty kilometers from here. Along with six others from our clan, I lived in a rented apartment there. We had no adult supervising us, we just watched over each other. When I look back on it, I can see that I was really too young to be away from home. But at the time I liked the freedom and the chance to see something more than Kufr Qara.

"The experience opened my eyes in a way. I became more of a free thinker. Religion stopped having any meaning for me. All the ritual—the praying and fasting—no longer made any sense to me, and I saw no point in pretending that it did. Also, I realized for sure that I could never be a *fellah* or simply stay in the village day after day. I wanted to be where the action was, in the cities and in the outside world.

"My parents didn't want me to be a *fellah* either at that point. They were glad to have me off studying. It was an honor to have your son as a student. They knew, my father especially, that the land was not extensive enough to have three sons working it and that education was a way of advancement. Look, in his time, if my father had been able to study outside, he would have gone, too. And with his mind, he could have been really something. So, in that way, he was glad to have me at high school. And when I graduated, he supported my going to university.

"The truth is, I was never that great a student in university. My mind was never fully into it. Some of my cousins whom I studied with in Nazareth went on to become doctors and lawyers. But that kind of career wasn't for me. What was for me? I didn't know. I knew I wanted to do something big, make some money. Just how, I had no idea. Anyway, I studied at Tel Aviv University for three years and then stopped. I never got a degree. The only thing I could do then was come back to the village and teach. You didn't need a degree then to teach in the village—now you do—so I was given a job teaching math in the primary school. I did this for ten years. Yes, *ten* years. I hated every minute of it. But I had a family to support and I had to have some money. What I also did to make money was to become a businessman on the side. Selling appliances, insurance, anything. And this I sort of liked. It took me out of the village, and I was very good at it. I knew how to sell things. Yet, again I could feel that it wasn't really what I wanted. I wanted to do something more exciting, something that had a bigger impact. And then finally, just by luck, I stumbled onto the thing that was right for me. Publishing books. That's a real story how that happened, but let's hold off a minute—"

Ahmad, who had been cooking the lamb chops on the grill, suggested we eat. His two daughters and Nufissa had put out a spread of homemade salads on the table (Nufissa was known as the best cook in the family), and we all began eating. Everyone except Ali was there; he had wandered off.

Ahmad was furious at him, and between gulps of food he kept lecturing Nufissa about the need to "straighten that boy out." Nufissa listened quietly, as did the daughters, who were seemingly unbothered by their father's harangue. When we finally finished eating and were drinking cups of thick, cardamom-laced coffee, Ali reappeared. But he quickly ducked into the house, and Ahmad, who had resumed talking, just ignored him.

"My lucky break," Ahmad said, "came when I went to the book fair in Frankfurt in October 1985. I was on vacation in Germany and just decided to visit the fair. There were books from all over the world there, including Palestinian books published by the PLO. These books were printed on fine paper, with attractive and expensive jackets—European-quality books, not like the cheap stuff in Arabic that we were used to seeing here. Well, a light flashed in my head. I was sure there was a market here for fine printed books on Palestine, and I figured maybe I could be the one to get into it first. Why not? It was worth a try. What I chose was the four-volume encyclopedia on Palestine that had just been put out by the PLO publishing house. I asked them to give me the rights and they did so gladly. I didn't even have to pay a shekel for it. Then I took a set with me in my suitcase and came back to Israel. Nobody at customs looked too closely, and I of course said nothing about what I was carrying. Was it legal to have it? I thought so, but I surely wasn't going to ask anyone right then.

"I decided to publish it secretly. Not go to the Israeli censor. Not ask permission from anyone. I found a printer—I won't say where—and immediately I went around to a lot of Arabs in Israel and the West Bank, and sold a hundred and sixty sets before we even started printing. That paid about half my expenses for printing two thousand sets. I was taking a big gamble, but if it worked I knew I had my start in the publishing business. And it worked! Those two thousand sets sold immediately and I made a real good profit. And we pulled off the most important publishing venture in recent Palestinian history. Not since 1948 had anything so important happened. Suddenly, out of nowhere, I became a name in the field. I felt great—really I did.

"As could be expected, though, the Israeli authorities came after me. People from the security services hauled me in one night at 2:00 A.M. They wanted to know where I printed the books, who bought them, and all that. By then I had checked into it and found out that as an Israeli citizen I didn't have to tell them those things. And so I refused. All they could do was to put a halt to my printing the books. And that they did. But by then it was too late. I had distributed them all. So, they kept harassing me, calling me into the office, making me wait there all day, humiliating me and calling me an *ibn sharmoota* [son of a whore], and things like that. I wasn't beaten, wasn't jailed, and while I had to pay a lot of taxes, I still made out real well. I had my start. From then on I knew I'd have the authorities watching over me, but it didn't matter. I was on my way."

Within four years Ahmad built his operation into one of the larger Arab-language publishing companies in Israel. Working day and night, he was a one-man show: editor, proofreader, accountant, and distributor. By 1989, he had published some thirty books, including reprints of works already published in Arab countries or by the PLO, translations of Hebrew books, and, more recently, some first printings of Palestinian authors.

He was not only making money, but, even more important in his mind, he had managed to enter the limelight, to become somebody who was known and worth knowing. Big-name local writers were courting *him* now, poets and novelists and other intellectuals, all of whom wanted him to publish their works. Several times a year he went on business trips to Europe or Arab countries (Egypt and Jordan), and he had even managed to hobnob with some of the big politicos in the Palestinian diaspora. Indeed, on one recent trip to Cairo, at a convention of Palestinian intellectuals, he had spent time with PLO Chairman Yasir Arafat—an encounter which, wisely or not, he flaunted when he returned to Kufr Qara.

As for his family, they were proud of his success, especially Umm Ahmad, who had prayed so hard and long that her eldest son would distinguish himself as she, above all, knew he could. Ghanem and Hassan, too, were glad for him, glad he was making a good name for the family and also glad he was doing well financially. In fact, the only one who seemed to harbor doubts was Abu Ahmad. He was pleased with his son's success and enjoyed reading, and even handling, the crisp new editions that Ahmad brought him. Yet he worried aloud that sooner or later Ahmad would do something to damage himself and, by extension, the family.

"I'm not worried about the government censors and the chances he has taken with them," explained Abu Ahmad. "He's a sweet talker and he knows how to cover himself there. What bothers me are his finances. He's too loose, and the income tax people have been after him before. He's made a lot of money. God alone knows what he does with it. I for sure don't know. The only thing I know is that my son, as smart as he is in business, is sometimes very foolish. I wish him all the luck in the world. But will he be able to stay out of trouble? I don't know. It's in the hands of God."

"My father worries for me, I know he does," said Ahmad. "Always has. I've given him some hard times, and he's thrown up his hands more than once and said, 'I want nothing more to do with you, go your own way!' Still, he's my father, and he's as strong-willed and opinionated as I am, and I know that beneath it all he's proud of me." Ahmad preened himself while looking in the rearview mirror of his Mercedes, and added, "And really, why shouldn't he feel proud? I *have* done something, no?"

We were driving along the Wadi Ara road on the way to a couple of villages where he had sold some books and was now collecting the money. Just over the ridge was the West Bank, and I asked him whether he did much business in the occupied territories. "Before the *intifada*, lots," he answered. "Now, almost none. I try to stay out of there. Not safe." And he began relating how only a few months before, while he was driving in the territories, his car had been stoned. The rock passed through the front window and landed in the back seat. "I could have been killed. The *shabaab* [youths] saw my yellow Israeli license plates—not blue ones like they have in the territories—and they started throwing stones." He forced a laugh. "If you're an Israeli Arab you get it from both sides. The Jews give you hell in Israel because you're an Arab, and the Arabs from the territories cause you problems because you're from Israel. Crazy, no?"

He tapped a Nelson on the dashboard and poked the cigarette into the corner of his mouth. "But I can't complain. Business these days is good enough in Israel. There are plenty of Arabs here with good educations and they buy books. I broke into the market at just the right time and I've made out real well. The problem is, you've got to stay sharp. Others see that there's a profit to be made, and the next thing you know they're moving in on your territory. That's capitalism, no?" He smiled maliciously. "And I'm a capitalist, right? I tell you, I have had to beat out more than a few competitors. Including even a guy who was a friend of mine. The son of a bitch was working for me as a salesman—on a commission basis, that's how I work it. The next thing I know, he's out there doing what I am, printing his own books. Well, friend or not, I crushed him. Don't ask me how. It wasn't a nice thing, but that's what you have to do to make it in business. Survival of the fittest, right?

"There are people who say I'm a son of a bitch, that I'm in it for the money and I'll do anything for the money. I know there's talk like this. And look, I'll be the first to tell you, money is an important thing and I like the good life. Good food, good drink, and fine clothes—though no screwing around. No other women for me except my wife. Surprises you? Well, it's the truth, and if I was a guy who swore on the Koran, I'd swear on the Koran that it's true. In this way I'm like my father. No women other than my wife." Ahmad put his hand with the lit cigarette across his heart and the ashes dropped all over his cashmere sweater. He brushed himself vigorously. "But money isn't the only reason I'm doing this work. I could make a bundle putting out pornography, but that's against my values. I won't do it. And Muslim fundamentalist literature—there's lots of money there these days. But I can't stand those guys, and I won't put out anything by them.

"When I got into this business, sure, I saw it as a money maker. Yet it's a strange thing that happens to you when you're in the book business. At least it happened to me. It's not like selling electrical appliances or insurance. In publishing, you meet the real cream of the society. Who was I? A nobody. And now I'm on a first-name basis with all these people. Poets, novelists, politicians. It does something to you. It makes you feel a certain responsibility. As a Palestinian, I mean. It makes you see that you've got a certain role to play. As a publisher of books, I'm in a position to do some good things for my people, meaningful things. And I do. Anyone who knows my company knows I do. The Israeli authorities for sure know it!" Ahmad pulled his car in front of the house of a schoolteacher who owed him several hundred shekels. He grabbed his leather briefcase, slicked back his hair, and added as he walked off, "And if I make a few shekels in the process, what's wrong with that? So much the better, no?"

7

ECHOES OF THE INTIFADA

IN DECEMBER 1987, a seldom used Arabic word entered the global vocabulary as well as the common parlance of Arabs and Jews throughout Israel and its territories: *intifada*, or uprising. After twenty years of occupation, Palestinians in the Gaza Strip and West Bank rose up against Israel. As so often happens, it was all triggered by a relatively minor incident. On the afternoon of December 8, a truck driven by an Israeli in the Gaza Strip swerved into a car transporting laborers from the area; four men were killed instantly and several more were wounded. Within hours of this incident, rumors began to spread throughout the Gaza Strip (population: 600,000) that the accident had been a deliberate act, a retaliation for the stabbing of a Jew two days earlier in Gaza's main market. Angry crowds gathered, rocks were thrown at Israeli army patrols, tires were burned—in short, full-scale riots broke out. But unlike other riots, these did not stop that night, nor the next day, nor the day after that. They just kept going and they spread.

Within days there were also riots throughout the West Bank (population 900,000), and in East Jerusalem (population 135,000). The Palestinians living there, generally more quiescent than their compatriots in Gaza, this time erupted in a similar fury. And there too, Israeli army reinforcements were called in to put out the flame, as they had been in

Gaza. But again they did not succeed. Casualties quickly began to mount, and as usual the media were there to catch it all: the *keffiyeh*-wrapped kids hurling stones and Molotov cocktails, and the Israeli soldiers pursuing them with batons and bullets. By the time the second week had ended, it was clear to most everyone that these ongoing riots in the West Bank and Gaza were something new—an uprising of the population, an *intifada*.

For the 700,000 Arabs living in Israel, these first two weeks of the *intifada* were a time of great excitement and turmoil. Like other citizens of Israel, they followed the daily events closely on TV and in the newspapers. Yet, unlike other Israelis, they were rooting for the *tifl el-hijreh*, the children of the stones. At the end of the second week of the uprising, on December 21, Arab leaders in Israel (specifically the National Committee of Arab Mayors and Local Council Chairmen)[1] decided to call for a general strike in solidarity with their fellow Palestinians in the territories. What happened then was a shock to almost everyone. Not only did the vast majority of the Arab population observe the strike, but in many places *in* Israel young Arabs carried out their own day-long uprising. Stones and even Molotov cocktails were hurled at vehicles, tires were burned, roads were barricaded, and Palestinian flags were unfurled. For a brief moment, it looked as if there might be an *intifada* on both sides of "the green line."[2]

However, for the Arabs within Israel, and particularly for the young people who took to the streets that December 21, their *intifada* would be short-lived. The National Committee of Arab Mayors and Local Council Chairmen imme-

---

[1]The National Committee of Arab Mayors and Local Council Chairmen is sometimes referred to as "the unofficial parliament" of Arabs in Israel. In addition to the heads of most Arab villages, towns, and cities, it includes in its plenum all Arab members of the Knesset (Israeli parliament), representatives from the Histadrut (the national labor federation) and the teacher's union, and a number of other important Arab figures.

[2]The "green line" is the borderline between Israel and the surrounding Arab states of Egypt, Syria, and Jordan during the period 1949–67. It is so called because on international maps this borderline was colored green. Today it is common to

diately denounced the eruption of violence and diplomatically promised to do their best to head off any further outbreaks. At the same time, reflecting the highly complex position in which they as Arabs in Israel found themselves, the National Committee made it clear that they would also continue to support the *intifada* in the occupied territories— by every legal means at their disposal. They would send food, medicine, and money. In addition, they would continue to speak out openly on behalf of their compatriots in the territories, who in their view were fighting the good fight.

This position, delineated by the Arab leadership in Israel during the first few weeks of the *intifada*, has continued to be the political beacon of almost all Arabs in Israel. To be sure, there have been a number of individual acts of violence since then, yet by and large the Palestinian Arabs in Israel (as they generally prefer to be called these days) have not resorted to extra-legal means; they have not attempted to bring the *intifada* to Israel. Instead, they have stayed on the sidelines, watching with a mixture of sadness and rage as they find themselves in the painful dilemma of— as some of them put it—"having my country at war with my people."

Abu Ahmad was a man of firm opinions—and not least of all on political matters. I had known him several months before he spoke about the *intifada*, and when he finally did, it was with heartfelt conviction. We were seated that day as usual in his *diwan*, and by his side was a copy of the Hebrew newspaper, *Yediot Ahronot*. He had just finished reading an item about an arson attack in the Galilee, in which local Arab youths had attempted to burn down the apple orchard of a Jewish settlement. The item obviously had upset him, and he sat there shaking his head back and forth. "No, no, it's not the way," he said and then added emphatically, "We

---

refer to Israel's pre-1967 territory as "within the green line" and to land conquered in the June War (1967) and still occupied by Israel as "across the green line."

in Israel cannot—absolutely cannot–use violence. Our leaders know it. And even Arafat himself has said it—Arabs in Israel must not use force. We must work *within* the system. Otherwise we'll only hurt ourselves, and hurt the *intifada* too."

He then went on to recall the explosive first weeks of the *intifada* and that day when the uprising briefly came to Israel itself. He, personally, had been against the strike call because he thought it might get out of hand. And unfortunately, he had been right. In the Wadi Ara area, a few kilometers east of Kufr Qara, "some fools" had thrown rocks and Molotov cocktails at passing cars and caused the main Wadi Ara road to be closed for two hours. When he had seen the TV footage of the incident that night, he had been ashamed—and worried. Why worried? Because if the violence had continued, there would have been severe repercussions for Israel's Arabs.

"I have lived here long enough to know what can happen," he said. "And I think I understand a little about what's going on in the Jews' heads. The *intifada* has them scared, and they're looking for a way to wipe it out. But they can't just go in and crush it with tanks and planes. The world is looking in, watching them closely. They, and the Palestinians too. Palestinians in the occupied territories *can* throw stones, like David fighting Goliath, but they can't use live ammunition. That is *their* limitation. And *our* limitation— I'm talking about Israeli Arabs—is that we can use no violence at all. No stones, no Molotov cocktails, no arson attacks. The moment we in Israel choose force, we invite the Jews to say, 'Look, we're being attacked by *all* the Arabs in the area. We have no choice but to crush them any way we can.' They're waiting for a chance to do this. And we would be fools to give them that chance. We'd hurt ourselves and the *intifada* at the same time.

"So what can we in Israel do?" Abu Ahmad continued. "A little, but not much. We can give the people in the territories money and food—things like that. In the early weeks of the *intifada*, a number of us in Kufr Qara loaded up a truck and brought all kinds of provisions over to this village in the West Bank. I know a few people there and I wanted to help them out. Since then, though, I've hardly been back. There's no point in it. Sometimes here in Kufr Qara people go around and take up a collection for some village over there. Or, at the mosques on Friday, money is sometimes collected. I give just as others give, but really that's about all we can do for them. We're with them in our hearts, of course, and personally I think they're going to win. I wasn't so sure in the beginning. Now—what is it, about fifteen months since it started?—well, I'm more sure. Arafat at last is playing his cards right, and there are one hundred and fifty countries who now recognize the PLO. Even the United States has begun to talk to them. So, in the long run it looks good. There will be a Palestinian state. Whether I'll live long enough to see it, I don't know. But it will come to pass, I'm almost sure."

As the *intifada* entered its second summer in 1989, it was clear to everyone, Jews and Arabs alike, that the uprising had become a war of attrition. And while there was much scurrying about by politicians representing both sides, it also became clear that no negotiated settlement was within sight. The PLO had won some important diplomatic victories, no doubt about it. But they had failed to convince the Israelis to sit down with them, and for the time being the Americans were placing little pressure on their long-standing allies to do so.

As the uprising went on, bloody day after bloody day, an ugly mood settled over Israel: exasperation and grief were everywhere, like a summer heat wave. Tension between the two communities, always there beneath the surface, was now fully out in the open. With the Arabs of Israel continuing to make no attempt to hide where their sympathies lay, many Jews—including a number of public officials—accused them of damaging, even betraying, the country. And incidents of frank racism, though repulsive to most Jews, nonetheless were happening with disturbing regularity.

In Kufr Qara, the mood was also bleak. One sensed that the *intifada* was never far from people's minds, though generally they preferred not to talk about it. Sometimes, however—usually after some major incident—they could not keep from talking, and then out came the stored bitterness and shared resentment.

One such incident early that summer was a racially motivated attack on three Arab bathers in Caesarea. According to the newspaper accounts (the incident was widely reported in both the Hebrew and Arabic press), a mob of Jewish bathers had attempted to chase the Arab men from the beach, and in so doing they had savagely beaten them. The following morning, as Hassan and I took a break from picking peppers, he began talking about "the outrage." Sitting with us was Samir, who had come by to borrow some vegetable crates from Hassan and stayed on when he caught the gist of the conversation.

"When you see things like this beach outrage," Hassan began, "it makes you feel like there's no hope."

"Hope?" Samir pounded his fist into a vegetable crate. "The only hope is to take a gun and go after those bastards. It's the only thing they understand."

Hassan shook his head slowly, but it was not clear whether he was disagreeing with Samir, or just expressing his disgust. "You can't even go to the beach anymore. These racist bastards are everywhere." Turning to me, he added, "I know people—quite a few really—that won't even go out of the village these days. Not even to Hadera to buy an ice cream. They're afraid, really afraid."

"Not me!" boomed Samir, thrusting his heavy jaw forward. "I'll be damned if I'll let them scare me off. Just three days ago I was there in Caesarea myself, along with Mustafa and Hammad. And we're going again tomorrow. I'd just like to see those Jewish punks try something!"

Ignoring Samir's remarks, Hassan continued, still speaking to me. "This may not sound like much, but I'll tell you something that happened to me just the other day. I was in Hadera, at this clothing store, buying a pair of slacks for the wedding. Me and Ahmad, we went together. The clothing store is owned by this Jewish guy. I've gone there many times over the last few years. Anyway, I pick out the slacks and go to pay the guy with a check, as usual. He tells me that he wants cash—that's the policy now. 'All right,' I

say, 'I'll get cash.' I'm about to leave when I notice that the
guy after me, a guy with a yarmulke, is paying for his clothes
with a check. 'Hey, what's going on here?' I ask the owner
after the guy with the yarmulke is gone. 'You took his check,
and not mine. How come?' The owner looks at me and, not
even embarrassed, he says, 'Look pal, that's the way it is
now. For Arabs, cash only. No more checks.' I tell you, I
couldn't believe it—"

"Believe it! Believe it!" Samir's face was flushed with
anger. "You should have beaten his ass."

"My brother almost did," answered Hassan. "He threw
the pants at the guy and started screaming at him, 'You
filthy, racist bastard! After all these years, you treat us like
that?' I had to pull Ahmad out of the store. I wanted no
troubles. I was angry as hell, but what was the point of
beating him? What would come out of it?"

Samir rose and started pacing about, more agitated
than I had seen him before. Hassan continued to sit for
awhile in silence and then went off to get some coffee. While
he was gone, Samir, still standing but somewhat calmer,
began talking about some things he had seen recently—not
in Israel, but in the West Bank. He still went there regularly,
he said, sometimes alone and sometimes with his father.
Unlike Hassan, he had relatives over there in several villages, including his father's sister, who had married a man
from a West Bank village before the war in 1948, and was
still living there.

"Because I've got family over there," Samir said, "I know
what's going on. Better than Hassan does. I've seen things
there the last year and half which I'll never forget. Never.
Like—just a few weeks ago—I was over there and I got
caught in the middle of one of those battles between the
kids and the Jews. Outside my aunt's village. The kids were
throwing stones and the soldiers went after them. With my
own eyes I saw them catch this kid. He couldn't have been
more than, say, eight years old." Samir glanced at Hassan,
who had sat down and was pouring the coffee. "I told you
about this, Hassan—remember? They threw the kid on the
ground and began kicking the shit out of him. Several soldiers, all at once. I thought they were going to kill him. On

and on it went. I wanted so much to help this kid. I think if I had a rifle with me I would have used it. But what could I do with my bare hands against all of them?"

"Nothing, absolutely nothing," affirmed Hassan solemnly. "You can't do anything."

"But I tell you, I admire those kids," Samir said. "They're out there every day with nothing but stones. And they're up against live ammunition. You think they're scared? Hell no! I don't know where they get the courage."

"Me neither," agreed Hassan.

"But courage they have. And plenty of it. They're real heroes, these kids. No doubt about it. Real heroes."

For Kufr Qara's farmers, the summer was a time when many hands were needed to harvest the vegetables. Tomatoes, in particular, required a good deal of manual labor—picking, sorting, and crating—and two or three people were simply not enough. Hassan had hoped that Ahmad's son, Ali, might be willing to pitch in. But Ali, just like his father, turned out to have no taste for farming (except for driving Hassan's tractor), and Hassan saw no point in asserting his rightful authority and demanding Ali's assistance. So he had to turn elsewhere to find help.

For the past two summers—in fact, since the start of the *intifada*—Hassan had found that his steadiest, and least expensive, help were a number of kids who lived over in the territories, in a village five kilometers away. Schools in the territories had been shut down since the early weeks of the uprising, and these kids, boys from ten to fifteen years old, were eager to have the work. Hassan, as well as other Kufr Qara farmers, had his "regulars" who came by each morning at the height of the harvest. And for the wage of ten shekels, plus all the vegetables they could carry home, the boys worked from 7:00 A.M. to 1:00 P.M. ("I wish I could pay them more," Hassan claimed. "But believe me, what they're bringing home is really helping their families. A lot of their fathers are out of work, and some of these people are living on nothing these days.")

They were a ragamuffin crew, these boys who came to

work in Hassan's fields. In their torn shirts and pants, their floppy shoes and their unkempt hair, they were immediately distinguishable from Kufr Qara's neat and well-groomed kids: the distinction, quite simply, between haves and have-nots. Yet there was also something else that was different about these boys from the territories. It was a difference that one saw especially in their eyes. At ten and twelve years old, they already had lost something of their youthful innocence, and when they looked at you there was a glint in their eyes that was both defiant and precociously shrewd.

As could well be imagined, they found my presence in Hassan's fields rather surprising. At first they were a bit suspicious of "the professor" (which is what they called me once they learned that I worked at the Hebrew University), but with Hassan's help their wariness gave way to good-natured curiosity. They asked all kinds of questions about America, including political questions: Why was President Bush so much in love with Israel? Did the Americans know about "our *intifada*"? Couldn't they see how the Israeli soldiers were criminals and murderers?

For my benefit, it seemed, there was also a lot of boasting about "our *intifada*," and had it not been for the look in their eyes, I probably wouldn't have believed any of it.

"The Israelis are no match for us. We stand right up to them," bragged a curly-haired boy, about thirteen years old, one morning as we were picking tomatoes together.

"Whenever the soldiers come, we run them wild through the village," said another boy right next to us, who was wearing a tattered red and white Coca-Cola tee shirt. "Mohsen, show him your arm," he said to the first boy. Then he added, "Mohsen here, he's got the hardest throw in the village."

Mohsen picked a green tomato off a plant, checked to make sure Hassan wasn't watching him, and then, with the rifle arm of a third baseman, he sidearmed the tomato a good fifty meters over the fields.

"Not bad, eh?" said the boy with the Coca-Cola tee shirt, smacking his friend on the shoulder. "Mohsen knows what he's doing. A professor of the *intifada*!" They both laughed wildly, their eyes filling with tears.

Moments later Mohsen said, "We're going to win, no doubt about it. This year, next year, we're going to chase the Jews out. And if stones don't do it, we'll get guns. One way or another, we're going to run them off."

"Right," agreed the Coca-Cola tee shirt boy. "Tell that to President Bush. Another year or so, it's a Palestinian state. No doubt about it. We're on our way!" And as if they were posing for a TV camera, both boys flashed victory signs with their fingers, and Mohsen picked another green tomato and tossed it down the row at some uncertain target.

Later that morning, as the boys had finished working and were loading up their plastic department-store bags with tomatoes and peppers, Samir came by on his tractor. He too had a few boys working with him that morning in the fields, and he came by because "there is one kid with me that you've got to meet. No questions, just come!" Samir told Hassan to come too, but he wasn't interested. So the two of us went off together on his tractor.

Samir's fields were located about a half-kilometer from Hassan's fields, and while we were riding there he briefly told me about Issa, "the most impressive kid I've seen—a cut above the rest." Issa came from the West Bank village of Barta'a. He had been working with Samir the past month. The previous two days, however, Issa had failed to show up, and this morning—after much prodding from Samir—he explained why he hadn't come. Issa, it turns out, was one of the leaders of an important *shabaab* faction in his village. Earlier in the week he had been given the task of printing up and distributing a leaflet. By accident, he had signed the leaflet with the name of the wrong faction. That night a group of masked *shabaab*, many from his faction, took him out into the hills and grilled him all night on his error, attempting to determine his motivations. He was pushed around and threatened for several hours. Finally, convinced that it was an accident as Issa claimed, they released him; but as a punishment, he was removed from his leadership position. Issa admitted that he had been shaken by the incident, and for a couple of days he had not felt like doing anything.

He was sitting there waiting for us under an apple tree,

a handsome athletic-looking boy of about fifteen, with close-cropped black hair and a thin moustache. Unlike other kids from the territories, he wore new clothes and tennis sneakers, and considering the ordeal he had described to Samir, he was remarkably calm. His eyes were without pain or defiance, but rather radiated an unexpected warmth and an evident intelligence. In another setting, an American one, I would have taken him for an honor student and perhaps a member of his high school tennis or track team.

Altogether, Issa and I talked for about an hour (Samir stayed out of it after having made the introductions), and to my surprise, he was frank and forthcoming. Yes, he acknowledged, it was true that he had been one of the *shabaab* leaders in his village until recently. He had been involved in the *intifada* since the beginning, and he intended to remain involved as long as it went on—or until he was arrested or killed. He said all this matter-of-factly, without the slightest swagger, and when I asked him if he was afraid, he immediately answered, "Of course I'm afraid. You cannot stand opposite someone who has live ammunition, and who you know is going to use it any time, without being afraid. But these are the risks we must take, and do take. We are willing to pay the price." And what kind of price had his village paid so far? "Nobody has been killed. We've been lucky," he answered. "But we've had forty or fifty injured, about ten of them seriously. About three or four of the *shabaab* are in jail now, another three have had their homes cemented shut, and one had his home blown up."

What did his family think of all this? Were they behind him? "I'm the oldest of seven," he answered. "My father and mother know I'm involved, but they don't know exactly how. They worry for me—that's natural. My father has the same feelings I do, he just doesn't get involved. He stays out of it, or tries to. Sometimes, though, you get dragged into it, even if you don't want to. Once, in the early days of the *intifada*, the soldiers came to our house and grabbed my father—he hadn't done anything—and in front of all of us, my mother included, they forced him to wash Palestinian slogans from the walls outside on the street. My father came back with his head bowed. It was very hard for me to see. If I could have, I would have killed those soldiers on the spot—wait, are you going to write that? Well, yes, go ahead and write it. That's what they deserve. I tell you, they do things like that and then they go and say they want to make peace with us. Is that possible, you tell me?"

Issa's face reddened as he said this, and for the first time his eyes lost their warmth. A certain brooding resentment came over him, and he sat for a minute or two in silence— though it felt like much longer—until finally, in a determined voice, he continued: "There is not going to be any peace. The Israelis don't want it, and neither do the Americans. They are not ready to give us our state, so what peace can there be? There will only be war. Iraq and Syria will fight against Israel. That's the way I see it. Eventually we will have our state. Either that, or we'll all die fighting for it. For us in the territories, there is no other way."

Issa glanced at Samir, who was listening intently, though his face was bent downward as he played with some small stones. Issa continued, "The only people I can't figure are the Palestinians here in Israel. They are our cousins and should be with us—not just in words, in deeds. But where are they?" Samir, uncharacteristically, remained without a retort and continued to look downward. In a tone that was more sorrowful than challenging, Issa then concluded, "They are a beaten people, these Palestinians in Israel. Not like us in the territories. Together we could really put up a fight. But no, they won't help us. I'm sorry to say this, Samir, but our cousins here just don't know how to fight. Something has happened to them. All these years living under the Israelis, I think. I don't know really why, but they just have no more fight in them."

And with that, Issa rose and politely said that he had to leave. Slowly and heavily, Samir rose with him. Then, flicking some stones off into the fields, Samir said to nobody in particular, "What can I say? The kid's right. Something *has* happened to us. What can I say?"

8

1947–1949:
IL NAKBA

THE PERIOD FROM NOVEMBER 1947 to July 1949 was the most decisive interval in the modern history of Israel/Palestine. The British decided in early 1947 to relinquish the mandate by which they had ruled Palestine since 1922, and the United Nations, on November 29, 1947, recommended partition of the territory into two states, one Jewish and one Arab. The result was war.

From the time of the partition decision until the British forces evacuated Palestine on May 15, 1948, a civil war raged between Jewish forces and Palestinian forces, who were aided by some five thousand irregulars from surrounding Arab states. On May 15 (the State of Israel was proclaimed on May 14), the regular armies of five Arab states—Iraq, Lebanon, Syria, Jordan, and Egypt—entered the battle. Fighting, interrupted by two truces, continued until January 1949, after which armistice agreements were signed between February and July of 1949. As a consequence of the war, approximately 370 Palestinian villages and towns were destroyed, and between 600,000 and 760,000 Palestinians became refugees. The western portion of the territory that had been earmarked for a Palestinian state in the partition recommendation was absorbed into the new state of Israel; the eastern portion was annexed by King Abdullah of Transjordan. In light of the results of this war, it is not surprising that the Jews refer to it as Milchemet Hashichrur, the War of Liberation. Nor is it surprising that for Palestinians this war and period are called by another name—il Nakba, the Disaster.

Kufr Qara, on the eve of partition, was a quiet place of about fifteen hundred inhabitants. Almost all were families of *fellaheen* who worked daily in their fields and whose contact with the outside world was minimal. Two Arab villages located two kilometers or so to the east, Ara and Ar'ara, were the closest neighbors. A Jewish kibbutz, Kfar Glickson, some three kilometers to the west, was the next closest settlement. The fields of Kfar Glickson abutted those of Kufr Qara, and over the years a few relationships had developed between farmers from the kibbutz and farmers from Kufr Qara, who worked, as it were, side by side. Abu Ahmad was one of these farmers.

When the partition recommendation was announced, it became clear that the border between the proposed Jewish and Palestinian states would fall, in the Wadi Ara area, smack between Kufr Qara and Kfar Glickson. The kibbutz, in other words, would be sitting across the border from the new Palestinian state; similarly, Kufr Qara would be sitting across the border from the new Jewish state. As happened in many places where Jews and Arabs had worked out a *modus vivendi*, pledges were made between individuals to not take up arms against each other, to protect one another.

But goodwill between individuals notwithstanding, when war came to the area, people inexorably became caught up in it. On May 8, 1948, in an attempt to conquer the Wadi Ara area, Jewish forces attacked Kufr Qara from the west. Women, children, and most men fled, but a small contingent of Kufr Qara's men stayed to fight. They were bolstered by a large number of Iraqi troops, who rushed to the scene and counterattacked in support of the interests of the Transjordanians (the Iraqi and Transjordanian kings were brothers). The net result was a standoff. And that's the way the positions remained until the end of the war: Jewish forces sitting on a ridge just a kilometer west of the center

of Kufr Qara, and Iraqi forces occupying another ridge a
few hundred meters to the east. The village itself became a
no-man's-land, its inhabitants scattered to wherever they
could find shelter. Most of them went to nearby villages that
were under the control of Iraqi or Transjordanian forces.

Eleven months later the war was over. As part of the
armistice agreement of April 3, 1949 between King Abdullah
of Transjordan and the new state of Israel, the king agreed
to turn over to Israel a large strip of territory in and around
the Wadi Ara area. Some fifteen Arab villages were located
within this area; Kufr Qara, on its northwestern edge, was
one of them. When Kufr Qara's residents returned to their
homes—and almost all did rush back in early April 1949—
they had no idea what would happen to them. Would the
Jews allow them to stay, or would they be driven off and
made permanent refugees? They had no way of knowing
that precisely then a debate was going on within the Israeli
government: whether indeed to abide by the terms of the
armistice agreement with King Abdullah and let the people
stay, or whether, out of "security reasons," to somehow force
out the Arab inhabitants of these fifteen or so villages and
thereby incur the wrath of the United Nations, the United
States, and King Abdullah. In the end, Israel decided to
allow the inhabitants to stay.

At the outset of these events, Abu Ahmad was twenty-nine
years old, and Umm Ahmad was twenty-two. They had two
children: Fatma, who was four and a half years old, and
Nihal, eleven months old. Together, along with Abu Ahmad's
mother and younger brother, Ibrahim (who had not yet married), they lived in the house where Abu Ahmad had been
born. Abu Ahmad was head of the family, and had been so
since 1944, when his older brother died suddenly of a blood
infection. Though quite young, he was also an important
voice in his clan and in the entire village. The role that he
played during the war was a pivotal one, and to this day it
is commonly said in Kufr Qara that if one wants to know
what happened there during il Nakba, he is the man to talk
to.

Abu Ahmad's recollections of this period were told to me over several days, though they appear here as a continuous story. Preceding them below are the recollections of Fatma and Umm Ahmad, the two members of Abu Ahmad's immediate family who remember living through this time with him.

FATMA:

"I was a small girl then, only four and a half years old, and my memories are not so clear. I was not sure what was going on. But still, I do remember some things exactly. Before the war actually began, there had been talk among the adults, especially from my grandmother. She talked about these people—Jews—who were going to make war on us, and if they caught us alive they would kill us. I was very afraid of this. But the truth was I had only seen one Jew in my life— one man and his family. This man was named 'Moti,' or something like that. He would come sometimes to visit my father. He'd bring his family, his wife and children. He was such a nice man and he had a nice family, so I was surprised to hear that his people, the Jews, were going to kill us. But I believed my grandmother when she said we would have to hide when they came.

"Then one morning I woke up and there was the sound of guns. My mother came over to me while I was lying in bed and said a blessing over me—*Ismallah alik*, may God watch over you. She told me that we would have to go quickly—me, my grandmother, and her—and, I think, my sister too. She said my father wouldn't be going with us right then because he was at work; but he would come later. I was too young at the time to know that my father wasn't really at work but had taken a rifle and was going to fight for the village. I guess they didn't want to frighten me.

"We went quickly, we had no time to take anything. I wore a dress and that was it. I went barefoot. My mother, seeing it was hard for me to walk over the stones, took me in her arms and carried me. There were gunshots all around and I was scared, especially because we had seen some people badly shot as we left the village. There were two or three of them as I remember, and I think they were either dead or dying. They were full of blood. But I felt my mother and grandmother would protect me. As we went, we met a man from some other village than ours, and he was a kind man. He let me get on his horse with him, and we all went to this other village, Ar'ara. I had an uncle living there and we went to stay with him and his family. My father, who had been working that day—really he was fighting—came home at night. He told us we couldn't go back to the village yet. So we stayed in Ar'ara.

"I remember the time in Ar'ara as a very bad time. I didn't like it there because we had to stay indoors almost all the time. The children in Ar'ara wouldn't play with us. They always chased us away, yelling, 'This is not your place, go back to your own village!' They didn't want us there. So we had to stay in the house, and mostly with my grandmother, who took care of us, played with us, and told us stories.

"Once in a while, my mother and grandmother would go back to Kufr Qara, and once they even took me. They went back to get things from the house, and also to harvest the grain and corn from the fields, our fields. But they couldn't stay there because the Jews fired at them and were trying to kill them. I had bad dreams about this. I would dream that the Jews were coming to kill us—there would be shots, and I'd wake up very scared. I wouldn't go to my mother because she had my younger sister with her, so I went to my grandmother and she told me everything was all right, and she hugged me, and I could go back to sleep again with her.

"After we were in Ar'ara for a while a bad thing happened. One day Arab soldiers came to our house and took away my father. They put him in jail and he was away for a very long time. We didn't think we'd see him again. I heard my mother and grandmother talking, and sometimes crying. They said my father had been taken away because he had been talking to the Jews. I didn't understand this. They said that the Arab soldiers were going to put him on a rope and hang him. I was very scared when I heard this. But then one day my father came back. The Arab soldiers had let him go. He had told them it wasn't true that he had talked to the Jews. They believed him and let him go. We threw a big *hafla* and were all so happy to have my father back. Soon after that we returned to Kufr Qara and to our house. Later I understood from my father that the one who had helped us go back was that 'Moti,' his friend. He and my father had talked, and he helped us come back to our house. I was so happy. I was able to go to school, and everything—or almost everything—was good again."

UMM AHMAD:

"Just before the war broke out, we knew something was going to happen. We had heard about things the Jews had done in Haifa and some villages in the north. Refugees came through here and told us how the Jews had thrown them out of their homes and villages. We feared it could happen to us. But we also knew that the Arab armies were large, larger than the Jews, and if they fought well they would win. So we thought. I had heard the men talking in the *diwan*, or when they came back at night from doing guard duty. So I knew how they thought, and they thought we'd win.

"On the morning that the war came, I had been heading out to the fields with some other women and children just before dawn. We were harvesting barley and wanted to get an early start. My husband was at home still sleeping, and Fatma was sleeping, too, with my money sash under her head like a pillow. I had the money ready to take, along with some other things, in case we had to flee suddenly. Two days earlier I had taken my youngest daughter, Nihal, to Ar'ara, where my husband's uncle lived. Anyway, as we were heading out to the fields that morning, suddenly there was a lot of noise and we were being shot at. A rocket or something hit one of the donkeys that a boy was riding. He was thrown off, but the donkey lay there dead. We all ran home. We knew this was it, the war had started. When I got home, I saw that my husband wasn't there, nor was his rifle. He had gone to fight. I grabbed Fatma, took the money, and with my mother-in-law began to flee the village. But someone from our clan said the women shouldn't leave then, it was too dangerous. They brought us to a huge building and put us there. I didn't believe it would be safer there, so I left along with some others. I wanted to save my daughter. My husband's brother, Ibrahim, caught up with us as we were leaving and came with us—my husband had sent him to escape with us. We took off in the direction of Ar'ara, away from the fighting. There were shots all around us, but, *il hamdu lillah*, nobody was wounded.

"It took about two hours to get to Ar'ara. When I got there I saw that Nihal was fine, and I got Fatma settled. But my mind was with my husband. He was in great danger. I didn't know what was happening in the village. I knew he was fighting someplace and that he had nothing to drink or eat. It was already mid-morning. So I decided to make food for him. I baked some pitot, made roasted potatoes and tomato salad, and filled a jar with water. I then headed back to bring it to him. But about halfway there, who do I see? Him. He and some friends were heading to Ara to get more ammunition. We sat down together in the shade of a tree, and the men ate and drank quickly. When he told me he was going off to get the ammunition and then return to the village, I told him not to go. I didn't want him to die there. He got angry and told me to go back to Ar'ara. I told him, 'Come with me.' We argued hard, but he said he was going back to fight. If he didn't, he said, the village would be lost to the Jews and we would never be able to return. What could I do? I told myself it's in the hands of Allah. I went back to Ar'ara and waited. I waited all day. Then that night he came to us. He said the Jews had been chased off. They were no longer in our village. Maybe in the morning we could go to Kufr Qara and fetch some of our things, *inshallah*, God willing.

"The next morning when we went back to Kufr Qara, it

was a great shock. Many buildings had been destroyed in the fighting. People were rushing about in great confusion, searching in the rubble for who and what they could find, weeping all the time. There were several bodies lying exposed, and some people were trapped in the ruins of their houses. In some places blood was on the walls, the floor, all over. Many animals lay about dead. I didn't know what condition our house would be in, but *il hamdu lillah*, it was still standing and our cow was there calling out to us. I was happy about that, but I couldn't feel too happy because so many of our neighbors had lost their houses. I didn't stay around very long. I took our cow, along with some provisions that were not taken the day before—oil, barley, animal feed, clothes—and I returned to Ar'ara.

"After that we stayed most of the time in Ar'ara. My children were fine, they had other children and people around to play with. My husband immediately found work selling sheep and we were able to have some money that way. Also, I had taken along our money, and my gold necklaces and bracelets, which I could sell. But how long could we last? We knew that in our fields the corn was ready to harvest and we wanted to go back and get it. This would be very dangerous, though, and we were afraid. Then we heard that some agreement was made with the Jews. We would be allowed to harvest the corn, but we could not return to live in our homes. So we went. I don't know what kind of agreement it was, because while we were harvesting we got shot at now and then. Some people got wounded and others got blown up when they stepped on mines that were in the fields. It was very dangerous, but we didn't know what would become of us and we wanted to be sure to have food. Eventually, what happened—this was after two or three months—the Red Cross came to Ar'ara and gave us some things. Just us, the people who had left their villages—refugees. We received flour, sugar, tea and coffee, and some blankets. It really helped. In Ar'ara the people even joked that it was a pity they hadn't become refugees so the Red Cross would help them out, too.

"We had enough to eat then and we were doing all right,

but then one day there was a knock on our door and some Iraqi soldiers came to arrest my husband. They took him away to Jenin along with several others. I didn't understand this. People were talking and they said that my husband had been in contact with the Jews. I knew that there were some men, one man especially, who was in contact with the Jews. He sold them sheep and made lots of money. But I didn't believe that my husband was in contact with Jews, nor was he selling them sheep. He got arrested anyway. He was in jail in Jenin many weeks, and after that in Nablus for many months. I was very scared. I didn't know what would happen to him or to us. My mother-in-law visited him often while I stayed with the two children. I was also pregnant then with Rafiqa. A few times I also went to visit. I brought fresh clothes and food, like bread and a stuffed chicken, cooked vegetables and dates—things he couldn't get in jail. I was only allowed to talk to him for fifteen minutes through a square in this iron door. What could we say? 'How are you?' 'How are the children?' There was no time to talk, and I tried not to show how scared I was. We didn't know when he would get out, or what would be the future.

"Then one day he was out, and came back to Ar'ara. Just like that. The Iraqis had discovered that he wasn't guilty and they let him and the others go. We had a *hafla*, and right after that we returned to Kufr Qara. Not only us— all Kufr Qara's people who were living throughout the area. All those months we had waited for this day. Yet once we got back, there was a problem. The Jews began shooting at us. When we went down to the well, especially, it was very dangerous. A number of people got shot and some were killed. We knew we couldn't go on like this, but we didn't want to become refugees. So my husband went to talk to the Jews, to see if he could get them to stop shooting and allow us to get water from our well. He told me later that the Jews had blindfolded him and put him in some kind of cell overnight. But he succeeded in convincing them. They stopped shooting and we were able to get water. They refused to let us return to our fields, though. Anyone out in his fields, they said, would be arrested or shot. Again I was very worried. What was going to happen? When could we return to our fields? How could we live? I was scared."

ABU AHMAD:

"From the moment I heard of the UN decision to partition Palestine, I knew there would be war. There was no way the Arab states would allow a Jewish state in the area. This I knew from the newspapers and especially the radio reports from all over the Arab world. They talked of wiping out the Jewish state and crushing the Jews. I was aware that the Jews had their own arms and ammunition, and that they were capable of fighting hard. But, really, I didn't think they had a chance against all the Arab armies and the thousands of volunteers who were coming to fight with us. I was sure we'd win. I wasn't imagining or hoping to throw the Jews into the sea. What I thought would happen is that we would establish one large Palestinian state and the Jews would agree to live with us as a minority. That was my belief and hope.

"Shortly after the partition agreement was announced, I went to visit a friend of mine in the nearby kibbutz, Kfar Glickson. His name was Mordecai—'Moti' I called him. He had lent me an insect sprayer to spray my squash and eggplants. I was actually the first in Kufr Qara to use one of these. Anyway, when I heard about the partition agreement, I decided I better go see him and give back the sprayer. I tied it on my donkey and rode to the kibbutz. I got a cold greeting from a lot of the people there. Not from Moti, though. We met in his room and he was friendly. We talked for a couple of hours about the political situation—how Kfar Glickson, according to the UN map, would be in the Jewish state, and Kufr Qara in the Palestinian state. He even joked that soon we would need visas and passports to see each other. But he suggested, more seriously, that for the time being it would be best if we didn't visit each other and waited to see what happened. One of us—I forget who—then asked what we would do if there is war. I said that if there is war, I will fight. He said the same. He didn't tell me, of course—I only found this out much later—that he was second in command of the Haganah [principal military organization of the Jews at that time] for the entire region. 'And what about our relationship to each other?' I asked. He said if war came he would protect me and my family. I said the same. I would let no harm come to him and his family. We embraced. I went home, certain that I would have to protect Moti and his people with my life.

"In Kufr Qara the next few months went on more or less as usual. We worked in our fields as always, including the fields that were next to those of Kfar Glickson. We greeted each other, talked a little, but there weren't any more visits between their village and ours. All of us knew that throughout the country there was fighting going on—in Haifa, Jaffa, Jerusalem. Some people thought that maybe, in our part of the country, war would not come. My view was that in any case we in Kufr Qara should be prepared to defend ourselves if and when war came. Many of us in the village had rifles which we had bought on the black market, after they were smuggled in from Egypt and Syria. We organized a village guard—I was in charge of it—and each night some of us patrolled just outside the village. We did not go to attack the Jewish settlements. I was against that. As long as there was peace in our area, I felt, we should not be the ones to break it. We should not fire the first shot. And we did not.

"The morning of May 8, 1948, one week before the British mandate ended, the Jews attacked. I was sleeping at the time. We had worked late the day before, preparing the fields over by Kfar Glickson for sowing tobacco seedlings. In my backyard I had the seedlings in wooden boxes ready to load onto the donkey. But an hour before I would have gone to the fields, at 4:00 A.M., the war began here. With mortars and rifle and machine gun fire, the Jews came, as we knew they would, from the west. It was a major attack. We had no battle plans, we just grabbed our rifles and ran to the houses located on the western side of the village. My brother, Ibrahim, wanted to come fight with me, but I told him, 'No, go with the family to Ar'ara.' I had only one rifle and a hundred seventy-five rounds of ammunition, and besides, if anything happened to me someone had to take care of the family.

"I didn't know at the time, but I realized later when I read the newspapers, that the Jews had us outnumbered more than ten to one. They had already taken part of the western section of Wadi Ara, and they wanted to drive through to Megiddo, twenty kilometers to the east. The newspapers later said that they had not been able to break through because they met overwhelming numbers. Nonsense! What overwhelming numbers? We were less than a hundred men those first twelve hours of the war. We fought with everything we had because we knew that if they conquered the village, it was the end. We fought a house-to-house battle, from one end of the village to the other. At one point, when there was a pause in the fighting, I went off to get more ammunition. I met my wife on the way coming with food. She told me not to return to the village, she didn't want me to die there. I tried to reassure her, but the truth is, I also thought I would die that day. More than that—I wanted to die *there*. I felt how badly we were outnumbered, and I knew that we couldn't hold on much longer. If I lost my home to the Jews, I didn't want to live. Kufr Qara was the home of my father and my grandfather, and without it life had no meaning to me. So I went back to fight. And to die there.

"But we survived. About 4:00 P.M., twenty-three Iraqi armored cars came to help us. The Jews must have seen them coming through their binoculars, because they backed off suddenly to a ridge just west of the village. They blew up about a dozen houses as they left, in order to make a lot of smoke and dust and partly hide their retreat. Some old people were still in those houses, and they were blown up in them. Altogether, we had lost about eight or ten people. We buried those we could find, and then were told by the Iraqis to go east. They mined the roads in the western area of the village and then took up positions on an eastern ridge. We were told that we could come back the next morning and fetch some things, but they wouldn't let us stay. We pleaded with the Iraqis, but it did no good. They wanted the village empty of people.

"The people of Kufr Qara scattered throughout the area, wherever they could find shelter. Some had no place to go, so they pitched tents in olive groves. Others were better off, relatives in nearby villages took them in. That's what happened to us. My mother's brother lived in Ar'ara, and we went to his house. I was able to work with my cousin, who bought and sold sheep, and I made some money this way. And my wife had taken along her gold, which we sold. So we had some money—enough to get by for a few months, anyway.

"Besides this, we had the crops in our fields, especially the corn, which was ripening. I hated the thought that we would lose it, and I figured that maybe we could go back and harvest it. We had no idea how long our situation would last and we wanted to be sure to have provisions. The only way to harvest was with the permission of the Jews, who occupied strategic positions overlooking the fields. I thought that maybe they would agree, particularly if I could make contact with Moti and some of his friends. So the way I went about it was this. I asked an Arab fellow who was selling sheep to the Jews to pass a note to them requesting a meeting. There were a few of these Arabs making good money by sneaking back and forth and selling sheep to the Jews. These Arabs were probably also passing on information to them, but that wasn't my business, I figured. I just wanted a meeting, and I decided that even if it meant taking a risk of getting caught by the Iraqis, I had to do it. I had to take the chance.

"The Jews sent me back a positive response, and a meeting was arranged. We met on a moonless night, in a field just outside the center of Kufr Qara. I went along with two others, but since they didn't speak Hebrew I talked for all of us. As I had hoped, the Jews who met with us were from Kfar Glickson—not Moti, but some of his friends, including one fellow who worked in the fields next to ours. They asked us what we wanted. I explained that we desperately needed to harvest the corn, that some of us—this was true—were

almost starving. I also said that although we had taken up
arms to defend ourselves, we were ready to live with them
in peace, and that we wanted, as soon as possible, to come
back and live in our village again as peaceful neighbors.
They said that they could not give us a firm answer then,
that we would have to meet again in a few days.

"We met again. The same way as the first time. They
told us then that there was no way we could return to the
village. What we should do, they said, is bring our families
and come with them. They would find us a new place on
their side. I said absolutely not, that for me Kufr Qara was
more dear than even a house in Mecca. Maybe they understood, maybe not. In any case, they did agree that for a few
days we could return to harvest the corn. We also decided
that in order that the Iraqis would not get suspicious about
some sort of agreement, the Jews would fire at us while we
worked. Not right at us, but above our heads. And that's the
way we did it. About half the village returned to harvest
their corn. Unfortunately, as we harvested, some of the Jews
fired a little too close, and a person or two was wounded.
My cousin's wife got shot through the shoulder. But generally the plan went well. We harvested a great deal of corn
in those few days, and the Iraqis didn't interfere with us
either.

"Not until a few weeks later, anyway. Then the Iraqis
came looking for me in Ar'ara. They arrested me and about
ten others. I discovered later that a few people had gone to
them and said I had been collaborating with the Jews. Lies!
I never passed on information to them. The sheep trader,
who *was* a collaborator, fled that same day we were arrested
to the Jewish side, and he stayed there until the end of the
war. I could have gone over too, it had been offered at those
meetings. But I wanted only to stay with my people and
return to Kufr Qara. So I wound up arrested as a collaborator! And for the next hundred and ninety-three days, from
September 9, 1948 to March 21, 1949, I was in jail—forty
days in Jenin and the rest in Nablus. I and the others were
accused of treason, which carried the penalty of death by
hanging.

"It was miserable in jail, of course. Lice, filth, cold, and little food. None of us knew what would be the end of it. We only knew that the Iraqis were preparing evidence to put us on trial, and maybe hang us. All we could do is sit and wait and hope. We had lots of time on our hands. And during this time I had a chance to think and try to understand what had happened in this war which we thought we were going to win, and which we obviously had lost. What I began to understand then—and later I became sure of it—is that the Arab countries did not really want to save Palestine. They could have, I believe, if they had wanted to. But all of them were under pressure from the West, especially America, not to destroy Israel. Their leadership was western-oriented and they went along with this pressure. Also, they all had their own selfish reasons for entering the war. Especially King Abdullah. He had the strongest army of all and he could have caused the Jews many problems, yet he was interested only in capturing eastern Palestine for himself. And the Egyptians and Syrians were more worried about Abdullah's expansion than anything else. Sure, nobody liked the idea of a Jewish state, and they all talked about destroying it, but they were not ready or willing to back up this talk. It was all noise. *Nobody* was interested in saving Palestine for the Palestinian people. I sensed all this then, and now, having read about what took place, I see that it was so. We were lied to and betrayed.

"All these thoughts I kept to myself while I was in jail. If the Iraqis, Abdullah's ally, knew what I was thinking they would have hung me just for that! As it was, if they could have proved that I talked to the Jews, that for sure would have been enough. But they couldn't prove it. We were brought before a military court, me and the others, but none of the witnesses came forth and testified. The Iraqis couldn't prove their case. They hung one Druse fellow, and they let the rest of us go. Just told us one day to get out, we were free to go home.

"I went back to Ar'ara and we had a big celebration. Then, a few days later, we returned to Kufr Qara. Word had gone around that the war was over, and all our people in the area came rushing back to the village. The Transjordanians who were sitting on the eastern ridge of the village—

they had replaced their cousins, the Iraqis—made no effort to stop us. The problem came from the Jews. They began firing on us, particularly when we went down to the well to get water. Several people were killed. It was obvious what their tactic was—to deny us water and thus drive us out. People began to panic. So we sent a delegation of elders to Jerusalem to speak to the Transjordanians and to see what could be done. There we discovered what had happened. The Transjordanians had just given the Jews the Wadi Ara area as part of the armistice agreement. They told our elders that Kufr Qara, according to the maps, was an empty village now belonging to Israel. The elders told them that they might have their maps, but Kufr Qara was *not* empty. The Transjordanians said they could do nothing. They told us to go slaughter a few sheep, arrange a *sulha* and try to talk it out with the Jews. That was it.

"When the elders returned from Jerusalem with this information, I knew we were in serious trouble. We were in a critical situation, just as we had been the day the war broke out. We couldn't go on without water and with people being shot. Our people were in panic and very soon, I feared, they would flee. And if they fled, and the village really was empty or almost empty, that was the end. We would never be able to return. I knew that something had to be done. So again I decided to go speak to the Jews. And again I had to do it without the Arabs—this time the Transjordanians— seeing me. If I was caught, I would be arrested and that would be it.

"I went this time with Hammad—yes, the same Hammad who is head of the village council today. He was seventeen years old then. He knew the way through the mines that had been placed on the dirt roads by the Iraqis. Really, I feared these Iraqi mines more than I feared the Jews. At one point, I stepped on some wire as we were walking, and I jumped in the air thinking it was a mine. Believe me, I was scared. We went through the thick grass in the fields. It was absolutely dark. When we approached the Jewish camp, Hammad said he was going back, he'd had enough. I told him he was staying with me. I was his elder, so he listened. Some shots were fired. I shouted at them in Hebrew that we were only two men from Kufr Qara and we were coming unarmed to speak to them. It was a good thing I knew Hebrew then. Without it we were dead. They shouted back to us directions on how to approach, how to avoid their mines. As we approached, they kept firing over our heads and all around us. I suppose they wanted to make sure we were alone. When we reached them, they searched us and asked who we were. I explained to them, and they let us into the camp. We sat down, and I pulled out a packet of expensive cigarettes that I had brought along. I was completely wet from walking through the fields, but at least the cigarettes had stayed dry. We all smoked. They asked us what we wanted, and I told them I was looking for Moti and his friends who I had made the harvest agreement with seven months before. They said that nothing could be done that night, we'd have to wait until the next day. We agreed. They put us in a room and put a guard at the door to make sure we stayed there.

"The next day we were driven to a camp further inside Israel. Waiting for us was this same fellow from Kfar Glickson who I had made the agreement with before. He was a captain. We talked for a while about what had happened to me since our agreement, what was going on in Kufr Qara, and so on. Again I told him that we were ready to live as neighbors in peace with them, just like before the war. He said he would do what was possible to stop the shooting, to allow us to go to the well. He agreed to speak personally with Moti, and he added—it was the first time I knew it— that Moti was a general, the second in command of our entire area. I mentioned that Moti was a good friend—he seemed aware of this—and I requested to see him. He said he'd do what he could. Then he told me to go back to Kufr Qara. In two days time, he suggested, I should return to the army camp outside the village and perhaps then I could see Moti.

"In those two days before I returned to the camp, the shooting suddenly stopped. People were able to go down to the well undisturbed. The panic stopped and many people who were about to leave decided to stay. I said almost nothing to anyone about what I had done. Not even my wife knew anything. Only later did I tell her a little. I feared that someone might find out and tell the Transjordanians, and I'd be arrested. I had to be very careful.

"Two days later, when I went alone to the Jewish army camp, there was no shooting. They apparently were expecting me. I was told that Moti was in the kibbutz, a couple of kilometers past the camp, and he had sent word that I should be allowed through. I went by foot, dressed in my usual clothes, *gallabiyeh* and *keffiyeh*. Nobody in the kibbutz said anything. Since I knew where his rooms were, I went straight there. I knocked on the door and he opened. We looked at each other, up and down, not able to talk at first. We embraced. I went inside and slowly we began talking. We talked about our families, how everything was with the children, and so on. Then we talked about the war. Mostly, I did the talking. He didn't want to say much about his role. It was not easy for him, I could see, to hear what had happened to me and my family. At one point, he even got up and went to his closet and brought back some money. I refused it. But what I did was to recall our conversation before the war. 'You have won and we have lost,' I said. 'What I ask now is that you help me—us—to return to our way of life together as it was before the war. That is what I want if you can do it.' Moti looked me in the eyes and said he would do everything he could to make this possible. I believed him then, and I still believe he did what he could. I thanked him, we embraced again, and I left.

"Ten days or so after this meeting, on May 22, 1949, the Jewish army entered our village and all the villages in the area. The Transjordanians had left their posts shortly before, as part of the armistice agreement. The Jews established a military police office in Ara. It was just one branch of the overall military government which was set up to rule almost all of the Arab citizens of Israel. We in Kufr Qara were told by the Jews that we could live in our village if we wanted, but we would not be able to return to our fields. We would have to find other work. We did not know at the time that most of our lands would be confiscated, that it would be five years before we could return to farming at all, and that for the next seventeen years we would be living under a military government. We had no way of knowing this, and if anyone had asked me I wouldn't have said it would go this way. In spite of the war, in spite of all that had happened, I felt the Jews were people that would treat us fairly, without cruelty. I don't know how many others believed as I did, but in May 1949, I personally felt that everything would be all right in Kufr Qara."

9

LIFE UNDER THE MILITARY GOVERNMENT (1949–1966)

WHEN THE WAR OF 1947–49 ENDED, the Palestinian population in the new state of Israel was in shock. Il Nakba had left them a minority in the country: the wealthy, the educated, the middle class—in short, their leadership—were gone. Those who remained were virtually all *fellaheen* or poor urban workers, the majority of whom lived in the hundred or so villages and towns that were still intact (some three hundred seventy Arab villages and towns had been emptied or destroyed). With the border between Israel and the surrounding Arab states now sealed off, the Palestinians in Israel were unable to visit their families and friends who had fled there, nor could they legally receive newspapers or listen to radio broadcasts from these places. The Arab countries continued to promise revenge, and *fedayeen* were slipping across the border and making hit-and-run attacks. Yet none of this offered immediate relief or salvation. Rather, it increased their misery, for it added to the Jews' tendency to view them as a potential "fifth column."

Nominally, the Palestinians in Israel—or "Israeli Arabs" as they came to be called—were considered as equal citizens in the new state. But in fact they were subjected to considerable discrimination. The vast majority of them, some 80 percent, found themselves living under a military government. The rule of the military over conquered Arab areas had been introduced by Ben Gurion during the war and was extended afterwards to include all the major areas of Arab population. The military government's authority was legally based on the British Mandatory Emergency Regulations of 1945, as well as on subsequent legislation passed by the Israeli government. These laws authorized the military governors of the various districts to exercise far-reaching control over the Arab citizens in their areas—control over their movements, their work, and their property.

Undoubtedly, the most painful of these laws were those that deprived the Arab citizens of their property. Some 870,000 dunams of land belonging to Arabs still living in Israel were confiscated by the state, and much of it was transferred to Jewish settlers—new immigrants as well as established kibbutzim and *moshavim*. The rationale was always the same: "security reasons." And while from the Jewish point of view these transfers were justifiable in light of the continuing threat from the surrounding Arab countries, to the Palestinians within Israel they seemed like a cruel attempt to deprive them of their livelihood. Indeed, from the Palestinian perspective, some of these laws seemed absolutely diabolical. For instance, one regulation—Article 125 of the Defense (Emergency) Regulations—allowed the government to designate large tracts of Arab land as "closed areas," thus making it impossible for Arab farmers to work them; and another regulation—Emergency Regulations (Cultivation of Waste Lands) Ordinance 5709-1949—declared that all land not cultivated could be reallocated to others, that is, to Jewish farmers. The Palestinian farmer thus found himself in the situation of not being allowed to go to his fields and then having these fields confiscated because he was not using them. Compensation was offered for the confiscated lands, but it seldom seemed adequate and only enhanced the farmers' feelings of being cheated out of their property.

These widespread land confiscations, coupled with

other restrictions on their lives—particularly travel restrictions—made the lot of Palestinians in Israel extremely harsh, even desperate, in those first years after the war. Some decided that life was simply too difficult, and they left Israel to join their brethren as refugees. Some joined leftist Jewish political parties and attempted to challenge legally the apparatus of the military government; they were often harassed. A few resorted to extra-legal means, forming clandestine nationalist groups, or even using arms; they were jailed or banished. And the majority, believing that there was little they could do to change the situation, chose to eke out what advantages they could from the ruling government, either by offering no opposition or by actively collaborating.

For the inhabitants of Kufr Qara, the period of the military government was especially painful. Some three quarters of Kufr Qara's twenty-four thousand dunams were confiscated, forcing many villagers to give up farming and look for work outside the village. But this was problematic. Special travel permits were required to go more than two kilometers outside the immediate vicinity of the village, and in the first few years these permits were not easy to procure. Moreover, as a result of its proximity to the Jordanian border—which *fedayeen* were crossing at night to attack Jewish settlements—Kufr Qara, along with all Arab villages in the Wadi Ara region, was placed under a nightly curfew; and this curfew (from 10:00 P.M. to 4:00 A.M.) remained in effect for thirteen years, until 1962.

For Abu Ahmad, these years were also extremely difficult and demanding. During this time his family grew from three children to ten, and he had the worrisome task of supporting them. For the first five years, until 1954, he had to do so by finding work outside the village. In addition, because of his pivotal role during the war, he emerged as one of the village leaders in the post-war period. By the time he was forty years old, he was head of his clan and a member of Kufr Qara's village council. This latter role brought him for a while into frequent contact with Jewish officialdom.

It is from this dual perspective, as father and village leader, that Abu Ahmad views the post-war military government period—a seventeen-year span which left its indelible mark on him, on Kufr Qara, and ultimately on all 700,000 Palestinians living in Israel today.

"The war had been a terrible time for our people. Kufr Qara had been emptied and we were scattered like leaves all over the area. We lived like refugees for eleven months, never knowing whether we'd be able to go back. When we finally did return, in April 1949, and the Jews let us go to our well and get water, I felt that our nightmare was over. Soon, I thought, life would go back to the way it was before the war. We would live with our Jewish neighbors as we did before the war—with respect and dignity. We would return to farming our lands and life again would be good. I know this sounds naive, but that's what I believed in those first days when we were back in Kufr Qara.

"It wasn't long before I could see that it wouldn't be that way. In May 1949—May 22, to be exact—the army came to Kufr Qara and to all the villages in the area, and the military government took over. They wasted no time in letting us know that life was not going to be as it once was. We could live in the village, they said, but we would not be free to go about when and where we wanted. In a way, they turned the village into a prison. No bars or walls, but still a prison. At night, we were under a curfew—at first from 8:00 P.M. to 5:00 A.M., and later from 10:00 P.M. to 4:00 A.M. In the first few years it was strictly enforced. Later they eased up. In the daytime, we were unable to leave the area of the village without special travel permits. Our well was to the north, a kilometer outside the main village area. We were allowed to go there as long as we walked on the dirt path and not one meter to either side of it. We could not go south of the main village area, or to the west, where almost all our fields were. All this was considered a 'closed area.' If you went there, as some people tried—like Samir's father— you got thrown in jail, as he did, for a month. The only way you could go was east, as far as Ara and Ar'ara, two kilometers away. A few Kufr Qara families had land in that direction, and they were fortunate. But all the rest of us were not able to go to our fields. We had to look for work outside the village, in the Jewish areas.

"To travel outside the area of the village, you had to have a special permit from the military government district office. The office was located in Ara. In the first year, these permits were hard to get. After that, they began issuing them more freely. But the permits were only good for two-week periods, and you often had to wait days or even weeks to get one. Anyone they suspected of having views against the Israeli government, or whom they disliked, was not given a permit. And that person was in real trouble. It meant he would not be able to earn any money to support his family.

"The truth is that in those first few years, the early 1950s, we were in a desperate situation. If it had not been for the Red Cross, which brought us some food—until about 1952—many would have starved. As it was, lots of people suffered from not having enough food. Many became sick. And when they became sick, since there was no doctor in the village, they were in trouble. To get to one, you needed a travel permit, and as you can imagine, many people suffered unnecessarily because they could not reach a doctor. Some even died because they couldn't get to a hospital in time.

"Things were so difficult in those early years of the military government that some people in the area decided to leave and go to Jordan. My uncle in Ar'ara, the man my family had stayed with during the war, was one of these. And he was not alone. Hundreds, maybe thousands, of people from villages just to the east of us went over the border to Jordan. The Jews did not oppose crossings in *that* direction! These people had spent the war in their own villages under the Iraqi army. They didn't know what it was like to be refugees. In Kufr Qara, because we had been refugees during the war, we knew what it was like. So, even though the situation was very bad, our people didn't leave. We stayed on. We were determined not to become refugees again.

"For my family these years were also extremely hard, but not as hard as they were for others. That was because of my Jewish friend, Moti. He helped us. He remained loyal to the agreement that we had made with each other before the war. Just as I had promised to protect him and his family if we won, so he had promised to protect me and my family if they won. And he did. At the end of the war, he became assistant commander of the military government district to the north of us. He was not in charge of Kufr Qara, but of course he was in close contact with the commander in Ara. It was Moti who arranged for Kufr Qara to be given the status of a refugee village, which enabled us to receive supplies from the Red Cross. That alone saved many people here. And to me personally, he was very helpful. He made it possible for me to have a travel permit right from the beginning, when they were almost impossible to get. He also got me permission to set up a business of selling animal fertilizer to Jewish settlements. From villages to the east, camel-loads of dung would be brought to Kufr Qara, and we'd load it onto trucks and bring it to the Jewish settlements. They needed it for their farms, and they paid very well. For me, it meant that my family was taken care of and had enough to eat.

"I was not the only one in the village who had a good connection with a Jew. There were about ten of us who had such connections. But in a way I was more fortunate than most. My friend Moti was a man of honor, and he helped me without requiring favors in return. This was not usually the case. In order to get business permits, or in the beginning, to get travel permits week after week, you had to provide something in return. You had to give them information, to collaborate. What kind of information? They wanted to know who in the village still had guns and ammunition, who was politically active in a nationalist movement, who was talking against the Jews. Also, they had a problem with infiltrators coming across the Jordanian border into Israel. Some of these people were just unfortunate souls, poor refugees trying to return to their villages. But others were armed *fedayeen* who were trying to set up cells and attack Jewish settlements. The Jews wanted to know who they were and where they were hiding out. And for all this they needed the help of collaborators.

"I have told you honestly everything that happened to me, and I want to tell you the truth here, too. In the early months of the military government, there was a point, a moment, when Moti *did* ask me for favors. It happened this way. He explained that the district office wanted information on infiltrators. If I knew of any, he said, as long as they were not members of my family or clan, would I be willing to give him their names? It was a horrible moment. I in no way wanted to betray anyone, and yet here was this man, Moti, who had helped save our village and my family, asking me to help him like this. I sat frozen, and then—to tell you the truth—I said yes. I do not know if I ever would have revealed anything, but what happened was that a few minutes later Moti turned to me and said, 'Look, forget what I just asked you. Our relationship has been clean up to now, and let's keep it that way. This information we can get from someone else. You don't have to help us.' And I didn't. From then on he never raised the matter again.

"What did happen is that after a few months I lost the fertilizer concession. Some of the district officers in Ara, who knew that I was making good money in this way, came to me and said that in order to keep the privilege, I would have to help them, to collaborate. I said no. So they took the concession away from me and gave it to two fellows from Ara and Ar'ara. I was left with no work. Moti, though, helped me out. He arranged for me to work as a guard in a *ma'barah* [temporary camp for immigrants] being built a kilometer or so to the west of the village. This work lasted for about a year. During the period that the camp was being built and for a few months after the new immigrants came, I did guard duty there. I made good money, enough to help my brother, Ibrahim, get married, and to pay for an eye operation for my mother so she didn't go blind.

"The guard duty work was easy, though once the new immigrants came there were some problems. They were all Jews from Iraq, about eighty people, and they had no idea what life would be like here. The Jewish Agency brought them one night in three trucks, and just left them with two lirot each, and water, bread, and beans. The camp was only a few shacks in a large clearing with a lot of thorn bushes around. They were all weeping and cursing Ben Gurion and the Jewish Agency. For three months before coming, they had heard lectures on how good it would be in Israel, and now that they were here it didn't look good to them. I told them they could come to the village and visit. 'What village?' they asked. 'My village, an Arab village,' I told them. Again they cursed Ben Gurion. 'They send us out here with nothing, and right next to Arabs who are going to harm us!' I had to calm them down, reassure them. I told them that they would be welcome in the village. They could buy sugar, coffee, eggs, and vegetables in the store there. If anything happened, I said, they could have my head. They weren't convinced, though. The Jewish Agency had told them not to trust the Arabs here, that we were all out to do them harm. So they didn't come to the village, hardly at all. And eventually I wound up losing the job. One of the immigrants complained to the Jewish Agency that *he* should have the job of guard duty, 'not an Arab.' And they gave it to him.

"That left me for a while with nowhere to go. Many of the men in the village were working then in a nearby rock quarry, twelve hours a day for about a half-lira—not enough to feed a family. It was real slave labor. I didn't want that, so I went to Tel Aviv, where my brother-in-law had a room. I was able to stay with him and come home on weekends. I found work in construction—simple labor. It paid one and a half lirot a day if you were an Arab and three lirot a day if you were a Jew. Since I spoke Hebrew well, I called myself Eli and made the three lirot a day. I never spoke a word of Arabic, not even with the Iraqi Jews I was working with, who mostly spoke Arabic. Nobody caught on, but I didn't like hiding who I was. And I didn't like the work or being away from my family all week. So after a few months I quit and went back to the village.

"For the next couple of years or so, I worked as a day laborer on Jewish settlements in the Hadera area, about ten kilometers from here. Jews there knew me from the time I was selling fertilizer to them, and even before. I didn't make much money, but I didn't have to call myself Eli and pretend to be a Jew. And at night I was home with my wife and children.

"After five years of working outside the village, I finally was able to go back to farming here. Not on *my* land—all that was confiscated—but on land that I was given as compensation. It happened like this. During those five years, the Jews had closed off almost all the farmland of the village and didn't let us go there. And according to this law they passed, because the land wasn't in use, they were able to confiscate it and then give it away. Did you ever hear of anything like that before? Well, that's the way it was. Our family's fifty-seven and a half dunams were given to Kfar Glickson and to a new kibbutz, Regavim. In 1954, the Jews offered compensation for the land they confiscated, either money or some other land instead. The money they offered was only a fraction of the land's value, and the land they compensated us with—no more than thirty dunams per individual family—was the worst farmland in the village. They had taken the best.

"Some people in the village refused to take compensation—especially those with large holdings. Their attitude was that the Jews had robbed them and they weren't going to deal with thieves. So they held out, hoping that someday soon the Jews would be defeated by the Arab armies, and they'd get all their land back. Or, in some cases, they really were just hoping that by holding out, the Jews might give them a better deal. Me, I could see the Jews were here for the foreseeable future, and I figured the deal they were offering right then, even if it wasn't fair, probably was the best we were going to get. And I was right about that. Anyway, when they offered my family and my brother's family together some fifty-seven and a half dunams of sloping, rocky land—in exchange for our fifty-seven and a half good dunams—I saw no point in waiting. I went to the men in the village whose families had owned that land and I said, 'This is what the Jews have offered me. Is it your intention to come to terms with them and take back this land?' They said no. 'In that case', I told them, 'we are going to accept the offer.' There were some hard feelings at first, but less than you might think. All of us were in a terrible situation. Hardly anyone got his own fields back. People understood that it was a question of survival and there wasn't much anyone could do about it.

"The land that I received was very poor, just a rocky

field. It's the land that Hassan is farming today. It still has lots of small rocks in it, but it is good soil now. In the beginning, when I took it over, I couldn't farm it. I had to rent a D-9 tractor that had an attachment which plowed to a depth of 1.2 meters. With that attachment I was able to get out most of the rocks and prepare the soil. I had no sons to help me. Ahmad was only one year old at the time. But my wife, who is very strong, worked with me, and my oldest daughters helped, too. At the end of six months, people couldn't believe what we had accomplished. We had turned this rocky field into farmland.

"Then what I did was organize a cooperative—along with forty others from my clan and related clans. We raised eight thousand lirot in cash, two hundred per man, and went to the bank and got a loan for fourteen thousand lirot more. With this money, we were able to get ourselves hooked up to the national water system, Mekorot, and to irrigate our fields. And that meant we had good yields year-round. Just like today, we grew all kinds of vegetables—tomatoes, cucumbers, green squash, eggplants, onions, peppers. And with a truck that we bought, we were able to bring our vegetables to the Jewish markets in Tel Aviv and Haifa. You still needed a permit to travel, but these were easier for everyone to get by 1955, and they were issued for six-month periods, not just for fifteen days like in the beginning of the military government. So all in all, life was easier for us—many of us. But for many others, who had lost their lands and got only money in return, or nothing at all, life remained hard. To survive, they had to work outside the village, in the quarry, in construction, or as farm laborers. Some of them even wound up working as farm laborers on their own lands, which belonged now to the Jewish settlements. For them, life was not so good, and the bitterness of il Nakba was harder to push away.

"I want to tell you now a little about the way politics worked at that time—during the military government period. Remember, even though we were under the military government and they confiscated our lands and treated us badly, we were still citizens of the State of Israel, which meant we could vote. Right from the first elections to the Knesset, we voted. And that gave us some influence. Ben Gurion's party, Mapai, was in power all those years. His people ran the government, including the military government. At election time his people would come to us in the village and sit with us drinking cups of coffee. They'd tell us that it would be wise to vote for them, that is, for an Arab slate associated with their party. In those years, until 1968, there were separate Arab slates associated with Mapai.[1] Ben Gurion's people made it clear that if we voted for them they'd be more ready to help us get roads and schools and water pipes for the village—or other things, like travel and business permits, and bank loans, and compensation for our land. But if we didn't vote for them, well, they wouldn't be helpful at all. Simple as that!

"In those early years, Meir Wilner, the head of the Communist party, came by here. He told us—I went to meet him—to vote for Rakah [the Communist party]. His party was the most outspoken against the military government. We should vote for them, he said, because they would fight against Ben Gurion's Mapai and against the military government. I said to him that I didn't like the military government either, but then I said, 'Tell me, do you or anybody else have enough votes to get rid of it?' He said no. I told him, 'In that case, I want the best we can get while the military government is here. And that you can't help me with. Only Mapai can. So I am going to vote for them.' And that's what I did—like most people in Kufr Qara. To me, it was the only thing that made sense. I made no apologies for it then, and I still think it was the right thing to do.

"During the period of the military government, I became involved in local politics. In 1958 we were told that we would be allowed to set up our local council in order to handle

---

[1]Arabs were not accepted as members of Mapai until 1968. The Communist party is the only Israeli political party that has had Arab members since the first parliamentary elections in 1949.

village affairs—you know, things like road and school construction, and tax collection. The first council was simply
appointed by the Ministry of the Interior, in consultation
with the military government. They told the village elders,
the heads of the big clans, to give them a list of candidates,
and they chose who they wanted. Naturally, they chose people from some clans and not others. That's how it worked.
Clans they didn't like or trust, they pushed aside. After the
first year, in 1959, we were allowed to hold elections in the
village for a nine-man council. Each clan put up a man or
two, and every adult in the village—men and women—
voted. People, of course, voted for their own clan or a related
clan. Most of the major clans got a person on the council,
and as leader of my clan, I got elected.

"I served on Kufr Qara's village council until 1963. It
was always an honor but seldom a pleasure. I had to hire a
man to help my family with the farm during those years
because I was busy with the council. During my five years,
we were able to do some good things for the village. We
paved the main road out of the village, and we got water
pipes installed to the houses. We didn't manage to get electricity, though. That took until 1972, after my time. Besides
this, I personally was involved in arranging business permits
and licenses and all kinds of paperwork for the people here.
On the council, I was the one who spoke and read Hebrew
the best, so I was dealing with lots of Jewish offices and
ministries. Bureaucracy then was no better than it is now.
And this work was truly no pleasure. But most unpleasant
was the problem of taxes. Our council had to collect taxes
from the people, and the people weren't used to paying
them. Under the Turks there hadn't been much to pay, and
the British had none at all. With the new Israeli government,
we were taxed on our land, our houses, and on other things
too. People who didn't pay had to be threatened and even
brought to court. This was an ugly business and I wanted
no part of it. By 1963 I was tired of all this work, and I
decided to get out and let someone else head the clan. I went
back to full-time farming, which caused less headaches—
and paid better.

"The final years of the military government—which ended in 1966—were not too hard. There were no curfews and travel restrictions were much less. Unless the military government was out to punish you, there was no problem getting permits to travel almost anywhere you wanted in Israel. In these ways we were freer. But we still had a feeling of being isolated—cut off not from other Palestinians in Israel but from Palestinians and all Arabs outside Israel. It was illegal to get newspapers from Arab countries and many books were banned. It was also illegal to listen to any Arab radio station except the Voice of Israel in Arabic. People did listen to broadcasts from Cairo, Amman, and Damascus. I did. But to do so was to break the law of *my* country.

"In the schools, too, there was censorship. Our children were made to study subjects as if they were Jews. They learned hardly anything about Arab history and literature. They studied Jewish history and literature instead. They were not even taught that they were Palestinians. It was forbidden to even use the word *Palestine* in class. Can you imagine that? Anything they knew about these subjects, they had to learn at home—almost secretly, you could say. And most parents didn't know enough, or have enough time, to teach them anything. It was a pity, but there was nothing we could do about it. The government wanted to keep us ignorant of who we were. They thought in that way they'd make us more loyal citizens. Or more quiet citizens, anyway.

"The truth is, the Israeli government never trusted us, and even while relaxing the military government restrictions, they always made it clear that they were watching over us. I could even say it this way—they let us know that we were at their mercy. Do you know what happened here in 1956? That was the year of the Sinai War. Have you heard of Kufr Qasim? Well, let me tell you. Just before the Israeli government went to war against Egypt, they decided to make a show of force to the Arab citizens of Israel. With heavily armed soldiers they surrounded the village of Kufr Qasim, which is near here. They announced that in a few hours there would be a curfew and anyone not obeying the curfew would be shot. Well, all the people who were in the fields then, or outside the village, didn't hear the announcement. When they came home past the curfew time, they were shot dead—forty-nine of them. And Kufr Qasim wasn't the only village where the army fired shots. In many other villages around here they also made sudden curfews and shot at people, though none were killed. That same day I also was shot at while working out in my fields at dusk. After the war was over and they had won, the Israeli government issued an apology to Kufr Qasim. But they had made their point. They let us all know that we were at their mercy. And I believe that if they had lost the war, or if it looked like they were losing the war, there would have been massacres here of Arab citizens.

"The same in 1967. The rule of the military government had ended a year before. But during the 1967 war, they resumed it for about two weeks, until the end of the war. They watched over us and let us know that we were at their mercy. Had it looked like they were going to lose that war, I believe the Jews would have attacked us and massacred many of us. I say this even though I know there are Jews of goodwill here. It was Moti, after all, who helped save my village and my family during the military government period. For this I shall always be grateful. But Moti, and people like him, were not able to prevent a lot of things that happened to us during those years. And anyone who lived through il Nakba, and the military government that came after it, learned one thing for sure—as Arabs in Israel, we have reason to be afraid. I am sad to say this, but it is the truth."

10

HASSAN'S WEDDING

EVER SINCE HE HAD BECOME ENGAGED to Zaynab in August of 1988, Hassan felt like things were finally going his way again. He felt calmer, happier, and once more himself. True, every day as he drove past the high school, for a second or two he recalled the horror of running over the boy; and every day he found himself glancing at the wall of his parents' salon, where Nabila's portrait hung as a reminder. He could not forget these things, and by now he realized that they would be with him for a long time to come, maybe the rest of his life. But they no longer were on his mind constantly, and he had begun to feel that once again his luck had returned.

How could he not feel happy? His house, which only a year before had been merely a set of concrete slabs sitting in trenches, was now fully finished. Well, almost finished. The lawn still had to be put in, some plumbing fixtures had to be installed, and Yussef still had to put the final touches on the living room cabinets. Apart from that, all the place needed was a thorough cleaning—and the rest of the bedroom furniture, and the traditional floor cushions which his parents were giving him as a present—and then he could move in. He *and* Zaynab. It made him almost laugh with joy to think of it. He and Zaynab in a house of their own.

By now he knew for sure that he loved her. She had

been the one, he realized, that had truly rescued him from the despair he had felt after those two disasters. She had taken something of a chance by becoming engaged to him. After all, a person with a run of bad luck such as he had— a person who had been cursed by the evil eye—was a definite risk. Her family had told her so. But she had had the courage to stick by her choice. And for this he was grateful. Moreover, as she had made clear to him after their engagement, she had been in love with him for the past several years. In fact, from the time she had been a high school sophomore, four years before, and had watched him riding by the school on his way to the fields, she had wanted to marry him. And on those days when he came to visit her brothers to do business with them, she had secretly watched him—and yes, she could finally tell him—with great excitement.

All this had come as a surprise to him; he had never realized the extent of her awareness and feeling. He had assumed she was quite ignorant of him (as he had been of her) until the sisters, his and hers, had made the suggestion that they become engaged. He had gone along with it because he was ready to marry and because his brother Ghanem—whose opinion he respected—had highly recommended her, and because he liked how she looked. However, it was not until after the *kitab* (marriage contract) was signed that he truly began to realize how lucky he was.

It was then that he started to take her out in the evenings—alone. Prior to that, they had spent almost no time alone; only a few minutes here and there at her parents' house. But with the engagement formally announced, he began taking her to Caesarea or Netanya in one of his brothers' cars. They would sit in a cafe by the sea all evening, talking and holding hands and even kissing. On some evenings they would stroll along the beach, and then if they could find a secluded spot they would kiss and hold each other more. All of this embracing, though, was a bit risky. They were inviting great trouble and gossip if anyone from the village accidentally discovered them. They knew this very well. Village mores had shifted a long way since their parents' time. It was now accepted that a couple might spend time alone, particularly once the *kitab* was signed.

(How hard it must have been in their parents' day, when couples were never left alone until the wedding night!) Yet being alone was one thing; sex on the beach, even if it wasn't full sex, was quite another. Zaynab's parents had been liberal enough in allowing them to go out in the evenings alone. Most parents in Kufr Qara would not have done so. Had they discovered what was going on at the beach, they would have been shocked and enraged.

But, God be praised—as Hassan found himself sacrilegiously thinking—they never did find out. He and Zaynab continued going out a couple of evenings a week, to Caesarea, to Netanya, and to the beach. They did, that is, until a few weeks before the wedding. Then, just to make sure there were no last minute slip-ups, they decided to see each other only at her house and only for brief periods. It was, they both decided (with a little pressure from her parents), the proper thing to do. And besides, with all the final preparations to look after, they no longer had the leisure or peace of mind to be running off in the evenings together.

Hassan was not the only one in the family who began to feel under pressure in those days before the wedding. Everyone, it seemed, was full of nervous expectation. They worried that something might go wrong at the last moment to spoil it all. It had been so difficult to find a common date when all of the hired wedding crew were available—the five-piece orchestra, the singer, the poets, the cook, and the video team. Summer, the dry season, was the most popular time for weddings throughout the country, and there was great demand for the services of such crews, especially for the good ones. What would happen now if the wedding suddenly had to be postponed? That danger always loomed. With such a large clan, there was always an older aunt or uncle who was near death's door. If one should die, God forbid, the wedding could not take place until a forty-day mourning period was observed. Indeed, there was one particular ninety-five-year-old aunt who was sick at the time; sick enough, in fact, that Abu Ahmad decided to go speak to the family, and it was agreed that should she die just before the wedding the death announcement would be delayed.

With all these worries flitting about like bats, nobody

was getting much sleep at night. And in the daytime, in an attempt to allay their fears, they busied themselves frantically with last minute activities. Abu Ahmad, who was fighting off a nasty flu, roused himself to supervise the cleaning of his half-dunam backyard, where the main celebration and entertainment would take place. Umm Ahmad and her daughters brought brooms and mops to Hassan's new house and cleaned it from top to bottom; when they finished this, the day before the wedding, they began converting some one hundred and fifty kilos of vegetables into homemade salads. Ahmad and Ghanem bought three sheep and two calves, which they spent a full day butchering; the meat, enormous slabs of it, was stored in three rented refrigerators which now occupied Abu Ahmad's kitchen and salon.

As for Hassan, he was giddy with anticipation. He tried to calm himself by finishing up the front lawn or picking some red peppers that were so ripe they were rotting on the vine. But it was hopeless. He couldn't work. A few times he dropped over at Zaynab's house, only to find that she too was jittery and was keeping herself busy by working around the house. It was hard to talk to her. Words no longer came so easily. It was better, he finally decided, to spend the last day or so away from her, with friends.

His friends kept stopping by to see how he was managing. They sat on the porch of his new house smoking and drinking endless cups of coffee. They humored him, teased him, reassured him. At one point Yussef came by to finish up the cabinet work, and inasmuch as he was a married man, a man with experience, he thought to give Hassan a little playful advice. Samir, sitting nearby, also got into the act.

Noticing that Hassan looked a little detached and edgy, Yussef began prodding him, "Come on, my friend, it's only your wedding you're going to, not your funeral."

Hassan forced a smile. "You know how it is, Yussef, I've got a lot on my mind."

"Yes, I do know. I remember what it's like. And I bet I know exactly what you've got on your mind!"

Samir chuckled and said, "Hassan's worried you're not

going to finish up the cabinets in time. The house won't be ready—"

"Right," interrupted Yussef. "It won't be ready in time for him to start screwing."

Hassan laughed half-heartedly and sighed. "I'm so tired right now. God knows how I'll be in two nights."

"You're tired now? Wait until the morning after. You'll be exhausted." Yussef sized up Hassan's reaction and added reassuringly, "A great night, the first one. You'll see, all night you'll be at it."

"Tell me, Yussef. The truth. How many times did you do it the first night?"

"Who can remember? A lot, say."

Samir slapped Hassan on the shoulder. "We'll have to give Hassan some injections or energy pills. Maybe we should have an ambulance nearby just in case."

Hassan feigned anger. "Come on, what do you take me for? I can go all night, I'm sure."

"Of course you can," said Yussef. "First night, it's no problem. Tired or not tired, you go all night."

"Same with the woman, right?"

"No problem. You can, she can. Especially in the beginning. The whole first year, she's ready all the time. After that, she's got a backache, or this and that. If she's not a virgin, forget it, even on the wedding night she's already bored—" Yussef halted, realizing Hassan might have taken this personally. He turned to me, explaining, "But here in the village, they're all virgins. It's not like America, or among the Jews."

"Right," Hassan affirmed.

"Mind you, they know about sex," said Yussef. "They talk to their sisters who are married. Sometimes to their mother too. It depends. But never to their husbands-to-be."

"Right," Hassan repeated firmly.

"Believe me, they've got sex on their minds plenty. Even more than we do. At least the first year. After that, well, you'll see. But in the beginning—just wonderful!" Yussef smacked his lips and rose to leave, his introductory lecture finished. Samir, flicking away the butt of his cigarette, got up to leave with him. Then, turning back, Yussef called to

Hassan, "What time does the *lelat il henna* begin? I got the invitation, but I forgot to look at the time. About eight, no?"

"Right, whenever," Hassan answered.

"Remember, get a little rest tonight. You'll need it!"

And Samir added, "I'm going to the pharmacy to get the pep pills now."

And they walked off as Hassan continued sitting on the porch, trying to laugh as hard as they were.

While family and friends had known for a couple of months exactly when the celebrations would take place, formal invitations were not made until a few days before. This was the usual way of doing things in the village, a precaution taken lest some untoward event in the final weeks cause a delay. Hassan's and Zaynab's families had printed up their own separate invitations, and as was typical, they each delivered them to their own invited guests. Altogether, more than a thousand people were expected, most of them from Kufr Qara.

The ceremonies were scheduled for two days, June 28 and 29. And while somewhat lengthy by Western standards, they were actually a streamlined version of the week-long festivities that had accompanied weddings a generation or so ago. No longer were there several days of singing and dancing prior to the *lelat il henna*, "night of the henna," and the wedding itself. People were simply too busy now, with steady jobs to go to in the morning; two consecutive evenings felt like quite enough and had become the norm. What had been retained was the traditional *lelat il henna*, a night of singing, dancing, and feasting, which culminated in the ceremonial decorating of the bride (now only her hand, not her face) with a sooty red dye, henna, as a symbol of good luck; it was now also common that the man be similarly decorated on the hand. The following evening was the wedding itself: another evening of singing, dancing, and even more elaborate feasting, after which the bride and groom finally went off to spend what was assumed to be their first night together.

All of this required so much preparation and organization that it was not surprising that the families were exhausted before the first guest even arrived. So it was, at least, with Abu Ahmad's family. They were all weary and spent, and there was a good deal of carping as they sought to finish in time. As it turned out, they were still hauling out red and white plastic chairs to the front patio and backyard, and still dicing up the lamb for *shishlik*, when the first guests began strolling in at about eight in the evening. Abu Ahmad, as yet unshaved, motioned for the male guests to sit down on the patio, as the women gathered separately in an area nearby.

Within a half hour the place was jammed with some four hundred people, mostly men. Bare light bulbs strung above the patio and out in the backyard lit up the crowd. Most of the women, as if warming up, were singing in stops and starts while beating an occasional tambourine or hand drum. The men, ignoring them, chatted with each other either on the patio or in the backyard. Small children, dolled up in party outfits, swooped back and forth between the adults, while boy and girl teenagers, just as dazzlingly dressed, stood in separate clusters, eyeing each other surreptitiously.

Wafting over the crowd was the smoke and smell of grilled lamb being cooked in a corner of the backyard. Ghanem had drawn this duty and he was dripping with sweat as he stood there adjusting the dozens of skewers. Standing next to him was his uncle, Ibrahim, a short heavy-jowled man with the belly of a sumo wrestler. Ibrahim had not come to help but rather to sample the goods, which he plucked into his mouth one after the other like M&M candies. Though he was Abu Ahmad's only brother and lived close by, I had hardly seen him during the first half year of my visits to the village; the rumor was that the two of them were at odds with each other. Curious to meet him and perhaps hear the story, I suggested that we go into the *diwan* and sit at one of the dinner tables. "What, eat salads in there?" he responded incredulously. "I've got the best spot right here—where the meat is right off the grill." He did suggest, however, that some other day I come visit him at his house. We set a tentative date, *inshallah*, and I went off to eat.

While the guests were still finishing dinner, Hassan prepared to go over to Zaynab's house where *her* party was underway, and where there were almost exclusively women guests. Going there was something of a break with tradition. Until recent times, the groom did not show up at the bride's party. But this new wrinkle had become more and more acceptable, and Hassan and Zaynab decided to do it this way—with their parents' approval, of course. Thus, with a small entourage of forty or so women from the family and a handful of male cousins and friends, Hassan drove over to Zaynab's house.

There he was greeted like a long-awaited movie star on opening night. The video crew that had been filming the proceedings for the past hour or so rushed out to greet him, their strobe lights glaring. And the five-piece orchestra seated on a makeshift wooden stage in the courtyard upped the tempo, as the singer crooned loud words of welcome. Zaynab, seated on an adjacent stage, smiled broadly through her makeup, and came down to greet him, delicately raising her floor-length white skirts.

Immediately, as though they had been waiting for this moment, the women from Hassan's family joined in the dancing, as did Hassan and a couple of his friends. Everyone danced alone, their arms raised slightly in the air and their pelvises gyrating sensuously. The older women in their ankle-length gowns, and the younger women in their bright cocktail dresses formed a circle around Hassan and Zaynab as the two danced opposite each other, scarcely touching. The video cameraman and his partner with the strobe lights dove in and out trying to catch every minute of the action as a third partner sat off to the side at a high-tech console, carefully editing the product. (Eventually there would be nine hours of videotape.) A few teenage boys and old men in *gallabiyehs* gathered around the console, more interested in watching the video than the dancing itself. And in a nearby pen several sheep bleated incessantly, not sure what to make of the whole spectacle.

Also standing off to the side, neither dancing nor singing, was Hassan's friend Samir, who had been reluctant to
come but at the last moment had trailed along to keep me
company.

"What do you think of all this?" he asked me at one
point.

"I'm not sure. It's the first time I've been to a wedding
like this," I answered noncommittally.

"Well, let me tell you, I don't like it," he said bluntly.

"No? Why's that?"

"Hassan, he's entitled to do what he wants. I wish him
all the best, really I do. But me, I think it's wrong to be
throwing big parties these days. You know, over in the West
Bank and Gaza, they've stopped having big parties now.
Since the *intifada*. There's no money and no taste for it.
People dying every day—how can you throw such a party?
Hassan doesn't feel this way, I know. He's got no family over
there like I do. But personally, I wouldn't do it. Not now, I
wouldn't."

Samir and I walked over to the other side of the courtyard, attempting to get away from the blinding strobe lights.
I decided to ask him whether he was, in fact, thinking of
getting married.

"Can't afford it," he answered. "No house, no money.
And no girl—not really." Then, nonchalantly, he nodded in
the direction of a tall, fleshy, full-breasted girl, with dark
skin and curly black hair. She was clearly the most sensuous
dancer in the courtyard as she gyrated her pelvis sugges-
tively while hardly moving her upper body except for a slow
seductive weaving of her hands and arms. Her eyes were
turned inward as if focused on some deep secret, and her
mouth was curved in a gentle come-hither smile. "Dances
well, doesn't she?" Samir finally said. "How old do you think
she is?"

"About twenty-five or twenty-six."

"Right, she looks like she's older. But she's only nineteen, Zaynab's age. And smart like Zaynab, too. They went
through high school together. I've had my eye on her for a
year now. I know her brothers. My family knows hers well.
I go over there freely, just walk in. Her parents and mine

would like us to marry. But I just don't know, I can't make up my mind."

"Not ready yet?"

"No, not really. But it's more than that. She's smart and pretty, but look at her—she's as dark as an African." Samir grinned self-consciously. "I know it's wrong. Against the Koran and all that. Still, I've got a thing in my head about Negroes. I want someone light-skinned like Zaynab, like me. I don't want my kids all coming out Negroes. I know it's crazy, and when I look at her out there dancing, I really feel nuts. I just don't know. I just don't know . . ." Samir wiped his beaded forehead. He suggested we move again, though this time it was not the heat from the strobe lights that was bothering him.

By now Hassan was saying his farewells to Zaynab and her parents, and his entourage was gathering around him to return to Abu Ahmad's house. The video crew, musicians, and singer were also packing up their equipment in order to go with him. Zaynab's brothers and male cousins joined Hassan, while the women of her family and her friends stayed with her to put on the henna, in a ceremony much like the one that would take place with Hassan a couple of hours later.

When we got back to Abu Ahmad's house, the guests, almost all men, were still sitting about, or in the case of Abu Ahmad's contemporaries, sprawling about, on thin mattresses that had been dragged out to the patio. There was no movie-star reception for Hassan this time. His entourage of women, along with the others who had stayed behind to work in the kitchen, filed out to the backyard and took seats in a corner—in the bleachers, so to speak. The men, about two hundred fifty of them, took the prime seats which faced the lit-up backyard. The video crew, evidently an experienced bunch, went quickly into action, and the orchestra and singer were soon at it again too.

For the next hour there was non-stop dancing—the *dubka* and *sahgi*, traditional male dances. Just as the party at Zaynab's had been primarily a women's event, the dancing now was an all-men's affair. Abu Ahmad's clan was known to have some fine dancers and the *dubka* put them to the test. Only young men were able to handle the rigors of this dance, in which a line of men with arms on each other's shoulders followed the spontaneous lead of the first dancer. Leaping at one moment, squatting at another, then limping in old-man fashion, the leader weaved forward as those in the line followed his improvisations. Several times the lead changed, with each new leader adding his own high-spirited tricks, and all dancing with a virile grace and power. The older men watched, their eyes gleaming wistfully, as the orchestra strummed out its hot, undulating rhythms. Eventually, as the young men tired, the tempo eased and the slower rhythms of the *sahgi* started. Middle-aged men rose to join in this circular dance, clapping and singing and slow-stepping along with the singer. Hassan joined in, along with Ghanem and Ahmad. Abu Ahmad, however, was nowhere to be seen, and I later discovered that he had taken ill and had been driven over to Ghanem's house. Umm Ahmad and her daughters and daughters-in-law were all there, though, sitting in the corner, patiently waiting to return to action.

Their turn came finally at about midnight, as the music stopped and almost all the men headed home. Only Hassan and a few friends stayed. The women came out of semi-hiding, and then, rather anti-climactically I thought, they performed the *henna* ceremony. About thirty or forty of them danced around Hassan, singing, trilling, and clapping. A plate of dark henna paste covered with daisies was brought out of the house, and an amateur artist—one of Hassan's friends—put some of the paste in a plastic bag and squeezed the henna through a small opening to painstakingly decorate Hassan's hand as if it were a cake. The design, simple in form and spirit, consisted of a heart pierced by an arrow in the center of the palm, Hassan's and Zaynab's initials just under it, and polka dots and curlicues on the fingers. When the decorating was over—it took a good half hour—Hassan was lifted onto the broad shoulders of Faisal, one of Ibrahim's sons, and for a few more minutes the women danced around them. Everyone seemed tired by now, with the exception of Umm Ahmad, who whirled about excitedly as if the night were just beginning. Hassan, his lavender shirt clinging to his body, was finally lowered to the ground. And then he and several friends strolled off arm-in-arm to a friend's house, where he would spend his last night as a bachelor.

The bachelor party lasted until dawn, and when his friends went off to work, Hassan slept for several hours. He awoke feeling rested and content. He lay in bed smiling to himself as he thought about how well the party had gone the night before. The crowd, he estimated, had been a large one, maybe five hundred people in all; for the first night, that was very acceptable. It meant that on the second night there would surely be a thousand or more guests. From Kufr Qara itself, a few hundred more would be coming, and then there were all those "respected ones," his father's friends, who would be arriving from surrounding villages and from the Galilee, and even from Jerusalem. So he hoped. Not only for selfish reasons—it meant he would get more gift money to offset the wedding expenses—but also because he wanted his wedding to bring happiness and honor to the family. This was the first wedding party since Nabila's death, and it was important that it go over well and renew them all. And so far, so good.

For Zaynab, who spent her last night at home, the morning had a painful sting. The *lelat il henna* had gone well, and it had been good to have Hassan come over to her house looking so handsome and happy. She looked forward to her new life with him, truly she did. But now the thought of leaving home—her father, her four unmarried brothers, and above all, her mother—filled her with an aching sadness. How could she bear no longer seeing her brothers every day? How would her mother manage alone without her? Her brothers had promised to visit often, and she could always go to see her mother, yet she knew, as every bride knew, that it would never be the same. She would be joining Hassan's family, raising her children as part of his family, and celebrating holidays with them. This was the way of her people, and she had known since she was small that one day her time would come to leave. And now that it had, she felt a grief deeper than any she had ever known.

Her whole family, in fact, had been trying to stifle their tears all morning and afternoon as they waited for the inevitable, which was due to happen, according to the plan, at 5:00 P.M. A generation or so ago, it would have been the duty of her father, and perhaps her brothers, to bring Zaynab over to Hassan's house, riding on a horse or a camel. But now things were done differently in the village: when both bride and groom lived there, as was often still the case, the groom's father along with other family elders went to fetch her—in a car.

And thus it was that Abu Ahmad, dressed in his smartest *gallabiyeh* and accompanied by half a dozen respected members of the clan, showed up at Zaynab's parents' house. Seats had been prepared for them in the courtyard, and bowls of fruit and cigarettes were set out on small tables. Zaynab's father, also dressed in a fine *gallabiyeh*, went out to meet them accompanied by his sons.

"*As-salaam aleikum* [Peace be upon you]," Abu Ahmad greeted them.

"*Wa aleikum salaam* [And upon you be there peace]," came the customary reply. "*Ahlan wa sahlan fikum, itfadalu* [Please make yourselves welcome]."

They all sat down. For a few minutes they smoked cigarettes and made small talk. Then Abu Ahmad turned to Zaynab's father and delivered the short, formal speech which he had silently rehearsed on the way over: "I respectfully request from you that you allow me to take the bride. For this, I shall be grateful. I also invite you to join us in the wedding celebration at my house. *As-salaam aleikum.*"

Zaynab's father formally replied, "*Wa aleikum salaam.* You are welcome. Please allow us now a little time so that we may go take leave of the bride." He and his sons rose and went into the house.

A few minutes later Zaynab emerged at the doorway. She was wearing her new wedding dress, a flowing white gown with winged epaulettes. She wore glittering earrings and a matching head-band, and looked like a queen going off to her coronation, except for the tears rushing down her cheeks. The grief that her family also had been trying to hold back all day now flooded them. They stood around Zaynab, weeping. Abu Ahmad, up to a point, had expected this; indeed, it was considered good form for the family to show some emotion when the bride left, in order to demonstrate that they were not eager to see her off. Yet what Abu Ahmad was witnessing here was genuine—even the father was weeping—and he himself could not help being moved by it.

While all this was going on at Zaynab's house, Hassan was winding up his own preparations at his friend's house. A barber hired specially for the occasion had cut his hair, shaved him, and trimmed his moustache. His friends, according to custom, gave him a prenuptial bath and doused him with cologne. They dressed him in his new black suit and dark tie, and brought him out to a chestnut horse that had been rented for the ceremonial ride to his parents' house, only a few hundred meters away. The women of the family, who had gathered outside, then followed the horse, trilling and dancing, as a friend held a decorated parasol above his head to shade him from the late afternoon sun. He arrived just as Zaynab did. The video cameraman (I couldn't help wondering if he were responsible for the perfect timing) was right on the spot to catch Hassan greeting her and then escorting her to the nearby elevated veranda of a neighbor's house, where she would sit the rest of the evening with most of the other women, peering down at the male party below.

"A real circus, no?" said Samir, coming over to me. He had been walking along with Hassan, next to the horse. "Fancy horses, dancing ladies with tambourines—the whole show." He looked weary, unshaven.

"You look like you didn't get any sleep last night," I said.

"Not a minute. I went at dawn from Hassan's party right to the fields. I've been there all day picking tomatoes. With the kids from the territories. That's how we got the horse for Hassan—rented from one of the kids."

"They're here?"

"No, they went home. What a mess! Last night in their

village the soldiers went on a shooting spree. You know—
some kids were throwing stones."

"Anyone get hurt?"

"No, not this time. But what a situation! My aunt's
village too—it's been under curfew all week. It makes my
blood boil. And what can you do about it? Nothing. These
kids are getting shot at and we're dancing. They're eating
rice and beans and we're throwing banquets." He shook his
head in disbelief. "It just drives me crazy what's going on
over there—" Samir stopped as another friend came by and
suggested we go into the *diwan* and eat. Samir declined,
saying he'd already had his supper, and then walked off.

Inside the *diwan* there was indeed a banquet set out for
the guests. Two long tables were set with plates and silver-
ware. Heaping bowls of salads, at least half a dozen varieties, lined the center of the tables. In large cooking vats
just behind the *diwan*, the hired chef had prepared a veal
stew and rice flecked with meat and pine nuts. Young boys,
all members of Hassan's clan, were bringing in huge platters
of the food to guests who ate voraciously, hardly talking,
and washed it all down with cans of sweet soda (as usual
no liquor was served, in keeping with Muslim strictures).
Upon finishing, the diners went out back, as others filed in
quickly to take their places and the boys brought fresh
mounds of food.

It took a good couple of hours to feed the thousand or
so guests, and by the time everyone had finished, the entertainment was already in full swing. The main attraction this
night was a well-known traditional singer-poet from Nazareth, Saud Assadi. He was working with a younger partner,
and the two of them sang in short shifts of about five or ten
minutes each. Sitting in plastic chairs that were set up in
long rows on the fringes of the backyard, the guests were
hanging on every word—especially when Saud Assadi sang.
He was clearly a spellbinder. Tall, silver-haired, and dressed
in a beige polished-cotton suit, he had the sweet, ingratiat-
ing air of an Italian movie actor. His partner was younger
and darker, both in complexion and dress, and while he had
a fine voice he lacked the charm of the older man.

It was clear from the beginning that part of the show

was a competition between the two men, old versus young,
to see who could best woo the crowd. This took place not so
much when they sang traditional and familiar songs but
when they improvised, creating, for example, their own
rhyming lyrics of praise for the village of Kufr Qara, for the
guests (many of the notables were singled out in special
refrains), and for their land, Palestine. The audience relished
the clever rhymes and word plays, and they clapped and
hooted them on. Several times, men rose to dance the *sahgi*
around the singers, chanting phrases that began to take on
a nationalistic slant—"*Bil hurriyeh u salaam, ehna bnaamin
fiha* [In freedom and peace, we all believe]; *Dawar ilfalak
dawar* [The world around us is changing]." The mood was
heating up. I wondered where it was all going. Then suddenly, as if on cue, the singers cooled down the tempo and
moments later turned off their microphones. They announced they were going on a break.

The crowd rose, itchy, and began milling about. People
went over to Hassan, who had been sitting in a plush arm-
chair in the front row, and pressed envelopes with cash into
his hand while kissing him on both cheeks. Abu Ahmad came
over to me and, grabbing my arm, insisted I meet "our
poets." He led me to the patio where Saud Assadi and his
partner sat, calmly sipping coffee. Introductions made, he
headed back to make the rounds among his guests.

I remained talking with them for half an hour or so,
during which Saud Assadi—he did most of the talking—told
me a little about his poetry and about himself. He had come
to the wedding, he said, at the request of Ahmad, who twenty
years ago had been his high-school student in Nazareth. He
still taught Arabic literature in high school there, but in the
summer he was constantly busy with weddings. This was
his passion. His father had been a singer-poet before him,
and he was teaching his oldest son how to perform; his
partner this night was a protégé, and one of his former
students in high school.

"Every people has its favorite art form," he said. "For
the Arabs, it is poetry. You see how the people out there
listen. They may not follow every last word and nuance of
the poetry, but they love the sound and its rhythmic beauty.

And it *is* beautiful, don't you think? For more than four hundred years, all through the Ottoman times and maybe longer, there has been a tradition of poets singing at weddings. How long this will continue in our electronic era, I don't know. But I'm glad that Jumaa here"—he tousled the young man's hair—"and also my son and others are taking it up.

"What we sing differs at each wedding. It depends on the mood of the people and on my mood too. And also on what is possible. You could feel out there, maybe, something a little political beginning, no? This is natural. Politics are on everyone's mind these days. But we must be careful. Just last week a poet friend of mine who also sings at weddings was arrested for having sung nationalistic songs. And I was in jail last year, after a wedding in the Galilee. I sang a poem which I wrote about the *intifada*, 'Children of the Stones.'[1] Well, the crowd went wild and began singing nationalistic songs and chanting slogans. Someone there must have told the police, because a few days later they arrested me, my son, the host, and seventy guests. And since everything is videotaped at these modern weddings, they had all the evidence they needed. They booked me for incitement, and I wound up spending five days in jail with my son. It wasn't a bad experience—we had fun singing there, too—but I'd prefer it didn't happen again." He stomped out the cigarette he had been smoking. "And it won't—at least not tonight. But we'll have some fun anyway. You'll see." And taking his partner by the arm, he strolled back for the final set.

---

[1]*Tifl el-hijreh* (Children of the Stones): "From over there afar,/From such a house,/A mother looks down at the street,/The street which is aflame.

She sees small children rushing all over,/And she cries out:/'Oh God who watches over the Ka'ba,/Please watch over them too!'

There is a boy stoning the patrol,/A boy who doesn't flee,/Despite the fire,/Despite the gas.

But then the boy is wounded in the head,/And he cries out:/'Oh my country, we have martyrs,/Whatever it takes, we shall provide!'

And at night his mother stayed by his bed,/Stayed with him until the end,/Till his last breath,/She stayed with him.

And now the boys and girls go to his funeral,/They sing him songs of his wedding,/And his mother buries him, then goes home,/And the very next day sends her very next son,/To join the Children of the Stones!"

Within minutes they were going at it again, singing short, pulsating lyrics in that same competitive manner. They stayed away from political themes, even though the men dancing about them were again chanting the vaguely nationalistic refrains. I looked at Abu Ahmad, who was sitting across from me, and his eyes were transfixed on the singers. So were those of everyone else. Then, as the competition became more and more blatant, the singers began flinging barbed phrases at each other. "Don't you dare cut into my song, old fellow/With my words I'll show you who is yellow," Jumaa hurled at Saud Assadi, who was glaring at him, and who then fired back: "Listen to my partner, young and brash/To hear some clapping hands, he'll say such trash." And on it escalated, all in rhyme, with the audience applauding each thrust and counterthrust of the strident younger man attempting to assert himself against his reproving mentor. The lyrics seemed to go right to the heart of this wedding night crowd of fathers and sons. At one point, Hassan's brother Ahmad rushed out to Saud Assadi, as if worried, and whispered in his ear; to which the poet responded into the microphone, "Don't ask me to let him go free right now/I'm going to finish him off, and how!" But Ahmad stayed, in mock persistence, and finally Saud Assadi allowed his microphone, which he had been pointing at Jumaa, to droop to his side. Rhymed reconciliations were offered, the two men again smiled at each other, and the audience howled its approval.

With the joust over, so too was the stag party. The men drifted off into the night. Abu Ahmad also went off, leaving Hassan and a few of the younger men to greet the women as they once again came out of hiding to cap off the festivities. Zaynab still looked fresh and radiant as two nieces, holding up her bridal dress, escorted her to the center of the backyard. A small wooden platform had been set up. Zaynab and Hassan mounted it while the fifty or so women from their families danced about them. Umm Ahmad, as might be expected, was the liveliest of the dancers. She whirled about with a potted green plant—a good luck symbol—mounted on her erectly held head. Her daughters were dancing, too, except for Maysa, who looked strangely forlorn. The video cameraman, still at it, panned the group and then moved in for final close-ups of Hassan and Zaynab removing the gold rings which they had worn on their right hands since the engagement party, and shifting them to their left hands. No prayers were said, nor were there kisses. The entire ceremony, a mere postscript to the all-male party, was over in a matter of minutes. And with no further fanfare, Hassan and Zaynab came off the mounted platform and walked quickly to Ghanem's waiting Subaru. Mercifully, the cameraman was no longer there to catch the anxious smiles that flickered across Zaynab's face as she settled next to Hassan and they prepared to drive off through the now empty village streets—past her parents' house, past the bleating sheep, to spend their first night alone in their new house.

11

MAYSA:
THE LAST CHILD

WITH HASSAN MARRIED, Maysa knew that her turn was
next. Indeed, in the weeks before the wedding, Umm
Ahmad had already begun turning on the pressure. "It's
going on too long now, you've got to choose," Umm Ahmad
had told her. "I still have time," she answered. "What time?
You're twenty-four. I want to see you marry before I'm in
my grave!" So it had begun. And with the festivities over
and Hassan gone, these proddings were sure to increase from
all her family—her brothers, her sisters, and maybe even
her father too. She could not hold out much longer. Soon
she would have to choose from among the several men who
had hinted or stated outright that they wanted to marry her.

And yet she was not ready. She still had not recovered
from Nabila's death, nor had she regained her zest for living.
She had felt this at Hassan's wedding. While dancing, singing, or trilling along with the other women, the sadness had
at times flooded her as she thought of Nabila and wished
that she were there. She had wondered if others could see
this sadness. She had such a childlike face—full cheeks, big
round eyes—and people expected her to always be smiling;
yes, the smiling, happy, youngest child of the family. But
try as she might, the smiles had not come easily, and during

those days of Hassan's wedding, Nabila had been with her as a constant companion.

The accident that had taken Nabila away from her happened almost a year and a half before, on February 23, 1988. Those days—it had taken two days before Nabila died—were as sharply clear to her as if they had just occurred. She remembered how she and Nabila had gotten up together in the morning. They had dressed together, put on their makeup together, and laughed and joked together. They also had made plans to meet at home at four that afternoon and to go together to Kufr Qara's women's club in order to organize a party for Mother's Day. But when four o'clock came Nabila, uncharacteristically, was not there. Nor was she back at five. Umm Ahmad had been terribly worried. "Something has happened, I just know it," she had said at first, and then ominously had added, "We've lost her." They had not been able to get through to Nabila at work, and then Hassan had heard on the radio of a serious automobile accident on the main Wadi Ara road. He had gone to the nearby Hillel Yaffe hospital in Hadera to see if it was Nabila. The next thing they knew, Ahmad was standing at the door with his whole family and it was written all over their faces.

They all rushed to the hospital—that is, after Umm Ahmad had been revived. She had fainted on the spot when she heard Ahmad say that Nabila was in the hospital. For the next forty-eight hours Nabila had remained unconscious, though she was still breathing. The doctors had operated on her in Hillel Yaffe and then transferred her to Beilinson hospital to operate on her again. The family had prayed day and night, hoping for a miracle. But no miracle came. On February 25 she died. Her swollen and disfigured body had been brought back to her parents' house. The village woman who usually washes the dead came, but Maysa insisted on doing the washing herself; the woman told her how to do it and which prayers to say. When she finished, the men took Nabila's body away to the graveyard—women did not go to the graveyard—and Maysa, who had not shed a tear until then, collapsed in grief.

Weeks, months, it had taken before Maysa had begun to return from the dead, from Nabila. At her new job, as a social worker in the municipality of Umm al-Fahm, she had barely been able to function. Fortunately her employers had been compassionate, otherwise she would have been fired. She felt so miserable that for awhile she seriously thought of seeking counselling or psychotherapy. But in the end she turned to friends and to her supervisor at work, and they had helped her. So too had Umm Ahmad. When she had felt so despondent that she could hardly get out of bed, her mother had talked with her and stroked her back to life. More than anyone else, her mother understood the enormity of her loss. And in a way, that was to be expected, because more than anyone else her mother knew what Nabila had meant to her—from the time they were both small children.

"We were the last children, Nabila and I," explained Maysa one afternoon shortly after Hassan's wedding, as we sat in her parents' salon with Umm Ahmad resting nearby. Nabila's portrait—the attractive young face of a college graduate—now hung on the wall above. "She was only thirteen months older than me, and really we were like twins. Right from the beginning we were always together. When we were children, we even slept together on the same mattress on the floor. There were not enough mattresses to go around and so the youngest children slept together, Hassan with Rana, and me with Nabila.'

"Of course we played together all the time, too. Hassan was sort of our ringleader. He'd organize all kinds of games. Like, we'd play 'store' or 'bank.' We'd bring make-believe money to the store and he'd give us make-believe food, or he'd open up a bank account for us in his bank. Always *his* bank, because he liked being the boss. We also played 'bride and groom' a lot, just like my mother used to play. Sometimes Nabila would be the bride, or sometimes me or Rana. Hassan or one of our cousins would be the groom. We were free to play like this together, boys and girls—not like in my mother's time, when boys and girls didn't play together at all, and certainly not the 'bride and groom' game. We took it seriously and did it like a real wedding. The bride would be brought through the back lanes around our house, and she'd come to the groom. Then there would be singing and dancing. We even had our own orchestra. It was like the real thing—except the bride and groom never went off together!

"Aside from all these games we played together, Nabila and I also went to school together. She was always a grade in front of me, and I followed her through grade school, junior high, and high school, just like a shadow. The teachers couldn't believe we were sisters because we were so different. She is a forceful person—*was* a forceful person. She was taller than me and very pretty, with this dark brown curly hair and sparkling brown eyes with long eyelashes. The teachers liked her because she was pretty and very smart, but she gave them a hard time. She was always questioning things, challenging things. Not like me. I was the obedient one and never challenged anybody. But we both did well in school, all the way through high school. And we both decided to go to the university, not just hang around the village and get married right away. That was fine with my parents. They're liberal in that way, both of them. They support the idea of higher education, even for their daughters. So Nabila was allowed to go off to the Hebrew University in Jerusalem, and a year later, again sort of like her shadow, I followed her there.

"Our family didn't have much money at the time, so both Nabila and I had to work in order to help pay for our education. I worked in the university cafeteria, the supermarket, the library, and as a receptionist at Hadassah Hospital, and even for a while as a cleaning lady. Everything. It was the only way both Nabila and I could afford to go to university at the same time. We also lived together in the same dorm room. That was very good for me, because she sort of protected me and helped me adjust to university life. So I didn't have the problems that a lot of Arab students have in finding their way in the beginning.

"You see, for many Arab students the shift to university life is difficult, even a little overwhelming. Particularly for those of us who come from villages, not cities like Nazareth or Haifa. It's not so much the idea of being around so many

Jews, because really Arab students hang around together just like in the village. It's more a question of being on your own for the first time, away from parental supervision. For the boys, who are spoiled rotten at home, suddenly they have to cook for themselves, wash their own clothing, and clean up. It's about time, really! Although—if I look at it through their eyes—I suppose it's hard for them. With us, the girls, there are no problems with these things. We've already had plenty of practice at home. Our problems are more in the area of choosing friends. Who do you hang out with? Girls from only your own village, or others too? For the first time, you are in daily contact with people who you haven't known all your life, whose families you don't know. It's a little frightening.

"And then there's the whole question of boys. In the village, you were never able to be alone with a boy. Not even in high school. In Kufr Qara, no girl dared being seen alone with a boyfriend. Her brothers or father would have beaten her up and locked her in the house. Or at the very least, she would have been severely scolded and shamed. So you can imagine what a shock it is suddenly to be free in the university, and actually go out with boys. Some girls don't know how to handle this freedom. They immediately start going out with some guy and having sex with him, and the next thing they know they're pregnant. When I was working as a receptionist at Hadassah Hospital, I used to see cases like this. They'd come for an abortion and they were terrified that their family or someone from their village might find out about it.

"But really, a girl didn't have to go that far to get into trouble. Depending on her village and family, she might get in trouble if word got back that she was just walking through the street alone with a boy. That by itself could cause her problems. My family is not so strict like some others, but still it would have offended my father and brothers to know that I or Nabila were, say, walking around hand-in-hand with some boy—even in a group. Nabila, she was a bold one, though. She didn't have many boyfriends in the university, only one guy who she went out with for awhile. She made no pretenses about it. He was her boyfriend and that was it. Fortunately she never got into trouble. Me, I was more cautious. I didn't have many boyfriends either, but there was one fellow that I started getting interested in during my second year. A fellow from Kufr Qara. Nabila was the only one who knew about him. I was very secretive. When we were with friends, I never held hands with him or did anything to indicate that he was my boyfriend. I didn't want anyone to know. Except Nabila. She liked him and told me that he is right for me and that I shouldn't let him get away. I still know him, but at the moment he's in Jerusalem and I'm here in Kufr Qara, and really, after Nabila's death, I wasn't interested in going out with anyone—"

Maysa stopped talking as Abu Ahmad came into the salon looking for the fan. She had been speaking in Hebrew. (Umm Ahmad did not understand Hebrew, but Abu Ahmad was fluent.) He asked the women to prepare some coffee for his guests outside, and Maysa went to do it. She returned shortly thereafter, and—after making a snide remark in Hebrew about her father's taking "our" fan—she continued.

"When I look back at it, I think that my experience at the university really changed my life. I went from being this very dependent girl to a much more independent person. If I think about it, I don't believe it was the contact with Jewish society and their ways which changed me. It was a matter of being free for the first time to decide things for myself. I had Nabila around to guide me and I *was* very dependent on her. But she believed in women being free and deciding things for themselves, and she was a big influence on me. When we returned to Kufr Qara to live—both of us graduated the same year—we were both determined to have more of a say about what we did, and with whom. Neither of us wanted to be pushed into marriage, even though our time had come. Particularly her time, since she was older.

"As always, she was bold and determined to do it her way. She didn't want to get married then, and she let it be known. She had graduated with a major in Arabic literature and sociology, and she found a job as a librarian in Givat Haviva. She liked the work and they liked her. The day before the accident she had received a promotion. She was making pretty good money. And do you know what she was saving up to do? To go live for a while in Spain. She had a girlfriend at the university from Spain, and she was planning to go live with her for a while. Real guts, she had! For a girl in Kufr Qara to do such a thing alone, without a husband, is really rare. But she had told my brothers and mother—not my father—that she was planning to do it. And she had almost convinced them to go along with it, to not oppose her. This was right before her accident. She had such plans. 'The world is so full of things for us to do,' she told me. 'And you'll see, Maysa, I'm going to do them!' That's what she told me, and I believe she would have, too."

Upon graduation from Hebrew University, Maysa had immediately found a job as a social worker in Umm al-Fahm, an Arab city some ten kilometers from Kufr Qara. Abu Ahmad would have opposed her remaining in Jerusalem or moving to another city in Israel, and she—unlike Nabila—was not willing to do battle with him. As it was, he was not enthusiastic about her traveling each day to Umm al-Fahm. But he figured at least she would spend her nights at home; and besides, her sister, Rana, lived there with her family, and so Maysa would not be altogether alone in that place.

Abu Ahmad did not like Umm al-Fahm—not at all. When Rana had made known her wishes to marry a man from Umm al-Fahm seven years before, he had refused. It was only after Umm Ahmad and all the sisters took up Rana's cause ("She's in love with him, and you'll ruin her life if you refuse") that Abu Ahmad had reluctantly given his consent. He considered Umm al-Fahm a den of iniquity, and even though Rana's husband came from a fine family, he did not want his daughter and grandchildren living there—how could you raise children in such a place?

Though only a short distance from Kufr Qara, the city of Umm al-Fahm does seem, indeed, like a vastly different place. It could even be in another country. A hilltop city of twenty-five thousand people, it is one of the poorest and shabbiest places in Israel. Sewage runs openly through the streets of many of its neighborhoods, and most people are sardined together in ramshackle housing. Unemployment, delinquency, and drug abuse abound, while a thin layer of the population (including Rana's family) live on its periphery in relative luxury. The only other sign of wealth in the city is its proliferation of mosques, seven in all, including a vast new domed structure that resembles Jerusalem's al-Aqsa mosque and is being erected by the Muslim fundamentalists who now dominate the city council.

Not more than a hundred meters from this ornate new mosque is a far less opulent building, whose basement entrance sign reads, in Hebrew and Arabic, "Umm al-Fahm—Department of Social Services." It is here that Maysa works. Abu Ahmad has never seen the place, and from Maysa's perspective that is just as well. Nor is he familiar with the work she does, and that too is for the better. "He'd be put off if he saw some of the places and people I'm dealing with," she explained. "The truth is, he'd prefer I got married and spent all my time in Kufr Qara. That could happen. But right now, I really enjoy the work. And the freedom."

We were sitting in Maysa's office, where I had gone to talk to her about her work. We sat alone—a point she noted. "Even to sit with a man alone in a room," she said, "is something I can't do in Kufr Qara. I mean, after university and all that, isn't it a bit ridiculous? But at least at work I am free to go about my business as I like—" Maysa paused to answer the telephone, and then with an air of authority she called in a male colleague and briefly discussed a case— as it turned out, a case of incest—which the two of them were treating together. "A nasty business," she said when he had left. "The police are involved now. It never should have happened that way, but sometimes that's the way it goes."

She walked over and closed the door so we would not be disturbed and then resumed talking about her work. "About half the time I spend with incest cases. I'm the so-called specialist here on that. The other half of the time I do general social work—with mothers or youth groups or orphans. But it's the work with the incest cases that I especially like and which I seem to be good at. God knows why or how. I didn't study this at Hebrew University. The only way I can explain it is that I seem to be good at talking to young girls in trouble. I always was, I suppose. Even when

I was in high school my friends used to come to me with problems. And I used to be a leader of youth groups in Kufr Qara and always the girls would talk to me freely. So in a way I've had lots of experience talking to kids with problems. Still, nothing really prepared me for this work—with incest cases, I mean.

"We get quite a few such cases here in Umm al-Fahm. More, I think, than in most places. This is simply because there are many more broken homes, with drug abuse or with the father away in jail, or things like that. There's often a lack of strong family ties and supervision, and people are crowded together. I know that incest cases can occur anyplace. Even in Kufr Qara there are a couple of cases which I am aware of. The files have come across my desk, though of course I have to keep my mouth shut about them. But in a place like Kufr Qara families are closer together and there's greater supervision, so you have far fewer cases. Here in Umm al-Fahm, I'm seeing an incest case almost every month. Already I've seen about fifteen.

"I've had to learn how to work as I went along. At this point, what I've learned is that you have to be flexible. Each case is different. Sometimes I deal only with the girl herself, if that is her wish. I'll meet her where she wants, in a park or some hidden place, and if she insists on not involving the family I'll go along. But sooner or later you usually have to involve the family. The people you *don't* want to get involved, if at all possible, are the police. Why? It's very simple. They immediately open a file on the family and the case gets publicized. This brings great shame to the family, and the girl herself is often more severely punished. Sometimes, though, you can't keep the police out of it. The mother or daughter goes and tells them. Like the case you heard me talk about now with Mahmoud. The girl herself went and reported her father to the police. A brave girl, maybe, but now the whole town may know about it.

"What I do most often is work with the whole family. I do what I can to reduce the shame of everyone. Although sometimes, I admit, I am deep-down furious at the father, if he's the one who's done it. But getting furious—for me anyway—is of no help. The main job is to get the family to work together to make sure it is stopped. And also to prevent them from taking out their rage on the girl. You see, even though she may be a very unwilling partner—even a rape victim of the father, brother, or uncle—she will catch the blame for having disgraced the family. And particularly if the word gets out, as often happens when she gets pregnant.

"Several cases that I've worked with are cases that come to the family's attention because the girl *is* pregnant. The first case I ever worked with was like this. A thirteen-year-old girl with lots of problems at school and with friends. She had had sex with her sixteen-year-old brother. She was very naive and didn't know she was pregnant. Not until her seventh month, when she began to feel ill one day and went to the hospital. There they discovered she was pregnant. She was sent to me by the hospital. The mother knew, yet she kept it to herself until the ninth month, and then she told the story to the rest of the family. The father took it fairly well, but her other five brothers were furious with her for having brought shame to the family. They were also furious with the brother who was responsible. He had run off to Eilat, and they went after him and beat him up. The girl herself would have been in real danger if she had been impregnated by someone outside the family. They might have killed her. As it was, they wanted her locked up inside the house and not allowed to ever leave. A life punishment, really.

"That's where I came in and could be helpful. I headed off this prison sentence. I worked intensively with the girl. I didn't start by going into any of the details of the pregnancy. Instead I asked her about other aspects of her life. Like her school work, her friends, that kind of thing. She began to open up to me and then her story came out. She was terrified at the time—this was before the father and brothers knew—that they would kill her. Later, when this didn't happen, the problem became the birth itself. With the family's agreement, I arranged for her to give birth in a hospital secretly and then have the baby adopted. The girl wanted to keep the baby, and it was hard for her to let it go. I had to work with her on that a good deal.

"Today I am still in contact with the girl and her family,

and she is doing all right. She is not being punished. The family has managed to keep the whole thing quiet. In fact, they are now even trying to arrange for her to marry. The problem is that she is no longer a virgin, and that alone— never mind the incest with her brother—might very well cause a husband to immediately divorce her. But fortunately, that too can be fixed. That's what I'm working on right now. There are doctors, Jewish and Arab, who perform the operation whereby they reform the hymen. Not just girls who have been victims of rape and incest go for this operation. Any girl can go. I should say any Arab girl, because they are the ones who go. It's not a legal operation, so it's a pretty good business for the doctors. They get about five hundred dollars for only a few minutes' work, and they don't have to report it. I prefer to deal with Jewish doctors on this because they are less likely to know the family, and the girl is less likely to be discovered. We have a guy in Hadera whom we deal with. No problem. Right now, as soon as the family arranges the marriage and gives me the go-ahead, I'll take care of it. Everything will be fine. And nobody will ever know."

Another day, later that week, we were back at her parents' house seated in the salon, Umm Ahmad sleeping on a floor mattress next to us, the fan whirring nearby. Maysa, wearing baggy slacks and a tee shirt instead of her pert business suit, looked a half dozen years younger—indeed the youngest daughter. Even her voice was less sure here, her authority seemingly left behind in Umm al-Fahm. I commented on this.

"Well, I suppose it's true," she answered. "There I'm a respected professional person. And here, well, I'm the doll-like little girl who supposedly needs protection. What can you do?" She shrugged her shoulders sadly. "I try to fight it in my own way, but I'm not a fighter. Not like Nabila was, anyway. She would take them all on, even my father. But I'm not made that way. I can't do it.

"The person I do occasionally get into battles with is my mother. She's real proud of me and glad to see me working as a professional person. She even knows a little about my work. I get telephone calls here and she sees me handle the cases. She even asks me about it, and sometimes I tell her. In a way, I think that I—and Jamileh too, who is a schoolteacher—fulfilled some of her own wishes. We did what she couldn't do in her time. *But* she's sixty-four and I'm twenty-four, and she has many thoughts of the old generation. That generation was brainwashed in a way, particularly about the role of women. And on these things we do disagree and we have some arguments.

"What kind of arguments? Well, take the example of children, boys versus girls. My mother would not have minded having ten boys, even if she never had a girl. I've heard her say it several times. Me, I want girls and boys. Both. To me, one is not more valuable than the other. But in my mother's eyes, girls can cause problems, or they can bring shame on the family—you know, sexual shame. And girls don't protect the parents in their old age. Boys do, supposedly. That's what she argues. I tell her, 'Mother, that's really nonsense. In our family, who causes more troubles, boys or girls? And who helps the family now?' She knows I'm right. She'll even admit it herself, that my brothers don't help them much financially. It's me who helps them now. The new washing machine and oven, they came from my salary. I make good money, thirteen hundred shekels a month, and I help them. Much more than my brothers. My mother knows this, but if you ask her if it's better to have girls or boys, she'll tell you straight—boys.

"Another area of disagreement, sort of, is in the whole business of getting married. After graduating from Hebrew University, there would have been real pressure on me and Nabila to get married, even though neither of us were ready. Because Nabila died, my mother stopped pushing it. She understood I was in no mood to think of marriage. Now the pressure has started again. My mother is better than many mothers in the village. She'll stand up for us with my father and help us to marry a man that we want—not just someone my father thinks is right for us because he comes from the right family. But she has this thing about getting married *soon*, before you get too old. To her, at twenty-four I'm already an old woman! 'Nobody is going to want you any-more,' she tells me. And I tell her, 'Nonsense, there are ten men out there who want to marry me. You've said it your-self.' And she answers, 'Good, then choose one of them. You've waited long enough. This year I want you to get engaged!'"

Maysa chuckled and glanced at her mother. Umm Ah-mad was still dozing, though she had a gentle, quizzical smile on her face, as if in her sleep she somehow understood what was being discussed. Then Maysa added, "I'd prefer to wait a little longer, but I just know that I won't be able to resist the pressure. Pretty soon I'll have to choose. I'm still not one hundred percent ready. I continue to think about Nabila and I'm still down a lot. But I know that it's no good to go on like that. My mother's attitude is that we have to go on, we cannot live in the past, we have to get over our tragedies. She's right, I know. She thinks that the best thing for me is to get married . . ." Maysa paused for a moment and then in a thin, contemplative voice said, "Maybe she's right. Maybe it is best. I just hope so, because it's going to happen. I can just feel it."

12

AFTER THE WEDDING

A GENERATION AGO, it was common practice for the women of the bride's and groom's families to wait outside the room where the new couple was having their first sex, and when the act was completed, for the mothers to display the bloodied sheet to the waiting crowd as proof of the bride's virginity and also the groom's prowess. Today there are still villages in Israel, and especially in the West Bank, where this practice is common. But in Kufr Qara this is no longer done. Instead, the groom's mother will sometimes come by the following morning, inspect the sheet, and let it be known to interested parties that all was as it should have been.

Hassan and Zaynab wanted no such ritual inspections, and so neither of their mothers showed up the following morning to offend them. They were left alone to "have the first one in the peace and quiet of our own place,"—as Hassan put it. It was only in the afternoon that Hassan opened the front door to the house, and a few close friends and Ghanem, taking the hint, came by to see them. Zaynab, dressed casually and once again with thick makeup, looked more relaxed than Hassan, who was unshaven and tense, as if the night of his dreams had not been what he expected. The men sat down as Zaynab, already assuming her housewifely role, went off to prepare coffee and fruit for them. Hassan and Ghanem discussed the work that needed to be done on the farm (Ghanem was replacing him for the next ten days), and they went over some of the unpaid wedding bills. Hassan was relieved to discover that the wedding costs—some twelve thousand shekels—were more than covered by the guests' gifts, and it even looked like he would have a few thousand shekels left over. "Not a bad profit," he concluded. "At least there's a few shekels for a honeymoon. I can't complain. Really, I can't."

In fact, Hassan and Zaynab had been eager to go on an elaborate honeymoon to Italy or Spain, but they could not afford it. The house and all the new furniture had cost more than they expected, and they were thirty thousand shekels in debt. So a trip to Europe was ruled out; they had to honeymoon in Israel. Somewhat disappointed, they left the following morning for Tiberias in Ghanem's Subaru, with their suitcases packed for a holiday of several days. They had booked a hotel near the beach. But as it turned out, the Sea of Galilee was a mistake. The whole area was crowded with Jewish tourists, the hotel was noisy, and the only place to cool off from the ninety-five-degree heat was in the sea, and neither of them knew how to swim. They wished they had splurged and gone to Europe after all. Now it was too late. Strolling around Tiberias that evening, sweating and discouraged, they realized there was no point in staying. Sometime in the future, they promised themselves, they would take that trip to Europe. For now it would be better just to go home.

They spent the next few days cocooned in their house, entertaining only an occasional guest or two. Mostly their friends and family left them alone. Nobody said anything about the abbreviated honeymoon, nor did they seem particularly concerned by it. Ghanem took over the field work and Umm Ahmad worked alongside him. There was much to do. Hassan had slacked off in the days before the wedding; the peppers were rotting on the vine and a fungus had begun to attack the unsprayed tomato plants. Ghanem did not mind the extra work. He secretly relished the chance to demonstrate that even though he had been a schoolteacher these past nine years, he still had the sturdy back—and soul—of a *fellah*.

One morning about a week after Ghanem had taken over, there was a sudden scream from the other side of the fields, where the thick, leafy pepper plants stood. It was Umm Ahmad. She came rushing toward Ghanem, holding her index finger, which was dripping blood. "I think it was a snake," she said, trying to contain her terror. Ghanem took out a handkerchief, wiped the blood, and looked at the wound. His face relaxed and he said, "No, it's not a snake bite. For sure. I can see by the mark. You only cut yourself on a plant or stone." Umm Ahmad, who knew she could trust her son, also relaxed a bit. They walked over to the edge of the fields, where Ghanem's wife, Latifa, and Ahmad's wife, Nufissa, were standing, their faces tight with worry.

"Thought it was a viper," said Ghanem, "but it's nothing."

"*Il hamdu lillah*, God be praised," said Nufissa. "Come, sit down, Umm Ahmad. I'll go get something to drink."

Umm Ahmad and Ghanem sat down under the fig tree in Ahmad's backyard. Umm Ahmad kept glancing at her finger and repeating "*Il hamdu lillah*." A few moments later Nufissa reappeared with some bottles of cola and Latifa brought out a tray of food—fried eggs, pitot, tehina, *labneh*, and homemade tomato sauce with olive oil. Everyone eyed the food, but with the exception of Ghanem, all were still too tense to eat.

"You had me scared, Umm Ahmad," Nufissa said to her mother-in-law. "Praise God, it was nothing."

"Praise God," everyone chorused.

"Nothing at all," said Ghanem. "Not the marks of a snake, I'm sure." And then, turning to Nufissa, he added, "On this I have some experience."

They all smiled uneasily and Ghanem began recalling the incident which had happened two years ago and which apparently was on everyone's mind right then. The family had been on a picnic at the Sea of Galilee—near the hotel where Hassan and Zaynab had gone for their honeymoon— when suddenly Nufissa was bitten by a snake which had somehow crawled into her blouse. Ghanem had had the presence of mind to go after the snake as it slithered away, and he caught it. Within minutes Nufissa was unconscious. They rushed her to the nearby Poriyya hospital, and because Ghanem had brought along the snake—a deadly viper—they were able to give her the proper antidote immediately and save her life.

"I never knew what happened," said Nufissa, "I only remember waking up in the hospital and people telling me that I had almost died. Praise God, Ghanem did what he did."

"Praise God for the hospital," Ghanem added. "We were just very lucky."

Everyone seemed more relaxed now, and the women joined Ghanem in eating the mid-morning meal. They ate quickly, with an unusual hunger. Nufissa went back into the house to fetch some coffee for Ghanem and me, and tea for the women (who by custom did not drink coffee with the men). Ghanem lit up a cigarette (the women did not smoke either), and the conversation turned to food, and particularly to the *musht* fish which Hassan and Zaynab had brought back from their one-day honeymoon in Tiberias and passed out to the family. What had drawn Umm Ahmad's attention was that Zaynab refused to keep any for herself, apparently unwilling or unable to clean them.

"Her mother never taught her to prepare fish," said Umm Ahmad to her other daughters-in-law. "One of us has to teach her."

"No problem," said Latifa. "I learned how and so will she."

"I'll take care of it," said Nufissa.

"Good," said Umm Ahmad. "She's a fine girl and not too proud to learn. She told me she'd done a lot of cooking with her mother, but she admitted she's still not very good at it. She's still very young."

Ghanem turned to me and explained in a voice that was loud enough for all to hear, "Nufissa and Latifa were also young when they married, but Nufissa was the oldest daughter and she knew everything about cooking when she came to us. Latifa, too, knew a lot. But, you see, each family has its own ways, things they like to eat, such as *maftul* [a wheat and bean soup], and the women have to learn these things. And not just this. How we are together as a family, how we help each other and work together—they have to learn all that. Zaynab's a fine girl. There'll be no problems, I'm sure." Ghanem leaned back and rested his head next to Latifa, but without touching her. The women continued their discussion on the preparation of fish, tittering as they recalled their own hesitant beginnings as cooks. Then as the group was about to leave, Hassan and Zaynab unexpectedly showed up, with Zaynab carrying a tray.

"*Yaatik il aafia* [May God grant you good health]," said Hassan, nodding toward the crate of peppers.

"*Allah yaafik* [God grant you the same]," answered Ghanem, in the customary reply.

Zaynab placed the sterling silver tray, a wedding gift, on the grass. On it were sterling silver spoons and several porcelain cups filled with pineapple and apricot slices. It was more fancy than the usual serving-ware, and Zaynab was dressed and made up more elaborately than usual. She sat down on the grass across from Hassan, carefully tucking her legs under her white summer dress. She seemed more uneasy than she had the day after the wedding, and Hassan also appeared fidgety. Everyone began to chatter excitedly. At one point a mangy mustard-colored cat came by and licked at Hassan's hand. Irritated, he dumped the remains of his coffee over its back, and it ran off frightened and strangely speckled as Hassan guffawed. Zaynab, who had watched this, turned to Umm Ahmad and said, as if joking though it came out sharply, "What's with Hassan? Is he some kind of delinquent?"

Umm Ahmad, who had also seen Hassan spill the coffee, feigned ignorance and answered playfully, "Hassan? A delinquent? Not at all, he's a fine one. No real vices. Doesn't drink, gamble, or chase after women!"

Zaynab looked at Umm Ahmad and said demurely, "Well, maybe he doesn't drink or gamble. But chasing after women—I know all about that. He told me himself."

"That was before he got engaged," said Umm Ahmad, straightfaced. "And he didn't chase after them. *They* chased after *him*."

Everyone laughed, including Zaynab. Then, as if suddenly reminded of something, Hassan blurted out that a
strange thing had happened to him the previous night. He
had had a crazy dream. Nobody said anything, though they
looked at him expectantly. He continued, "It went like this.
I was in with this large crowd of women. It was all foggy
and there was a lot of commotion. I don't remember exactly
what set me off, but somehow I was all upset and angry. I
went to take a swing at someone, and just as I was about to
make contact, I woke up and I was in terrible pain. I had
hit *myself* right in the you-know-where!" He clutched his
hands over his crotch. "Can you imagine that?"

Zaynab, who evidently was hearing this for the first
time, broke into laughter, while trying to cover her mouth
with her hands. Everyone else laughed too. Then, as if relieved by this impromptu group therapy session, they all
rose and walked off. And as they did one of the women said
softly to Zaynab, "*Diri balik ala Hassan* [Go easy with Has-
san]. Everything will be just fine."

But everything was not fine. While the women of the
family and Ghanem were hearing the hints and echoes of
his troubles with Zaynab, it was to his cousin, Rafiq, that
Hassan turned to openly pour out his unhappiness. Rafiq
was not one of the more frequent visitors at Hassan's house,
but he and Hassan shared an important kind of intimacy:
with each other they could discuss sex. Rafiq, who was about
a year or two younger than Hassan, had become engaged at
about the same time and was planning to marry in another
month. The two of them had taken to discussing their problems and worries with each other, as well as their sexual
explorations with their fiancées. Thus, in those first few days
of his marriage, when little was going as expected, Hassan
went to consult with Rafiq. What could he do, he asked
Rafiq, so that Zaynab would warm up to him? He knew very
well—both he and Rafiq had discussed it—that there might
be some difficulties in the beginning. Women were sometimes like that, even if they had already indicated that they
liked sex. But he had not taken advantage of her, he had
held off until his wedding night to have it all with her. And
what was his reward? Nothing, or almost nothing.

"I waited so long," he said to Rafiq. "What am I supposed to do now?" Rafiq, who was surprised by Hassan's
difficulties, sought to calm down his cousin. "It's all in her
head," he reassured him. "She's scared. She likes sex just
like any woman, and as soon as she stops being scared it'll
all go fine. Take it easy with her. Don't give up, but take it
easy. Just give her a little time and everything will work
out."

Comforted by Rafiq's words, but not fully convinced, Hassan
returned to the fields and during the next few weeks he
attempted to lose himself in work. Zaynab too busied herself
around her new house, attempting to appease Hassan by
conscientiously cleaning and polishing every surface until it
glistened. Guests began coming by more frequently, including Zaynab's brothers, who, as promised, managed to visit
almost every day. In front of them, Hassan and Zaynab
carried on as if all were well, laughing and joking and entertaining them. They did not want to alarm them and
thereby arouse the hovering concern of Zaynab's parents,
and above all her father, who had never been too keen on
the marriage anyway.

In the evenings, Hassan returned to playing cards with
his friends Samir, Faisal, and a few others. They were all
bachelors and had been concerned that Hassan might be
lost to them once he was married; they were heartened to
see this wasn't so. And in their company Hassan was able
to forget his woes. Seated out on the porch—the inside of
his house was too hot—Hassan and his friends played round
after round of hearts, and chatted on into the night. Hassan
resisted the temptation to go join them on escapades to
Netanya or Caesarea, but he was glad, even relieved, to have
them come over and while away these muggy summer evenings.

One evening as he sat on his porch alone with Zaynab,
one of his pals showed up breathless and agitated. "You
ought to see what just happened," he said excitedly. "A fight!
Samir, Faisal, they were all in it. A real blood bath!" Hassan

rose as if to go off, but the friend added, "It's all over now. Nothing you can do about it. I got there late myself. But I heard a lot of guys were really messed up. Nothing we can do now, they've all gone home. Tomorrow we'll go see Samir and Faisal. Right?"

The following morning as he was mounting his tractor to go to fetch Umm Ahmad, Samir and Faisal came by shouting for him. They were both smiling, though Faisal had a nasty bruise on his cheek.

"You missed a good one, Hassan," Faisal said triumphantly.

"What happened?"

Samir pummeled Faisal on his thick bicep. "Old Faisal here is going to be boxing champ of the country," Samir said. "You should have seen him—a real warrior."

"Against who?"

"A bunch of wiseguys from Baqa al Gharbiya," said Faisal. "We taught them who's king here in Kufr Qara."

Samir sniggered and began explaining what had happened. The past three nights, as part of the holiday celebration of Id al-Adha (Festival of the Sacrifice), a temporary amusement park had been operating in Kufr Qara, with rides and refreshment booths and enough neon lights to attract people from the entire area. The night before, a group of about thirty young men from Baqa al Gharbiya, an Arab town ten kilometers away, had come to have some fun at Kufr Qara's expense. Drinking beer and wine, they started whistling at a few Kufr Qara girls and even made passes at them. Within minutes a crowd of Kufr Qara's z'lam (guys) showed up and there was a brawl. Three men from Baqa al Gharbiya were seriously wounded. There would have been even more injuries, said Samir, but the Jewish military police from a nearby army base came by and dispersed the crowd. "Our own *intifada*," concluded Samir sarcastically. "Except instead of fighting the Jews, we're fighting each other!"

"I enjoyed it anyway," gloated Faisal. "You need to have a little action sometimes."

"Right," agreed Samir. Then to Hassan he added, "You

see what you miss out on when you're married, Hassan? No more fun and good times. A boring life being married, isn't it?"

The truth was that in those last few weeks of summer married life at last began to look good to Hassan. He didn't know exactly how to explain it. Maybe Rafiq's advice had helped, and maybe Zaynab had been talking to her sisters or sisters-in-law. What was sure was that his problem with Zaynab was no longer there. Everything was going at last just the way it was supposed to go, *il hamdu lillah*.

But, alas, life was strange: no sooner did you solve one problem, than you created another. Now he could hardly focus on his work. He wanted only to be with Zaynab. He would look for excuses to take the day off with her—to go to Haifa (to arrange a bank loan), or Tel Aviv (to exchange a living-room chair). And once they were there they'd sit in cafes or stroll along the beach, enjoying a day or so of the honeymoon they had been deprived of before. In the fields he found himself thinking of her constantly, feeling her presence close by, and sometimes he would just stop work and disappear into the house, emerging an hour or so later with a sheepish grin on his face. All this was great fun and exactly what he had hoped for, yet the fact was that the farm was going to hell. Ghanem and Ahmad, even if it wasn't really their business, began to criticize his laziness. Crops were rotting on the vine, bacteria and fungi were having a picnic on the plants, and the fields were overrun with weeds. Umm Ahmad, who was often left to work alone, chose to overlook Hassan's lapses, and she urged his brothers to do the same: there would always be another summer, and by then, if not sooner, Hassan would surely settle down.

As summer turned to winter (there was only a brief autumn) the rains came, and Hassan had good reason to stay indoors. He had managed, with Ghanem's help, to plant the winter vegetables—cabbage, cauliflower, carrots, squash, and some parsley and dill. But his poor harvest in the summer had left him in even greater debt, and there were days that he didn't even have the cash to pay for groceries. Fortunately, Ahmad's publishing business was doing well, and while he did not give Hassan any cash, he did put him to work selling books. So on his off-days—and in the winter there were many off-days—Hassan would occasionally leave Zaynab and go up to the Galilee to sell books.

For her part, Zaynab also decided to find work. Once or twice a week, she began to substitute as a teacher in the village kindergarten. She had not trained for this, but in the village no special credentials were needed for substitutes, and she had a natural feel for working with children. Hassan encouraged her to go. The money helped, and besides, she seemed to enjoy it. "She's a smart girl," he reasoned, "and I think it's good for her. Before she married me, she had thought of going to university, but I was against it. Where would that have left us? I told her, 'Later, you'll get your chance, you'll find something.' Maybe she already has. As long as it doesn't take her away too much, why should I mind?"

If asked whether she still entertained hopes of going to university, Zaynab would answer coyly, "I'm going to the University of Hassan"; then she would add that while leaving Kufr Qara was not possible, she still had other ideas. She and Latifa—who also married young and didn't go to university—had come up with a plan. They were going to form their own preschool. Two evenings a week they both were attending a course offered by the Ministry of Education in the neighboring village, and in two years they would have certificates enabling them to work as preschool teachers. Assuming Hassan didn't mind, they were planning to open up the preschool right there on the bottom floor of her house.

As she thought about all this, Zaynab could barely believe her good luck. After those early weeks of marriage, when she and Hassan were so miserable with each other and she had been so frightened, now suddenly everything was working out. As she thought about it, she realized that what had helped her through was not only her love for Hassan but also the encouragement she received from the women in his family. Before she married she had heard that Latifa and Nufissa, and above all Umm Ahmad, were not like some others. They pulled each other up, not down. She was well aware of the biting Arab proverb, "Dogs will enter paradise before the mother-in-law and daughter-in-law will love one another." Indeed, it was like that for her friend Zahra, who had married about the same time. Poor Zahra already had become her mother-in-law's slave, cooking and cleaning and washing up for her. But Umm Ahmad had been so different. Umm Ahmad cooked for *her* on the days she had to go to class or work, and because Umm Ahmad had a washing machine, she had volunteered to do *her* wash. And more than that: Umm Ahmad was someone you could talk to. When she believed that her son was in the wrong, she wouldn't automatically take his side as so many mothers-in-law did, she'd defend her daughter-in-law. Like that business of Hassan's playing cards late at night with his friends—when she heard about that, Umm Ahmad went straight to Hassan and told him to cut it out, it was no way to treat one's wife. And he had stopped, or mostly stopped, and there was no longer that problem between them.

Actually, as Zaynab thought about it, the only problem remaining between them, if you could call it that, was the question of how many children to have.

"Ten! We're going to have ten!" Hassan was insisting.

"Three, maybe four!" she'd answer.

"Come here, you, we're going to make one right now," he'd tease her. "I want to have a son."

"And what's wrong with daughters?"

"One daughter—and nine sons. I need help in the fields."

"All daughters, no sons. You'll see!"

On and on they would argue, half in jest, and half seriously, with both wishing that, *inshallah*, the first would already be on the way. And then one watery day that winter Zaynab knew, as sure as the rain on the roof, that it was.

13

Ibrahim and Ismail: Abu Ahmad's Brother and Nephew

IF Hassan's wedding had brought happiness to his immediate family, it also had caused, or at least brought into
the open, a schism in the wider family. Only a few days after
the wedding, Abu Ahmad and his brother Ibrahim had a
heated exchange. The two men were no longer speaking to
one another. According to Ghanem, who first told me the
story—though he tried to make light of it—the argument
revolved around a missing electrical cable. Apparently Ibrahim had lent Abu Ahmad a cable for the orchestra's use, and
when the wedding was over Abu Ahmad failed to return it,
apologizing that he had lost it. Several days later, however,
when Ibrahim's wife visited Abu Ahmad's house, she saw,
or thought she saw, the cable lying in a corner of the kitchen.
She informed Ibrahim and—"as is my uncle's way," said
Ghanem—he came charging over, cursing Abu Ahmad and
Umm Ahmad, and saying he wanted nothing more to do
with them. Insulted, Abu Ahmad had told his brother to
leave and not come back. And so things stood.

A couple of weeks later, I was sitting alone with Abu
Ahmad in his *diwan*. Curious to hear his version, I asked

whether he would be willing to tell me about his dispute with Ibrahim. A pained expression came across his face and he indicated that he didn't want to talk much about the matter, though he agreed to provide a few details. "That business about the cable is just an excuse," he said slowly, waving his hand in disgust. "My brother has been a good younger brother over the years. He's listened to me and been loyal. But he's got a bad temper, and now and then he blows up. Weeks or months later, he comes and makes up. What happened here had nothing to do with the electrical cable. That's nonsense. My brother is mad at me because Hassan wouldn't marry one of his unmarried daughters, that's all. He's got three left, and he wanted Hassan to marry one of them. I understand him. I wanted it that way, too, and I asked Hassan to consider it. But I couldn't force him. Hassan wanted Zaynab, and in the end I went along with it. So Ibrahim is angry at me. He figures I should have used force. But he, above all, ought to know that when a son is bent on doing something, it's not easy to force him. Sometimes you have to go along."

Abu Ahmad's brother lived diagonally across the main square, right next to the mosque. Together with his second wife (his first wife had died in 1973), their three teenage children, and the unmarried daughters from his first marriage, Ibrahim inhabited the cramped downstairs quarters of one of Kufr Qara's older houses. Immediately upstairs, connected by a perilous stairway, his oldest son, Ismail, was living with his wife and three small children.

Although Abu Ahmad and Ibrahim had cut off mutual visits, their sons kept in contact. Hassan, who enjoyed playing the role of pacifier in family quarrels, made a special point of staying in close touch with Faisal and Ismail. He also encouraged me to visit his uncle. "He's basically a good guy. I'm sure he'd like to talk to you," claimed Hassan, adding with a psychological touch, "He's had a hard life, he's the youngest brother and all that—but he's got a good heart, really."

Ibrahim had not been especially receptive when I had

tried to talk to him at Hassan's wedding, but when I showed up at his door several months later he was effusive. "My friend, you are most welcome in my home," he greeted me. He was just sitting down—actually, lying down on the floor mattress—to a mid-afternoon meal. He beckoned me to join him. He lay on his enormous globe of a belly and, as if peering over it, he dipped into the platter of meat and vegetables before him on the floor. I sat next to him and we ate in silence for a quarter of an hour. ("My uncle lives to eat," I remembered Hassan saying. "That and maybe one other thing—he has sixteen children.")

When he finished eating, Ibrahim rolled over on his side and again repeated his effusive welcome. "Why have you not come sooner, my friend?" he wanted to know, squinting at me with partially glazed eyes. He had a large fleshy face, and on the center of his forehead was a red scaly callous, an emblem of reverence that had grown over the years from prostrating his head to the ground five times daily in the required prayers. "You honor my house now that you are here," he insisted. "*Ahlan wa sahlan.*"

He began rolling a cigarette from loose tobacco stored in a blue Danish cookie can, and while he did so he started talking—without any prompting—about his life. He was well aware that I was writing a book about the family and he wanted me to hear "a few facts" from him. He was the youngest, he said, or at any rate the youngest of the surviving brothers. Abu Ahmad (Ali, he called him) was five years older. He, Ibrahim, had been his father's favorite, and when his father died it had felt to him like the world had come to an end. Only a few years after that, his oldest brother had died, too, just as suddenly, and from then on Ali was in charge of the family.

"I was twenty-one at the time and he was twenty-six," Ibrahim explained. "But I was like a son to him. Ali told me what to do and I listened to him—in the work around the farm, in politics, in everything. We got along real well. At least for a while we did. The first big argument I can remember us having—" He spat out some loose tobacco that had stuck to his tongue. "It was during the war in 1948. We had a big fight over who was going to use the family rifle.

We only had one. I had just come off guard duty that morning when the Jews attacked and I had the rifle with me. Ali
wanted it. He said he knew how to use it better. A pack of
lies, I told him. I could use it just as well as he could. We
got into this fight over who would use it, until others came
along and said, 'Give Ali the rifle. He's the older one and
he's got the calmer head.' What could I do? They were right
about his having the calmer head—I'm hotheaded sometimes—so I gave in. Instead of defending the village, I had
to take our mother and Ali's wife and children to Ar'ara. I
felt bad about that.

"After the war we returned to the village, but we
couldn't go back to farming right away. I suppose Ali's told
you all about what happened then, hasn't he?" I described,
in brief, what Abu Ahmad had mentioned about that period.
"But he didn't tell you about me and him?" he asked. He
shook his head in disbelief. "About the problems between us
back then, he didn't tell you anything? You know, of course,
that there are problems between us still, no?"

I answered that I was aware of the blowup between him
and Abu Ahmad. And I added that it was my understanding
that there had been a dispute over an electrical cable and,
further—I felt it best to level with him—that there was
"some misunderstanding" over Hassan's choosing Zaynab
and not one of his cousins.

"A pack of lies!" Ibrahim erupted, his ears reddening.
"All lies! Let him keep his sons. Who wants them? Who needs
them?" He spat out some more tobacco. "The electrical cable, yes, he took the cable and didn't return it. What does
he expect me to do, forget it? My wife goes over to his house
and sees that his wife is now using it for the washing machine. And Ali says it's lost! Sure I got angry. Who
wouldn't?" Ibrahim leaned back against the water-stained
wall and began rolling another cigarette. "But look, the electrical cable was just the last straw. It's the way things have
always been between us. He's the older brother and he takes.
I'm the younger brother and I give. That's the way it's been
between Ali and me. I'm fed up with it.

"Back forty years ago, when the war was over, it started.
We were all living together then. Me, Ali and his family, and

our mother. Those were hard years, we had to scrounge around to make ends meet. He worked. I worked. And all the money went into a common pot. *His* pot, of course. Never mind, though. He had a wife and children. I didn't. So naturally he needed the money more. But do you think things changed when I started to have a family? Not at all! We all continued to live in the old house up the street, and Ali and I farmed our fifty-seven and a half dunams. I let him take care of the money. Then one day my wife comes to me and explains—mind you, I was a fool, I didn't notice it—Ali's wife, Fadwa, was using all the money for *their* needs and *their* children. They were buying clothes and furniture while we had nothing. So I went to Ali and we had a fight over this. We decided to split up. He was building a new house and he moved there, along with Mother too. This was in 1954. I moved to another house, this house here. We split all the household possessions, all the accounts, and went our own ways, each farming his own land.

"Ali wasn't happy with this arrangement. It was hard for him to work. He's got this bad leg. And he was getting involved in local politics, as head of our clan. So one day he came to me and said, 'Let's get back together.' My wife was against it, she felt we'd do better if I didn't join up again with Ali. All I was doing, she said, was taking from my children's mouths and giving to his children. She was right again, yet I didn't listen. I told her to stay out of it—we'd live in our house, they in theirs, but Ali and I would be back in business again. I felt I had to do it this way. Look, in the whole world there's billions of people, and out of all of them I've got only one brother. He wants me with him, so I couldn't say no. Besides, at the time he had lots of enemies, political enemies. They were people from other clans and they were out to get him. They came to me and asked me to go against my brother. I wanted no part of that rot and told them to get lost. I decided to line up again with Ali, just the way he wanted.

"Politically, I've stayed with him through thick and thin. He'll tell you that himself. I've always gone with his judgment. He understands these things real well. If he says vote for the Labor party, it's best for our people, I go along with him. Always have. But in other things I've learned not to trust him. After I went back with him in 1958 or so, it wasn't long before he started again with his old tricks. Actually, not so much him as his wife. That Fadwa, she may talk like honey, but she's a sneak. Ali and I were making real good money on the farm in those days. Prices for vegetables were good then, not like now. All the money once again was going into one pot, and that Fadwa, she was dipping into it with both hands. My family again got screwed. It made me furious. I tried to ignore it. Believe me, for several years I tried to keep the peace so Ali and I could stay together. But finally I couldn't ignore it any longer. His children were getting so much, and mine so little. So I told Ali, this is it. I'm going my way and he can go his. No more working together, no more family business for me."

Ibrahim rose from the floor mattress and went over to an armoire in the corner of the room. He returned with several crumpled sheets of paper that were fastened together at the corners by a safety pin. "Since the late sixties, when Ali and I broke off, I've been keeping my own records of what he owes me. You see these figures here—" He handed me one of the yellowing papers and pointed to some numbers. "That's what he borrowed twenty years ago, and that's what he's paid back. He still owes me all this—1,893 lirot! Believe me, if he'd been fair with me, I'd never do this. I would have emptied my pockets for him whenever he needed. But now I wouldn't give him a kilo of sugar—nothing. That's how mad he's made me."

Then, leaning forward, his glazed eyes looking past me, Ibrahim said, "Take a look at my eyes. You think I can see you clearly? I can't. That's what all this anger has done to me. It's made me half blind. Anger, the kind of anger I have, kills you. I'm no doctor, but I know a thing or two. Some people get diabetes, some get heart trouble or cancer. That's what anger does to you. Me—it's destroyed my eyes. I can't see clearly anymore from all this anger that's built up inside me. And when I think of that, it makes me even angrier. That's the truth, my friend, the real truth."

Living directly overhead, in an apartment built six years before, was Ibrahim's oldest son, Ismail. At thirty-five, Ismail seemed like a younger replica of his father—the same fleshy face and barrel belly, and the same raucous voice, which periodically restored order amongst the children. Unlike his father, however, there was something playful about Ismail. He enjoyed telling jokes and amusing his friends, and while he was quick to anger, just like his father, he wrapped it often in the educated garb of sarcasm and irony; Ismail, unlike Ibrahim, had had the benefit of a college education.

Ismail was also something of the political black sheep of the family. He was a Communist, a card-carrying leader in Kufr Qara's Rakah (Communist) party—for seventeen years, and proud of it. He and Ibrahim had fought bitterly over this in the early years, with his father threatening to disown him. In the end, however, Ibrahim had managed to patch things up with him ("A son is always a son, no matter what stupid things he's done," affirmed Ibrahim.) And when Ismail needed to build his house, Ibrahim suggested that he construct a flat just upstairs, which Ismail agreed to in part because the family could not then afford a fancier place such as those his cousins had.

I had first met Ismail not at home but out in the fields, while working with Hassan. Ismail was a physics teacher in Kufr Qara's high school, and in the afternoons he would occasionally work in the fields, relieving his younger brother, Faisal. With his young sons for company, he'd stop by on his tractor and have some coffee or a cigarette with Hassan. On one such occasion, while we were discussing politics, he invited me to visit him at home. He wanted me to hear, he said, some things he was sure that his uncle and cousins were not telling me. "They've got their view, I've got mine," he said provocatively. "Why not come hear mine?"

It was not so easy catching Ismail at home, however. Twice I showed up as agreed, and twice he was not there. This was not so uncommon among the villagers, and with Ismail it was standard procedure. On the third time, when I did find him at home, he was, just like his father, effusively welcoming. He sent his wife off to make coffee, and with a flick of his heavy hand sent two of his children scurrying into the next room. He was ready to talk. After a few comments about the upcoming Land Day demonstration which his party cronies were preparing for, he agreed to talk about the Communist party, and particularly about how he had chosen that direction.

"Now the whole family accepts that I'm a Communist," he began. "Now it's not so unusual. Hundreds of people in Kufr Qara vote Communist these days, so it's more acceptable. But back twenty years ago, when I first got involved in it, it was taboo here. Hardly anybody dared join up. How did I get involved? Well, it's a long story, but I'll make it short. It started, I think, back when I was ten or twelve years old, in the mid-sixties. My father, my uncle, were all Mapai [Labor] party supporters. They supported this Zionist party, the party of Ben Gurion, because they thought they'd gain advantages for the village by doing so. They were opportunistic, pure and simple. Me, I was too young to really understand all that, but I knew that my people were oppressed— *everyone* knew that—and that Ben Gurion's party was heading the government of the oppressors. So I couldn't see supporting them—no way. Then one day there was an open-air meeting here in Kufr Qara, with some members of the Communist party giving speeches. Many adults went to hear them, and me and a few friends also went along. Nobody made us leave. I was surprised to see both Jews and Arabs giving speeches together, and even more shocked to hear what they were saying. They denounced the military government, denounced the discrimination against Arabs in Israel, and denounced Ben Gurion's government. It made a big impression on me, really it did, though I said nothing to anybody. Certainly not to my father.

"I continued to go to these rallies whenever the Communists came to the village, as they occasionally did. And by the time I was in high school, in the late 1960s, the first party branch opened here in Kufr Qara. That was in 1968, and there were only a handful of members. After school I would sometimes sneak over to one of the party members' houses and read *al-Ittihad*, the party newspaper. I didn't dare bring it home, my father would have beaten the crap out of me. But I read, I absorbed, and without telling anyone, I was already in my heart with the Communists. As far as I could see, they were the only party speaking up for the Arabs.

"Where I got even more involved was at the Hebrew University. I went there in 1972, and what I found was that my friends, the people I was naturally drawn to, were usually Communist party supporters. It was a little dangerous to be involved because the Israeli government had its eye on the Arab students, through the Shabbak,[1] and if they found out that you were a Communist they'd open a file on you and might cause you problems. But I didn't care. I was a bit reckless. I was more worried about my father catching me than anything else. He never did catch me then and never knew that I was one of the organizers of the first branch that opened at the Hebrew University. Word did get back to him through someone's sister, but when he confronted me on it, I did what I had to do. I lied to him.

"And that was the last he knew for a while, because the following year I had to leave the university anyway. That's another story altogether. My mother died—suddenly, in her sleep—and my father was left with twelve children still at home. He told me that he needed me to come home and help him. Naturally I came. I dropped out of the university and came back to the village to work. It was a bad time for the family and a bad time for me, too. I figured my chances of going back to school were finished, that I'd be a laborer the rest of my life—that's it. I got a job for a while as a truck driver. I worked on the farm and also in a factory. And I joined the Communist party branch here in the village. I knew my father would eventually find out because as a party member you had to distribute copies of the party newspaper. Sooner or later he was bound to catch me.

"As it happened, it was my uncle, Abu Ahmad, who caught me first. One day he saw me distributing the paper.

---

[1]Shabbak is an acronym for Sherut Bitachon Klali, the Israeli internal security services.

'Are you crazy?' he asked me. 'What kind of garbage are you handing out?' I told him it was worthwhile in my view. 'You're going to wind up in jail, you know,' he said. I shrugged. And since he didn't think I was taking him seriously enough, he yelled at me, 'Don't come to me for help when you're locked up. I won't help you—you can rot there!' And that wasn't the end of it, of course. My father got into the act, too, threatening me and cursing me for ruining my life. He told me I was heading for trouble, that the Shabbak would finish me off, and that I was naive and a political ignoramus." Ismail sighed and glanced at his wife, who had entered the salon with coffee and some homemade cake. "He was right in a way, or half right. I was no political ignoramus, but I was a bit naive about what could happen to me. That's for sure."

Ismail took the platter from his wife without introducing her and resumed his narrative. What he began talking about, in some detail, was the machinations of the Shabbak. Over the years, he said, he had come to know quite well how they operate, though back in the early 1970s he had not yet had any run-ins with them. They were "sneaky bastards," he claimed, and "smart as hell"; they knew how to intimidate and how to keep people afraid.

"People don't know about this so much outside Israel, do they?" he asked rhetorically. "They're not aware that in every Arab village the Shabbak has its agents. Here in Kufr Qara they have maybe a dozen people. We know who some of them are. But even though we know, it doesn't stop them from operating. It's not like over in the occupied territories where they kill off collaborators. Here they swim about freely, sniffing at what's happening and reporting it. Why do people collaborate? Simple. They get paid for it, or they get some favor for it. Say, for example, you want to open a business and you need a license, or want to get clearance from the Ministry of Education to teach in the school system. Say, also, that you've got something against you on your record—you were, or are, a Communist like me. Then they might come to you and say, 'We'll ignore your background, *but* we want you to give us some information.' So to get the license or the clearance you're made to collaborate.

"Look, I'll tell you what happened to me—my first run-in with these bastards. It happened when I was working in a paper-making factory in the mid-1970s, after my mother died. I was working at this place in Hadera for several months, pushing around heavy rolls of paper all day. One day there was an announcement on the factory bulletin board that they were looking to promote some of the workers to the job of supervisor. Why not apply, I figured? What have I got to lose? Maybe I can be some kind of mini-boss. So I signed up to take the exam. Weeks went by and I heard nothing. Then one morning my supervisor told me that a company officer wanted to see me. It wasn't in my mind then, at least not until I got there, that maybe this was some Shabbak setup. Yet once I met this so-called officer, I knew. How? Because he knew all about me. He knew that I was a Communist, that I distributed newspapers in the village, and so on. He told me that he'd arrange for me to take the exam soon, I could be a supervisor, *but*—I was waiting for the but—I had to meet *our* friend tomorrow in Hadera. 'I have no friend in Hadera,' I told him. 'And besides, I have to work tomorrow.' He answered, 'Never mind, we'll punch you in.'

"I was almost sure that I was being set up to be re-cruited, so what I did was go back to my Communist friends in Kufr Qara and ask their advice. Should I refuse to go? No, they said, I should go along. So I went the next morning to a cafe where I was told this guy would be. I didn't go alone, exactly. A friend accompanied me part of the way, and I told him that if I didn't reappear, he should inform them in the village that I'd been taken away. You see, I was afraid. Anyway, I went to this cafe, and when I got there the owner seemed to know who I was. He sat me at a nice table in the corner, brought me a free pack of Marlboros, and went off. After a while along came this guy, a James Bond type straight out of the movies—tall, blond, with sunglasses and a briefcase. He greeted me in perfect Arabic. I asked him who he was and he said, 'Abu Faris'—the name of a famous Arab poet. 'And besides that?' I asked. He answered, 'Enough for you to know that I am in charge of the Wadi Ara district.' Well, we talked for about two hours. The guy was no fool. He talked about Marx and Lenin and communism, and how he is a socialist just like me. He really knew his stuff.

"Finally, after all the ideology talk, he got down to business. He wanted me to help him with information on Arabs in the Communist party. I told him that I thought that was what the meeting was all about, but no, I wanted no part of it. He then began to reason with me, so to speak. I'd actually be helping people, he said. Someone might be about to get into real trouble—say, by planting a bomb. If they were discovered beforehand, they'd only get a few years in prison, not life imprisonment, and nobody would get hurt. Better for everyone, right? On and on it went in this vein, until finally I made it clear that I wasn't going to collaborate. Then he leaned on me harder. He reminded me that I might not get the promotion at work, might not even keep my job, might not be able to return to university, and might even wind up having to report periodically to the police. 'Think about it,' he said. He handed me his white card. I refused it. 'Take it,' he repeated. I refused again. I went back to work that day and quit—before they could fire me. I knew it was only a matter of time. And I was right. Because a Communist pal of mine, who worked at the same factory and was subjected to the same thing I was, stayed at the job. He didn't want to lose the money. And he was fired ten days later."

Ismail paused when he finished relating this run-in with the Shabbak. Sweat glistened on his forehead, as if he were reliving the incident. We sat silently. For a few moments, the afternoon stillness was pierced by the call to prayer, "*Allahu akbar*," from the mosque next door. Gazing at the street below, we watched Ismail's father walking arm-in-arm toward the mosque with his brother-in-law.

I turned to Ismail and asked whether his being a Communist had caused him any further troubles with the Shabbak. He shrugged his shoulders and said sarcastically, "Well, it might have been easier if I were a Muslim fundamentalist. Although, these days you can be sure the Shabbak has them covered, too." He then went on to say that actually, if he were to tally it up, he personally had gained more by being with the Communist party than it had cost him. However, he added jokingly, "I've got a file with the Shabbak now at least as wide as I am.

"But if it hadn't been for the Communist party," he

continued, "I'd never have finished university. The family had no money to send me. My father had remarried and no longer needed my help so much, but how could I pay for the education? Fortunately, the Communist party helped me out. Each year, through their party connections in Eastern Europe, they send Arab students on scholarships to study there. My year, thirteen Israeli Arabs got selected and all went to Czechoslovakia. I don't know why they chose Czechoslovakia. They just did. Each of us was free to pick what he wanted to study. I wanted law, but my father talked me out of it. 'All lawyers are crooks,' he told me. 'They turn lies into truth and truth into lies, all for the sake of money. No son of mine is going to be a lawyer.' I didn't want to fight him on this one, so I chose something else—mechanical engineering.

"And off I went. I didn't speak a word of Czech, and I didn't even know where the place they were sending me was. I only knew that I was glad to go abroad and have a chance to learn. Frankly, it was a hard time—and a good time. Seven years I was there in this small town, Kosice. It took me two years to understand enough of the language to really follow the texts, and another five years to get the master's degree. In between, I also had a good time. The Czech girls are very nice and free, like Jewish and American girls. No complaints. I probably could have stayed on and worked there, but I was eager to get back home. I was almost thirty years old then, and I wanted to settle down.

"When I came back I was in for a bit of a surprise. I had been hopeful of getting work in my area, as an engineer, but nothing was available. I had been naive, foolish. Because I was an Arab and a Communist, everything was closed to me. I realized then—and to this day I regret it—that I should have studied law after all. Then I could have requalified here and worked in the Arab community. With an engineering degree, however, you have to work with a Jewish company, and there's not an outfit in the country that's going to hire an Arab Communist as an engineer. I had screwed myself. The only thing that seemed possible then was to teach, math or physics, in the local high school. And here again I had problems due to my background. Like I told you before, you have to get a security clearance from the Ministry of Education in order to teach, and the ministry goes to the Shabbak and checks you out. By then I already had a sizable file with them.

"How did I wind up teaching, anyway? That's a complicated story, but it came down to this. The Ministry of Education recommended that I *not* be allowed to teach, but I had political pull on the village council, and that saved me. You see, I've never done anything illegal. Belonging to the Communist party is not illegal, and as far as I know, refusal to collaborate with the Shabbak is not illegal either. Nonetheless, the Ministry of Education every year informs the local high school that they would like my contract terminated. But the high school principal has supported me, and also—this is crucial—a close member of my family is an important person on the village council. He and I don't have the same political views, yet because of the family ties he supports me. So thus far I've been retained as a half-time teacher of physics. It's not much of an income, though I'm not complaining. I could easily have wound up with nothing.

"As for the Shabbak, they pretty much leave me alone these days. They know who I am, and up to a point I know who they are. They know what goes on in the village, and I make no secret of my doings. Like the upcoming Land Day demonstration, you can be sure they have their people in on our organizational meetings. But really, they're not so busy now with us, the Communists. It's not like fifteen years ago. Today the Shabbak is most worried about Palestinians in the territories and what's going on there. So for the time being all of us here in Israel have a rest. As long as we're not hoisting Palestinian flags or picking up stones and joining the *intifada*, they're not too worried about us. They keep their informers around, but the real action is over there in the occupied territories. We, the Palestinians in Israel, are taking a breather."

•   •   •

As an addendum to this chapter I would like to add here some information that I gathered after speaking to

Ismail. The reader may be wondering, as I was, just how accurate Ismail's perspective was regarding the operation of the Shabbak in Kufr Qara. He was neither the first nor the last to speak about their operations. And indeed, I think it fair to say that there was a widespread understanding or belief among Kufr Qara's people that the Shabbak is well plugged into what is happening in their village, and for that matter, the entire Palestinian community in Israel.

To check Ismail's information, I got in touch with a Jewish individual who at one time was a high government official and also had formerly been a top operator for the Mossad (the external security services, or roughly the equivalent of the CIA). This individual, as it happens, is a relative of a close friend of mine. He was aware that I was writing a book, and because of my friend, I think, he agreed to talk to me with the understanding that I neither name him nor quote him directly.

What he told me, in essence, corroborated Ismail's story. He explained that while he did not know specifically what was happening in Kufr Qara—and of course he wouldn't tell me if he did—he did know in general about the Shabbak's operations. According to him, the Shabbak has its agents in every Arab village in Israel. They use local people who collaborate with them. Collaborators are essentially of two types. There are those who do it solely for the money, and there are those who have fallen into some personal difficulty and need help in clearing it up. For example, someone may have problems with the income tax authorities, or someone may have a blemish on his record that interferes with his attaining something he wants—a license, a security clearance, or a government job. The Shabbak then clears up the problem in exchange for the individual's cooperation.

Once the Shabbak has recruited an individual, that person reports periodically to them. Meetings are held outside the village. The kind of information that the Shabbak is seeking differs from time to time. These

days, among Arabs in Israel—my source speculated—
the Shabbak is primarily interested in who might be
actively supporting the *intifada* by participating in violence or advocating such participation; passive participation—that is, sympathy with the *intifada*—is not
likely to concern them. Apart from this, the Shabbak
maintains its presence in every village simply to let the
Arabs know that they are there, to have them think
twice before doing anything against the state. Collaborators operating in Israel, unlike those in the territories,
are in no physical danger. It takes an organizational
force, as exists in the territories (the PLO, or the Muslim
group, Hamas, for example), to kill collaborators. The
Shabbak has not been able to root out such forces from
operating in the territories, but within Israel the Shabbak has the situation well under control. Collaborators
can operate freely and usefully even if they are known;
and they are most certainly operating now, as always.

14
LAND DAY

O N MARCH 30, 1976, for the first time since the establishment of the Jewish state, Arabs in Israel called for a
general strike. The immediate trigger was a recent government decision to confiscate twenty thousand dunams of
Arab-owned or Arab-worked farmland in the Galilee, for
purposes of building Jewish settlements and a military
training ground. These intended confiscations were a painful
reminder to Arabs in Israel of the enormous land expropri-
ations of the 1950s; and beyond that, since the Jews talked
openly of "Judaization" of the Galilee, they served to stoke
Arab feelings of being a vulnerable minority. With organizational backing principally from the Communist party—
which was strongest in Arab cities, though it had considerable support in most Arab villages, too[1]—a strike was held
throughout the country. Marches and demonstrations, some
planned and some spontaneous, took place from the Galilee
to the Negev. The Israeli army and police wound up clashing
with the demonstrators in several places. And to the shock
of Arabs and Jews alike, by the day's end there were scores
of injuries and six Arabs had been shot dead.

[1]In the previous elections to the Knesset in 1973, the Arab vote for the
Communist party nationwide was 37 percent and in Kufr Qara it was 33 percent.

From that year on, March 30 has been a day of protest for Arabs in Israel. Known as Land Day, it has become their national day. The vast majority do not go to work that day, and typically there is a demonstration in each of the three main areas of Arab population in Israel—the Galilee, the central area or (the Triangle), and the Negev. In the last three years, since the *intifada,* Palestinians in Gaza and the West Bank have also called for a general strike on Land Day in solidarity with those in Israel. And not surprisingly, it has become a day of high tension, as the Israeli army and police seek to prevent what are called in Hebrew *hafarot seder,* disturbances of order.

In Kufr Qara, a village known as a quiet and orderly place, that first Land Day in 1976 came as a shock. The local village council, like the great majority of village councils that first year, took a formal position against the strike call: they did not close the schools and they urged people to go about business as usual. Nonetheless, a large number of Kufr Qara's people—above all, those who did not work in the Jewish sector and hence did not fear retaliation—decided to strike. Intent on further ensuring that the strike was a success in the village, the local branch of the Communist party came up with its own action plan. And one of those who was involved in these plans was Abu Ahmad's nephew Ismail, a leader of the Kufr Qara branch.

Today, fourteen years later, Ismail remembers that day as a high point in his political life and as a "watershed point" in the political life of the village and country. "Nobody could have imagined that it would turn out as it did," he said as we sat in the salon of his apartment overlooking Kufr Qara's central square. "We knew there was widespread feeling in support of the strike, but we also knew that many people were afraid. The local council was afraid, too. They did not want to confront the government. They thought it would only bring reprisals, so they opposed the strike. What we did, our group of fifteen or so in the party, was to go against the council. That morning several of us got up early and went to the taxi and bus depot and tried to convince people not to go to work. 'Today they're confiscating land in the Galilee, tomorrow who knows what they'll take,' we told them. Some listened and some didn't, though almost everyone agreed with us.

"But we didn't stop at that. The main thing we did was go to the schools. If we could close them, we figured, then we'd really achieve something. So we went first to the high school as the students were arriving. I had a brother who was in high school then, and we cornered him and his friends and told them, 'Let's close down the school!' They were afraid, but they agreed with us. And the next thing we knew, scores of students were around us saying, 'We won't go!' Soon it snowballed and we had hundreds refusing to enter the school. We then began marching back to the village, about three hundred of us, and as we marched people joined us, including some older people. We went to the junior high. The principal must have heard we were coming because he had locked the iron gates. But people were excited now, and we tore the gates out of the ground and poured into the school. In minutes we emptied it. We were singing and chanting and came marching back through the center of the village. You should have seen it—one after the other the stores closed, until all of Kufr Qara was shut down. Except for the post office. The postmaster was a crazy man, and he came to the front of the post office waving a knife, saying he'd slit the throat of anyone who tried to shut him down. We could have overwhelmed him, but we let him go because we all knew he was such a crazy guy.

"As we were marching through the village, at one point my father came running up to me. I was right in front, and he embarrassed the hell out of me insisting I come home. 'The army is going wild,' he said. 'They're killing people in the Galilee and around here, too. I heard it on the radio. Get yourself home!' I didn't believe him. And anyway, I wasn't about to let him embarrass me that way. So I kept right on marching and singing until the whole thing broke up about an hour later, with Kufr Qara completely shut down. Then, when I finally got home, I turned on the radio and heard it for myself—six Arabs shot! I couldn't believe it at first, and then I felt really angry. How dare they shoot us down like that! I was furious. But more than ever I could see that we had been right to join the strike. We had to stand up for our rights—even if the government was going to make us pay a price for it. There was no other way."

The weather forecast had been for high clouds and possibly rain on March 30, 1990, but at noon the sun burned down on Kufr Qara's central square where small clusters of young men in shirt sleeves already were gathering. On their chests were small red stickers which bore the inscription "People of Kufr Qara Join Together to Support Land Day." And as villagers passed by, the young men occasionally stopped them, attempting to persuade them to join the caravan that was heading for the 2:00 P.M. rally in Taibeh, half an hour away. Ismail seemed to be the principal organizer as he moved back and forth between the men, his paunch protruding as usual from his shirt, and his thick hands punching out exclamation points as he directed the troops. Most of the men—I was to discover later—were friends from the Communist party, though there were also a number of "independents" who had come to participate. There were no women, and hardly any men past forty years old; there was not a *keffiyeh* or *gallabiyeh* in the crowd.

Seeing that we would not be leaving for a half hour or so, I walked over to Abu Ahmad's house. He was resting inside while the women sat on the mattresses on the hot outside patio. Umm Ahmad, along with her daughters Fatma, Rafiqa, and Maysa, had spent the morning gathering *zaatar*, wild thyme, out in the hills to the north of the village—hills that used to belong to Kufr Qara before the confiscations of the 1950s. The silvery-green leaves lay spread out on a straw mat drying in the sun. The women, all wearing bright ankle-length dresses except for Maysa, who wore jeans and a red blouse, were drinking glasses of lemonade as they hovered over a photo album from Hassan's wedding. They laughed excitedly, and I thought I heard a couple of them say something about a forthcoming engagement party, "*inshallah*," God willing. I was not sure, but assumed they were talking about Maysa's engagement, which, as she had indicated to me a week before, was now "a real possibility," though at the moment nothing was certain because both families—really both fathers—had raised objections.

I drank a glass of lemonade with them (there was no further talk of an engagement), and then went inside the house, where Abu Ahmad was lying on a floor mattress, reading a Hebrew newspaper. He poured me a small cup of thick unsweetened coffee and then asked what I thought of the demonstrations planned for that day. I began telling him that they seemed to make sense to me and that in any case I was going because I was curious to be there, but he suddenly interrupted me.

"They're a mistake," he said flatly. "It's not the way."

"Why?"

"We don't need confrontations and violence here. It's fine to go on strike, I'm all for that. Stay at home, observe the day quietly, and that's it. But demonstrations will bring us no benefit. Let those in the occupied territories make demonstrations and throw stones. But we, the Arabs in Israel, cannot afford to use force. And once you start demonstrating, anything can happen."

I asked him whether his view was shared by his sons, and he said that it was, except for Ahmad, maybe, who once in a while "joined up in these things." Ghanem, anyway, was down in Eilat vacationing with his family; and Hassan was out in the fields working, not even observing the strike. "But you go along and see for yourself," he said to me. "Just don't let anyone lead you into trouble. And today, I have a feeling, there could be trouble."

Back in the main square, a crowd of between one hundred fifty and two hundred was still milling about as Ismail, his face glistening, directed people into cars and a bus. He pointed me to a white sedan. The car belonged to Riad, a fellow in his early thirties, one of Abu Ahmad's neighbors. Riad, like Ismail, was a leader in the Communist party, and while Abu Ahmad had been willing to forgive such transgressions in his nephew, he could not overlook them in his neighbor. The two of them were barely on speaking terms. I, however, had chatted with Riad a number of times, found him interesting, and was glad to go with him.

Soon the caravan of cars and the bus were pulling out of Kufr Qara and down to the main Wadi Ara road. Opposite the entrance to the village, partly obscured by a thicket of trees, were an army truck and two jeeps.

"Protecting the village," said Riad sarcastically, nodding in their direction.

"May they go to hell!" said one of the men in the back seat, a portly red-cheeked fellow.

"Every year the same thing," added the thin bespectacled man beside him.

"You'll see," said Riad, "every Arab village until Taibeh will be guarded like this. If any villagers decide to throw a spontaneous demonstration, the army will stop them. *Hafarot seder*, disturbances of the order."

And indeed, as we drove along the road toward Taibeh, every Arab village did have an army truck or a couple of jeeps sitting outside its main entrance. The villages, from what could be seen, were all shut down like Kufr Qara. Stores and workshops were closed. Except for a few *fellaheen* out in the fields, nobody seemed to be working.

The fields all along the road were ablaze with the short-lived colors of spring. Plum and peach trees flowered pinkish white, and yellow daisies sprouted wildly in the olive groves. Large rectangular tracts of barley, their grained tops shimmering white in the early afternoon sunlight, checkered the landscape along with smaller plots of vegetables—lettuce, onions, and green squash. A lone turbaned shepherd boy, oblivious of the day's import, crossed his flock of black goats over the main road as cars came screeching to a halt and had to wait for him to clear the way.

A few kilometers further along there was another interruption—this one, apparently, more expected. Several army jeeps were standing alongside the road, and brown-bereted Golani soldiers were randomly waving over cars. Our car got waved to the side.

"Oh hell!" said Riad, under his breath. "Here we go again."

A blond soldier, maybe twenty years old, came walking up to the car, a rifle strapped over his shoulder and a baton on his belt. "Your identity card," he said coolly to Riad. And then as Riad was searching through his wallet, he said to the rest of us, "All of you, identity cards." We pulled out our blue Israeli identity cards, but he only inspected Riad's. "Your driver's license and car registration," he then said. Riad handed the documents over and the soldier quietly inspected them. Then, returning the papers, the soldier tapped on the window and said gruffly, "*Sa!* Drive on!"

There was a moment of silence as we drove off, and then the red-cheeked fellow in the back said, "Just like we were some kind of criminals. Damn them!"

"Never mind. It could have been worse," said the man next to him. "You saw the people waiting outside their cars getting the full inspection, no?"

"I wouldn't take any crap from them," boasted the red-cheeked fellow.

"Who are you kidding? Of course you'd take their crap. What, you want to get slapped around and arrested?"

"I'd slap them right back!"

"Nonsense. Who are you trying to impress?"

Riad turned to me and said, "The soldier wasn't nasty, but he made his point. He's got the power and we don't. We're citizens going to a legal demonstration—"

"What do you mean *citizens*?" interrupted the red-cheeked fellow. "There's no such thing as *citizens* in this country. Just Arabs and Jews, that's it."

"Forget it, it could have been a lot worse," the thin man repeated. "Look, the soldier is only a kid. All of them, just twenty years old. And all week they hear their political leaders telling us to watch our step. Just the other night on TV—there was Arik Sharon publicly warning Arabs of Israel what could happen to us. So what do you expect from these kids? Respect for us?"

"I'm telling you, I wouldn't take any crap from them," repeated the red-cheeked man.

"Of course you would. We all would, and do. That's the whole point—to let us know that they have the power and we don't. It may be *our* Land Day today, but it's *their* land every day. And they don't want us to forget it."

The two fellows in the back seat were quiet for a while and then began talking of other things. Riad, however, still had his mind on the soldier, and he said to me, "What took place there was nothing—*if* it was an isolated incident. But it's not. Believe me, it happens all the time in different ways." He then began to relate how he had been stopped dozens of times over the years—"because I look like an Arab"—and asked for his identity card. He could be walking along a street in Tel Aviv or Jerusalem, alone or with his wife or with friends, or he could be waiting on a line for a bus, or at the movie theater. A soldier or policeman would come over and ask to see his identity card. Sometimes it was done harmlessly enough—like today—but at other times it was done in a humiliating manner. And there was nothing one could do about it.

"I remember one time at the Tel Aviv bus station," he said. "The police yelled at this dark-skinned guy with a moustache to come over. But the guy either didn't hear them or just ignored them. 'Hey you, get your ass over here!' they screamed at him. He came walking over slowly. I thought they were really going to do something to him. But then the guy says, 'Hey, I'm a Jew. What's the problem?' The police immediately got polite with him, looked at his identity card politely, and said, 'Excuse us.' I guarantee you if he had been an Arab, it wouldn't have ended that way. He would have had real problems, and none of that 'Excuse us.'"

By now we were only a kilometer outside of Taibeh, and traffic began to slow down. There seemed to be a backup. Overhead, for the first time we noticed a helicopter, and in the distance was a row of blue and white police vans on the shoulder of the road. As we inched forward, cars began coming in the opposite direction, from Taibeh, and the drivers shouted to us that the entrance to the town was blocked. "Some rock throwing," one of them said. So we too turned around and headed for a dirt lane that entered Taibeh from its outskirts.

Driving on a street that paralleled the main road, we soon arrived at a spot about a hundred meters from Taibeh's main entrance, and there we saw what had caused the roadblock. About forty or fifty youths, all wearing *keffiyehs* which hid their faces, were gathered in an empty lot and hurling stones at the police vans parked across from the entrance.

It was a scene from the *intifada*, now within Israel itself. The policemen stood there shielding themselves from the barrage and looked about ready to counterattack. Riad shook his head and mumbled, "Doesn't look good. Any minute it's going to explode." But like the other drivers, he did not wait to see what would happen, and instead continued on to a parking area far down the road, where a crowd of several hundred were assembling with placards and banners. This was the planned—or in any case, the legal—demonstration.

We all joined this crowd, which soon began marching toward the center of town, away from the direction of the stone throwing. The contingent from Kufr Qara walked loosely together, and with them, I noticed, were Ahmad and his son, Ali. He apparently had decided at the last moment to attend, and for the first time had brought along Ali, who was the only youth in the entire Kufr Qara group.

"Did you catch the scene at the entrance?" Ahmad asked me.

"Yes."

"Bad stuff," he said. And then, as if he were quoting from his father, he affirmed, "Stone throwing is not what we need. Not the Israeli Arabs."

Ismail, who was walking next to us, jumped in, "What do you expect when the police stand outside the entrance? They intimidate—and the kids respond. No police, no stone throwing. Simple as that."

Ahmad agreed, but repeated, "It's no good. No good."

"Of course it's no good," said Ismail. He mopped his forehead with his shirt sleeve. "Let's pray the police have the sense to stay out of the town. Otherwise this could get ugly."

"They'll stay out," said Ahmad, though without conviction. "It'll go all right. Except for the stone throwers." He looked at Ali, who was taking in every word, and added, "It'll be all right, you'll see."

The procession of a thousand or so continued through the streets of Taibeh, gaining participants and enthusiasm as it went. Along the street, as well as on the balconies and rooftops of the two- and three-story apartments, stood old men and women, many in traditional clothing and some flashing victory signs to the marchers. The latter were almost all younger people in Western clothing, and except for one group of teenage girls, all were men. Hand-drawn placards and banners sprouted everywhere, with slogans such as "All Support to the *Intifada*," "Unite Against Repression," and "Two States for Two Peoples—Israel for the Jews and Palestine for the Arabs." There were even a few banners written in Hebrew, carried by a sprinkling of Jews who had come along. At the head of the procession was a fellow with a bullhorn, who led the crowd in chanting nationalistic refrains, and for the entire kilometer-long march he never let up for a minute, nor did the contingent of men and teenage girls chanting along with him.

The march ended in Taibeh's center, at a treeless park with concrete benches—a place known as the Park of the Land Day Martyr, in memory of the young man who had been shot dead there during the first Land Day demonstration. At the park's entrance was a prominent memorial stone festooned with flowers and a handwritten sign that read, "In Everlasting Memory of March 30, 1976." Surging into the park, the marchers pushed forward to the speaker's dais, and as they gathered they sang the illegal Palestinian national anthem, *"Baladi, Baladi"* ("My Country, My Country"). Overhead, at a height of about a hundred and fifty meters, a helicopter circled a couple of times rather menacingly.

"Put your hat on," said Ismail to me. "They're taking pictures."

"Come on!" I did not believe him.

"I'm serious. They've got a camera up there."

Ahmad said, "They're looking for Palestinian flags—the red, white, black, and green colors. It's illegal. They see any, the police get called in."

I looked around and there were no flags to be seen, though I had noticed as we entered the main plaza a newly whitewashed door with a curious painting of a white-cloaked, red-turbaned Islamic fundamentalist riding a black horse and carrying a green banner that read, "There is no God but Allah." I mentioned it to Ahmad.

"That they can't see," he said. "Only flags. And as you can see the demonstration is well organized. Not a flag in sight."

The helicopter made one more pass at no more than seventy-five meters and then flew off toward the main road, where the stone throwers were. Tapping the microphone and pretending not to notice the helicopter, the master of ceremonies shouted out elaborate greetings to the crowd, who now numbered at least twenty-five hundred. "And a special greeting," he said, "to our brothers from the occupied territories, who, despite the army, managed to get here!" The crowd clapped enthusiastically, and Ismail whispered to me that the army had cordoned off the West Bank and Gaza from Israel. "They try to divide us," yelled the man with the microphone, "but we are one—all of us one people." More cheers. And then he called for a minute of silence in honor of the "six martyrs who fell on the first Land Day, and also all our brothers and sisters in the occupied territories who have fallen in the *intifada.*"

For the next hour or so half a dozen speakers, representing the spectrum of Arab political opinion, gave brief speeches. ("I think they're cutting it short today," said Ismail, "because of what's going on outside on the main road.") Among the politicos were the mayor of Taibeh, two members of the Israeli parliament, the head of the united local councils in the Triangle area, a leader of the Histadrut (the national labor federation), and the principal Muslim fundamentalist leader in Israel. All were Arabs this day, though in years past Jews had been included among the speakers.

Most of the speakers read from notes, and the crowd responded with tepid applause. One after another they called for the Israeli government to end the occupation, recognize a Palestinian state, and grant greater equality to the Arab citizens of Israel. At one point a telegram from PLO chairman Yasir Arafat was read ("All success to the nationalist efforts of the Arab citizens and to the forces of Jewish democracy in their just struggle"), and the audience clapped and whistled its approval. Ironically, just as the speaker finished reading the message, the helicopter returned in a low swoop and drowned out the cheers.

It was not until the final speaker, however, that the crowd came fully alive. From the moment he grabbed the microphone, it was apparent that this fellow, the Muslim fundamentalist leader Abdullah Darwish, knew what he was doing. He talked without notes, and unlike the other speakers, who all were clad in neat sports clothes, he wore a rumpled brown cloak, as if his agenda had no place for frivolous grooming. "Brothers and sisters, how good it is to be with you to celebrate our holy Land Day," he began, his large face beaming as he panned the flock. "It is good to be here together—all of us united. . . . The state of Israel looks upon our unity as a punishment from above, and not as a chance to sit with us in dialogue. They want us divided and weak. They threaten us with their tens of thousands of new immigrants from Russia. But I have news for them. Last year in Gaza alone, tens of thousands of new Palestinians arrived—to their mothers. *They cannot replace us!*" The crowd roared. "They must live *with* us! And stop threatening us! . . . That big man in the Israeli government, Arik Sharon—yes, a very, very, big man indeed—" Peals of laughter as Darwish mocked the rotund strongman of the Israeli political right. "He keeps telling us to remember 1948, and beware. Well, *effendi* Sharon, we *do* remember. What were you up to in 1948, *effendi*? Do you think we have forgotten?" He wiped his brow and concluded, "And the very fact that we're here for Land Day proves that we will always remember. And we will defend our rights. We will have our day, brothers and sisters. We will succeed!" The audience applauded loudly as the cleric replaced the microphone and bounded off the dais with two of his aides following him. The show was over.

As we headed out of the plaza, Ismail, Ahmad, and Riad were shaking their heads in disgust and bemoaning the speeches, which they agreed had been more slogans than substance. But above all, they were angry about Darwish's speech—"his act" as Ahmad called it.

"The guy can talk, I'll grant him that," said Riad. "He's used to addressing a crowd every Friday in the mosque—"

"Just garbage," interrupted Ahmad. "All words with no program, no nothing."

"He's dangerous, though," said Riad. "He knows how to play to the crowd. You saw him."

"All nonsense," said Ismail. "He's got nothing to say. They just shouldn't have let him have the last word, that's all . . ." Ismail paused and we all looked overhead. The helicopter, lower than ever, was circling over the crowd as it made its way to the parking area. "I wonder what's with the police and the kids," said Ismail. "Probably all over by now."

"I knew they wouldn't enter the town," said Ahmad.

Ali looked at his father and blurted out, "But see the smoke! Tear gas, right?"

"I think he's right," said Ismail. "Tear gas and burning tires. Something must have happened."

While driving out of town (I joined Ahmad and Ali), we passed the area where the youths had been hurling stones, and where the police evidently had made their charge. There was not a kid or a cop around, but tires and tear gas canisters were still smouldering in the area. Ali craned his neck to take it all in, his ten-year-old's face brimming with curiosity. Ahmad turned on the radio, hoping to catch some news. But when the news summary came on at five o'clock, there were as yet no reports—except for mention of Land Day itself and the fact that fifty-five hundred additional police had been on duty throughout the country to protect against "disturbances of order."

It was only a couple of hours later, when we were back at Abu Ahmad's house, that we finally found out what had happened. According to the newscaster, it had been "a relatively quiet Land Day" in the Galilee and the Negev; only a few people arrested for displaying Palestinian flags, and one small clash among the demonstrators themselves—Muslim fundamentalists versus Communists—in the Galilee village of Arrabe. However, in the central region, in Taibeh, there had been a serious confrontation between police and stone-throwing masked youths. The police "had shown restraint," said the newscaster, until two petrol bombs were hurled at them; then they responded with a tear gas and baton charge, driving the youths back toward the town. An estimated twenty people were injured, including seven police, and twenty-two were arrested. Among those detained were youths from Taibeh, and also several from nearby villages on the West Bank, who had apparently come over to Israel for the day.

"So unnecessary. So stupid," said Abu Ahmad when the newscaster finished. He glanced at his son and grandson, and shook his head slowly.

"At least the police stayed away from the main demonstration," said Ahmad.

"At least," said Abu Ahmad. "But why go looking for trouble? Why give them a chance?" Ahmad and Ali were both quiet. "Ali, you were there?"

A smile flitted across Ali's face, and he answered stiffly, "Yes, grandfather."

Abu Ahmad shook his head again. "It's not the way. Not for us, the Arabs in Israel. Let them throw rocks in the territories, but not here." He pointed his thick finger to his head and added in Hebrew, "*Lo b'koach, rak b'moach*—with brains, not brawn."

"Agreed," said Ahmad in a subdued voice.

And then softly, to nobody in particular, Abu Ahmad said, "It's no good. Rocks, petrol bombs here. It'll bring us nothing. Just problems, nothing more. In Israel, we need no *intifadas*."

15

MAYSA'S ENGAGEMENT

JUST AS MAYSA HAD ANTICIPATED, once Hassan was married and out of the house Umm Ahmad did not stop reminding her that her turn was next. And not only Umm Ahmad. Her sisters, too—though more delicately—started pressuring her to make up her mind. "Sooner or later you're going to have to choose," one of them said, "so why not choose *now?*" Maysa was prepared for all this. Yet what took her by surprise was a shift in her own feelings. She found herself much less resistant. Perhaps, she thought at first, she just couldn't stand up to all the badgering. But no, it was more than that. Something in her *had* changed. For the first time since Nabila's death, she found herself paying attention to her appearance. She bought some bright-colored blouses and new slacks, she began putting on lipstick and eye-shadow just as she used to do, and she again went regularly to the hairdresser. True, there were days when she lapsed into a sudden sadness, but these days were fewer now. And most of the time she was her old self—or almost.

In the natural way that these things happen, a number of potential suitors began to sniff the change, and in customary fashion they let it be known—usually through a sister or mother—that they were interested. Maysa was pleased by all these offers. As she began to contemplate seriously the possibility of becoming engaged, there was one man in particular who she felt drawn to. This was Fawzi, the young man from Kufr Qara whom she had secretly dated when she was studying at the Hebrew University. Fawzi was still in Jerusalem, finishing his fourth year of medical studies. Over the past two years, he had occasionally and discreetly dropped by Abu Ahmad's house when he was in Kufr Qara. Even in her sadness, Maysa enjoyed seeing him; perhaps because Nabila herself had been so fond of him and had encouraged her to "hold on to Fawzi."

In the months after Hassan's wedding, Fawzi, who was also a friend of Hassan's, came by several times to the new house. Maysa managed to be there at those times. She also managed, on several occasions while on professional business in Jerusalem, to visit Fawzi in his dorm room. Without anyone knowing it, the two of them had renewed their "close friendship," as Maysa tactfully put it. And they even had begun talking—again, without anyone knowing it—about the possibility of getting engaged. They wanted each other, they felt, *but* would their families go along with it?

In order to get engaged they needed their fathers' consent, and each knew that his or her own father would be opposed, albeit for different reasons. Fawzi's father was a successful businessman, but he had just put out a great deal of money to set up one of his older sons in a dental practice. He could not afford right then to pay his share of the expenses for an engagement party, and also pay for the construction of a new house for Fawzi. Moreover, there was another brother, two years older than Fawzi, who had not yet become engaged; if anyone was entitled to press the father, it was he and not Fawzi.

For her part, Maysa also knew that Abu Ahmad would be against her choice. It was not a question of liking or not liking Fawzi; Abu Ahmad did not base his decision on such things. It was simply that Fawzi's family was from a small, uninfluential clan, and there was little honor in marrying one's daughter to that kind of people. This obstacle might be overcome, she believed, because Fawzi's father was personally successful and several of his sons, Fawzi included, were well-educated men. Abu Ahmad could respect that. What he ultimately would not respect was the thought, the possibility, that Maysa and Fawzi had been "close friends" before the engagement party, and further, that this arrangement might persist after the party, before they were married and respectably settled in their own home. If he had any inkling of such things, he would flatly oppose Fawzi. Or so Maysa feared.

Aware of these obstacles, both Fawzi and Maysa gingerly set about the complicated process of winning their fathers' approval. Fawzi, as a man, was able to do so more directly. He first approached his brothers, and especially the older brother whose turn was rightfully next, and he won everyone's agreement. He then went to his father and made his case. As expected, his father said no, he could not afford it. However, Fawzi did not give up. And, lo and behold, several weeks later, with his entire brotherly band behind him, he convinced his father to go along with it—with the understanding that the new house, and hence the actual wedding itself, would be delayed two years, until Fawzi finished medical school.

While Fawzi was conducting these discussions with his family, Maysa set into operation her own, even more delicate negotiations. She could not go directly to her father. Instead she went to the women of the family, her sisters and her mother. They were overjoyed for her, and quite relieved that she had at last decided. No question, they would be on her side. Then she let her brothers know. Both Hassan and Ghanem were with her, too, even though they had some hesitation about the long wait between the engagement and the wedding itself. (At the engagement party, the *kitab*, or marriage contract, was officially signed; according to Israeli law the couple was then legally married. But in the eyes of the villagers—that is, according to local mores—the couple was considered married *only* after the wedding itself.) During the long interim, both brothers wondered, would Maysa be going to Jerusalem to visit and go out with Fawzi? They were not naive and knew that this was likely. But after all, they figured, Maysa was a wise girl and she could be trusted to not do anything shameful. The one who did not agree with this assessment was Ahmad, who, as the oldest son, took upon himself the role of safeguarding the family's honor. Once he realized that everyone was supporting Maysa and that his father had already been informed by Umm Ahmad, he resolved to bring his opposition out in the open.

This confrontation, which eventually would decide the fate of Maysa's engagement plans, took place one evening at Abu Ahmad's house. Ahmad came by to visit his father, and as it happened his mother and Maysa were there, too. They were watching television, but immediately turned it off as Ahmad began addressing his father. As if the women were not there, Ahmad laid out his objections to the engagement: Maysa and Fawzi would be waiting a long, long time before the wedding itself and things could happen; people might see them together, say, in Jerusalem, and how would that look? Besides, Fawzi was not really from such a respectable clan, so why all the impatience to get engaged to him? Ahmad talked slowly, elaborating each point in its most sinister light. Abu Ahmad lay there silently puffing on a cigarette. Umm Ahmad said nothing. And Maysa too, knowing it was wisest to hold her tongue, managed to do so for fifteen minutes or so—until finally she could take it no longer.

"How can you say such things, Ahmad? How *can* you?" The words erupted from her mouth with a force that surprised even Maysa herself. "It's *me* you're talking about. It's *my* life, not yours!" Ahmad looked at her angrily, but was too astonished to counter her. Umm Ahmad and Abu Ahmad also seemed taken aback. Maysa hesitated a moment and then went on, looking now at her mother.

"Always you are reminding me, Mother, I'm not a child anymore. Well, that's right. I *am* grown up! I've been to university, I've lived there four years on my own—with Nabila. And now I'm holding down a responsible job and making money. Isn't that true?" Umm Ahmad nodded ever so slightly, but continued her silence.

Maysa resumed, this time daring to face her father and Ahmad directly. "Fawzi is the man I want. No other. I am marrying *him*, *not* his family and clan. Just Fawzi. If you say no to me—if you forbid me—where will I be? Years it'll take to find another. And besides, I'm not interested. If I can't have Fawzi, I want nobody. Nobody at all!"

Maysa sighed deeply, not quite believing what she had just done. Abu Ahmad did not say a word, but rose from the floor mattress and, leaning on his cane, went off to the other room. Umm Ahmad followed him. Ahmad shook his head, still astonished by what had taken place, and abruptly left for home. And Maysa continued to sit there softly shaking, sure that this thing that she had just done—this challenge that nobody except Nabila would have dared to make—had just ruined her chances of marrying Fawzi, whom, she realized at that moment, she wanted more than ever.

Several days after this episode, Hassan and I were working in the fields, pulling the last of his carrot crop from the soil. It had rained the night before, and the soil was moist and workable. Hassan was feeling buoyant that morning, knowing that he was going to "catch a price" with these early-April carrots. While he worked, he talked gaily of one thing and the other, and then at one point I asked him what he thought of Maysa's confrontation with Abu Ahmad. By then it was common knowledge throughout the family and everyone had his own opinion about it. Hassan smiled knowingly, as if he had expected the question, and said slowly, "Well, I'll say this, she's got guts. That's for sure."

"But what'll come out of it?" I asked him directly.

"Hard to say at this point. It's up to my father. He's sitting on it right now. We'll know soon." Hassan wiped his wet forehead with his forearm and suggested we go drink some coffee.

Seated under the fig tree, whose young leaves provided little relief from the punishing sun, Hassan began talking about Ahmad's concern that Maysa might bring dishonor to the family. "I understand my brother, really I do," he said. "And believe me, I have a better idea what's going on than he does. But I look the other way. I prefer to trust that Maysa and Fawzi, whatever they do, they'll do it without drawing attention. That's the point, the main point. You don't want people to see you together acting in the wrong way. The word gets around and it's an *aeb* for the family."

Hassan chuckled uneasily and then went on to describe

an incident that had taken place some ten years before in Kufr Qara and had brought *aeb* to one particular family. It involved a case of adultery. "It's not the only case of adultery that's taken place here," he said by way of a preface. "There's other cases, I'm sure. But the difference with this case was that everyone knew about it. It even made the newspapers. The couple wasn't discreet, not at all! And so the family had to do something about it."

The incident, Hassan said, involved the wife (actually, the former wife) of one of his neighbors—which neighbor, he preferred not to say. This neighbor had a close friend from the nearby village of Ar'ara. Almost every day, this friend used to come and visit. Nobody thought anything of it. Then one day, suddenly, the man's wife was missing. This was an obvious and serious thing because she had five small children and she had left without them. But a few days later they found her. Where? She was attempting to cross the Israeli border into Lebanon together with the husband's close friend from Ar'ara. It turned out that the two of them were lovers, had been for some time, and they were trying to escape. What happened then was that they were both arrested for the offense of illegally attempting to cross the border. However, the police soon realized they had a more serious problem on their hands. They knew that if they simply released the woman to her family, she might be murdered. Therefore, what they did was called her husband and all the men from her family into the police station. They compelled each one to sign a statement that he, personally, was responsible for the woman's life. Then they released her to their custody. The men debated about what to do and decided that the husband should kill her anyway. But he was unable to do it. He simply divorced her and sent her back to her family. They held her under "house arrest" for six months, until finally they married her off to an old man from the West Bank, who then took her to live with him in Saudi Arabia. Since then, she's never seen her children, and all of her family now lives in a permanent state of *aeb;* none of her sisters can find a husband. Nothing ever happened to her lover, and it is not known where he is right now. Her

husband is remarried, though he too has been partly shamed
by the incident.

"And why all this tragedy?" Hassan asked in conclusion.
"Because it became a public scandal. What she did was
wrong, a sin. But she's not the only one who's committed
adultery in Kufr Qara. And she's not the only one who's had
sex without being married to the man. These things do happen. This woman did it, though, in a way that exposed her
family to great shame. Those poor people can hardly show
their faces in the village now. Nobody wants that to happen
to them. And so you do what you can to make sure it doesn't
happen. You see?"

"And you're worried about Maysa in this way?" I asked,
somewhat incredulously.

"It's not the same thing, of course," Hassan answered.
"But she *is* our sister, and so the thing comes up. If she and
Fawzi aren't married, they have to be careful. I trust her—
believe me, I do. And I think my father will go along. My
mother will convince him, and so will Ghanem and I. But
it's a problem just the same."

Hassan had correctly anticipated Abu Ahmad's decision.
About a week after the confrontation, he passed word
through Umm Ahmad to Maysa that he agreed to her choice
of Fawzi. He had made up his mind after listening to the
entreaties of Umm Ahmad (she had begun speaking with
him the very night of the confrontation) and also after consulting with his other sons, Hassan and Ghanem. It was
Ghanem, especially, who had convinced him. Abu Ahmad
trusted the judgment of his second son more than that of
the others, and when Ghanem firmly stated his confidence
in Maysa as well as in Fawzi, Abu Ahmad decided to go
along with it. Not that he was happy about the decision, but
he knew that in the changing world in which he was living
a veto would cause more family upset, probably, than it was
worth. So, with reservations, he gave his approval.

That done, there remained only one more formality to
dispense with before an official announcement could be

made: the setting of the *mahr*, or bride price, which would be a part of the *kitab*. A generation ago, this *mahr* often involved a hefty sum. It was meant to compensate the bride's father for his loss, and much of it (the pre-*mahr*) was paid over immediately at the signing of the *kitab*; the remainder (the post-*mahr*) was paid only if there was a divorce.[1] Nowadays it was usual to ask for only a small, symbolic pre-*mahr*, and to defer any substantial payment, a post-*mahr*, to the contingency of a divorce. Abu Ahmad, as a gesture of good will to Fawzi's family, decided to ask for no pre-*mahr* at all; not even a symbolic sum. But he did request a post-*mahr* of $25,000—not an unreasonable amount by today's standards—and this met no objection from the other side. And so the last hurdle was overcome quickly, and Maysa and Fawzi, to their considerable relief, were at last free to announce their engagement.

Having waited so many weeks, and under such tension, for the clearing of family opposition, they were eager to set the date of the engagement party as soon as possible. They picked the next to last Friday of the month and, as was customary, they announced that the event would take place at Abu Ahmad's house. This left them only two weeks to complete all their arrangements.

In a typically hysterical rush—which everyone cursed but secretly loved—both families went about the numerous preparations that such an occasion naturally entailed. Fawzi's people took care of contacting the *sheikh* who would perform the ceremony, as well as arranging for the musicians and video crew, and purchasing the gold rings that Maysa and Fawzi would exchange that day. Maysa's family was in charge of providing the food and the setting, which meant that Abu Ahmad had to clean up his backyard (since Hassan's wedding it had once again become cluttered with weeds and junk) and Umm Ahmad had to make arrange-

[1]For a discussion of marriage and engagement practices in Palestine in the 1920s—including the ritual of setting the *mahr*—see the pioneering study by Hilma Granqvist, *Marriage Conditions in a Palestinian Village* (Helsinki: Societas Scientiarum Fennica, 1935), vol. 2.

ments to serve food to three or four hundred invited guests. In addition, the guests had to be informed, and for Maysa and Fawzi this involved visiting dozens of homes and personally inviting people, even though written invitations were also sent.

All this last-minute scampering about filled everyone with excitement, and by the morning of the party there was a sense of frenzied anticipation. Only Abu Ahmad, who was whiling away the morning as usual in his *diwan*, seemed calm and unruffled. Umm Ahmad rushed to and fro with a mop and pail. The brothers were busy in a corner of the backyard, butchering three sheep. And all five sisters, who seldom appeared together, were at work making the salads. Maysa herself had gone to the nearby village of Baqa al Gharbiya, where the area's best seamstress put the final touches on her pink-and-white floor-length satin gown, and where she had her hair coiffed and her makeup professionally applied.

She returned home shortly after one o'clock, an hour before the guests were due to arrive, and as she walked into the house her entire family gawked at her as if she were a member of some unknown royal family. That look from all of them, that frozen moment of non-recognition, seemed to undo her. She rushed into the salon and collapsed into sobs, with Umm Ahmad and all the sisters hovering over her, some of them sobbing with her. It had finally hit them: Maysa, the last sister, was going off—and Nabila, whose turn it should have been, was not there with them. The men, who were all standing outside, knew well enough not to interfere. Exchanging puzzled glances, they went back to pushing a few more chairs into place in the *diwan*, where the *sheikh* would shortly be conducting the formal ceremony.

"That hour before the guests came was the hardest in my life," Maysa would later explain. "I couldn't stop crying, and I even felt like I couldn't go through with it. Somehow it wasn't right. I looked up on the wall and saw Nabila's picture, and I so much wanted her to be with me. She was the one who had told me to choose Fawzi. Now that the day had finally come, she wasn't there. I couldn't stand it. My sisters too—especially my oldest sister, Fatma—understood just what I was feeling. It was terribly sad. Here all the guests were arriving and I was sitting in the house crying my head off. I didn't feel I could face all those people right then."

As it was, Maysa did not have to face them—at least not for the next half hour or so—for the ceremony in which the *kitab* was officially signed was an all-male affair. The women remained apart, a few in the house with Maysa, and most out in the backyard. The ceremony itself was conducted in the *diwan*, with some seventy-five men, principally older men, seated there as witnesses. At the outset of the ceremony the *sheikh* did appear in the house with Abu Ahmad and two witnesses, just long enough to obtain from Maysa the customary consent that a man, in this case Abu Ahmad, would serve as her representative at the official ceremony. The *sheikh* then returned to the *diwan* and began the proceedings.

The *sheikh*—a balding, professorial man in a sportscoat and tie—kneeled on a straw mat on the floor, with Abu Ahmad seated cross-legged to his left and Fawzi seated similarly to his right, facing Abu Ahmad. The other men sat on the floor or in plastic chairs all around them. Abu Ahmad was wearing his finest gray wool *gallabiyeh* and a silk *keffiyeh*, and Fawzi was dressed in a dark blue suit with a matching dark blue tie. After opening the ceremony with a short reading from the Koran, the *sheikh* enjoined Fawzi and Abu Ahmad to clasp each other's right hands, and in turns to repeat after him: "I, Abu Ahmad, agree to give to Fawzi X—— my daughter Maysa, with the following *mahr* to be paid." And then, "I, Fawzi X——, agree to take Maysa ——, and to pay the following *mahr*." Both men then signed the marriage contract which the *sheikh* had brought with him in his briefcase. Finally, turning to the assembly of men, the *sheikh* closed his eyes, extended his palms—as did all seventy-five men—and in unison they recited the Fatiha, the brief opening chapter of the Koran. And with that, the official ceremony was over. Bowls of fruit and biscuits were passed around while the men continued to sit chatting with each other.

Just outside the *diwan* late-arriving guests had to dash

for cover as a downpour suddenly pelted the area. Muddy
rivulets flowed through Abu Ahmad's backyard, and the
plastic chairs set up there filled with water. The party would
obviously have to be delayed or transferred elsewhere.

"A rotten bit of luck," said a familiar voice off to my
side as a hand came thumping down on my back. I turned
to see Samir's face smirking at me. I hadn't noticed him in
the *diwan*; he apparently had rushed in to take cover. "Maysa
and Fawzi took a chance having the party at this time," he
said. And then he added philosophically, "Sometimes it's
better to be patient and wait. Until the summer, say."

"Is that what you're going to do?" I kidded him.

Samir's face reddened. "Well, yes. That's right. How did
you know?"

Surprised, I admitted that I knew nothing.

"I thought maybe Hassan told you. He's one of the few
who know I'm about to get engaged."

I congratulated him and asked whether he had finally
decided on the woman who seemed to be dancing for his
benefit at Zaynab's henna party.

"Oh, her—no," he answered, as if barely remembering
her. "She was too dark, like an African. I'm getting engaged
to this woman I met a couple of months ago. My brother
pointed her out to me. She's always coming to his grocery
store. She's from a good family, one that's connected to
mine. I arranged for an invitation to her house, met the
parents, met her, and . . . well, that was it. She's a beautiful
girl, and smart too. And white as snow. I'll admit it, I wanted
a light-skinned girl, and she's even lighter than me."

"When's the party?" I asked.

"Soon. We just have a few more details to settle and
we'll announce it. Sometime in the summer, when there's
no chance of rain. Only beautiful skies overhead." He smiled
broadly. "You don't want to take any chances. Me, I want
no rain-outs."

Fortunately, the thundershower that had arrived so suddenly disappeared just as quickly, leaving a steamy mist
over the backyard. The backyard itself was a muddy bog.
So the party was transferred fifty meters away to a neighbor's house, where the sloping gravel courtyard was wet but
serviceable. Two small wooden platforms with red and black

awnings were hastily set up, one for the musicians and the other for Maysa and Fawzi. The video crew, eager to make up for lost time, immediately plugged in their gear, and the women of both families, young and old, began dancing enthusiastically in a circle in front of the platforms.

The party went on for the next two hours. During that time the dancing and music continued nonstop, and the guests went off in turns to have *shishlik* and salads in Abu Ahmad's *diwan*. Maysa and Fawzi, though, remained on stage, descending only on occasion to join in the dancing. Fawzi seemed to be enjoying himself, laughing as he danced and laughing again as guests came by to buss him on the cheek and thrust envelopes of cash into his hand (by the day's end, he and Maysa would have eighteen thousand shekels, enough to lay the foundation of their new house). Maysa struggled to maintain a smile, but—as the video would later painfully reveal—it was a sad smile that kept reappearing, one made all the sadder by the glittering makeup that framed it. All five of her sisters periodically came up to the platform and attempted to cheer her up, but to little avail. Only when she and Fawzi finally exchanged rings, near the end of the party, did she seem truly cheerful. Fortuitously, the video crew also captured this sequence for posterity.

As a reluctant late-afternoon sun came flickering through the low clouds, the party ended and the guests drifted off. Several of the grandchildren, led by Umm Ahmad, began the cleanup. Fawzi and his friends and brothers, still full of party spirit, decided to return to his house and continue the celebration. But Fawzi did not want to leave Maysa alone. Even though it was against custom, he told her to come with him. Abu Ahmad and the three brothers, however, would have none of this spontaneous irregularity: she could not, and would not, go to any all-male party. Having had her fill of battles, and realizing that she had won the most important one of all, Maysa chose not to challenge them. Fawzi went off alone. And Maysa went back into Abu Ahmad's house, got out of her slightly mud-splattered gown, and threw herself onto her bed, where she remained undisturbed, asleep, until noon of the following day.

16

GHANEM, THE TEACHER, AND A VISIT TO THE HIGH SCHOOL

A S A MEMBER OF A FAMILY and a people who were passionately gregarious, Ghanem was that unusual individual—
a private person. His father, his two brothers, and the
women of the family were most happy when gathered with
others, many others. Whereas he, the middle son, seemed
most content when alone or with his wife and two daughters.
Then his staid and somber face would leak a laugh and he
was good for a joke or two.

Of the three sons—for that matter, of the ten children—
Ghanem was clearly Abu Ahmad's favorite. It was to Ghanem that Abu Ahmad ultimately turned for advice (Should
Maysa marry Fawzi? Should he, Abu Ahmad, visit a doctor?). And it was on Ghanem that he leaned when some
delicate or demanding family task had to be done. "Ghanem's the most trustworthy and reliable and the cleanest of
my boys," said Abu Ahmad. "He's never let me down and
always listens to my voice."

In a way, it was surprising that Ghanem had not followed in his father's footsteps and become the family farmer.
He surely was more physically suited to it than Hassan.

Stocky and heavy-muscled like Abu Ahmad, and as reliable as dawn itself, he seemed the likely candidate. Indeed, during his four-year stint as the principal farmer, from 1973 to 1977, the family had done exceedingly well; all outstanding debts had been paid off and the farm was turning a decent profit. Moreover, Ghanem knew then that nothing he ever did in life would give him the pure satisfaction that he took from farming. Yet he also knew that he lacked a quality that farming demanded: he was not a gambler. Looking to the future and the time he would be supporting a wife and children, he wanted a steady paycheck. "I wanted my two thousand shekels a month," he stated, "no matter whether it rained or hailed, or what the price of tomatoes was in the market."

So Ghanem headed off to Tel Aviv University with the sober aim of acquiring a B.A. and returning to Kufr Qara as a teacher. In this he had Abu Ahmad's blessing as well as his financial assistance. Abu Ahmad, who had been thwarted as a boy in his own educational aspirations, was eager that at least one of his sons attain a university education. He knew that Ghanem, unlike his older brother, Ahmad, would finish what he started. And he did. Four years later, diploma in hand, he returned to the village and promptly found work as a junior-high teacher—of Hebrew.

"In the university," said Ghanem, "I focused on Hebrew literature and language. I knew there was a need for Hebrew teachers in the local school system. The kids are studying it from third grade right through high school. So it was the practical thing to do. And maybe, too, my father had some influence on me—his experience, I mean. You know that he was the first in the village to learn Hebrew. For him, it always came in handy. He valued it. And over the years, I came to value it, too. In this country you have to know Hebrew to get along."

One of the immediate benefits of the job ("my biggest fringe benefit to date," as Ghanem drolly put it) was that he met his wife-to-be in his first year of teaching—she was one of his students. "But I don't want you to get the wrong idea," he added. "I didn't go after her *while* she was in my class. The fact is, at the time Latifa was my student I was still involved with a girl I had met at the university. But that relationship broke up. Three years later, when I was looking to get engaged, I thought of Latifa. She had grown even more beautiful over those years. A lot of guys were also interested, but I had an inside track because I was a close friend of one of her brothers and our mothers are distant cousins . . . and maybe she liked me back then as a teacher. I don't know. *That* you'll have to ask her."

"A lousy teacher. He was terrible," Latifa teased, blushing as she glanced at Ghanem. She had bright emerald eyes and high cheek bones, and was still as pertly pretty as a teenage fashion model. "No, seriously, all the kids liked him. He was kind and didn't yell—not often, anyway. Even if you were an average student, like me, he tried hard to teach you. But did I think then that this was the man I'd marry? Oh no, never. I was only fourteen years old. Boys were off limits. And Ghanem was this . . ." she grinned at him, ". . . this *old man* in his twenties."

We were sitting in Kufr Qara's only park, a grassy acre that had just been planted the year before to cover the boggy remains of the village's old water-well area. Ghanem and Latifa, after much prodding from their two young daughters, had finally brought them down to the new park with its slide, swings, and freshly painted refreshment stand. The girls scampered off immediately to the swings, and Latifa lithely ran after them. "She's the best thing that's happened to me," Ghanem said with uncharacteristic enthusiasm. "Seven years of marriage and it's all been good. Lucky, no?"

We sat silently for a moment as a swarm of gnats, no doubt longing for the old well, circled overhead. Ghanem took out a pack of Marlboros, his father's brand, and he and I began talking about the local school system. Some days earlier I had expressed an interest in visiting Kufr Qara's junior high–high school complex. In addition, I told Ghanem that I would be curious to hear how the schools had changed in the last twenty years—that is, since he was a student. He seemed eager to talk about this, and so had invited me to accompany him and his family to the park.

"I've been thinking about the question of how things have changed since I was a student," Ghanem began, a bit didactically. "And it's interesting. Because in a way, some things haven't changed much at all, while other things are vastly different than they used to be. Take, for example, the way the boys and girls relate to each other socially. You've seen them walking to school in the mornings, I'm sure. Boys walking with boys, and girls with girls—never mixed together. That's the same way as when I was a student in high school. We didn't dare talk one-to-one with girls then, and to this day they don't either. They attend classes together, yes. This isn't Iran and Khomeini-style here. Not yet anyway." He chuckled to himself. "Outside of class, though, boys and girls go their own ways. No respectable girl would be caught talking alone with a boy. Her parents would come down hard on her. And I'll tell you the truth—" He paused as Latifa and his daughters came running over toward us. "I'm not so sure I'd want my daughters to be any different. They're still young, but I'm pretty much traditional on this one."

His daughters flung themselves onto Ghanem as Latifa stood above them, her hands on her hips. The girls said they wanted money to buy some hot dogs and sodas. Ghanem looked hesitant, but when Latifa nodded her consent he took out his wallet and handed them the money. He then resumed.

"It's not so much in the area of boy-girl relationships that things have changed. At least I don't think so. What really has changed is the kinds of things that are taught in school and the openness you see today. Of course if you ask the students themselves, I imagine some of them will have complaints. But really, the freedom they have to discuss political things, and the material they learn in school, are . . . well, it's like night and day compared to when I went to school."

Ghanem went on to explain that when he was a student in junior high and high school, he and his classmates were grossly uninformed about politics, and what is more, the educational system was designed—he could now see—to keep them that way. Few students during that time thought of themselves specifically as Palestinians, and fewer still knew anything of the history of the Palestinian people. Rather, they thought of themselves as Israeli Arabs, and more broadly, as part of the Arab people. But there was no pride instilled in them about their Arabness, and the truth was they felt a certain shame about who they were. And the school system, he now realized, was something of an instrument for perpetuating this sense of shame.

"I entered junior high school back in 1967," he recalled. "It was right after the June War. And I graduated in 1973, right before the October War. That was a terrible period for our people. The Jews had won that war—the Six-Day War, they call it—and our people were walking around with their heads bowed. Our hero, Nasser, the man we'd been counting on to rescue us, had failed miserably. We were ashamed. But do you think we talked about any of this in school? No, never. It was forbidden. Not once in junior high school did we ever discuss in class what was going on politically in the area.

"What did we discuss? The same curriculum as always. And what a curriculum that was! There was no such thing as Palestinian history because there was no such thing as Palestine. Really, that's the truth. The word *Palestine* was never mentioned in class, and you weren't even allowed to write it in your notebook. The teachers feared the Ministry of Education would have them fired. And they would have, too! I remember once in music class the teacher asked us if we knew any folk tunes. One boy rose and began singing something he must have learned at home—a Palestinian nationalist song. Well, the teacher went crazy. He leaped up on a chair and started screaming, 'What are you doing? You're going to get me fired! Stop at once!' It's shameful, but that's the way it was. The teachers were frightened to even mention the name of their own people.

"We learned nothing of the modern history of this whole area. Only the ancient history, with a great emphasis on the Old Testament and the Jewish presence here—and a little about the Muslim world in the Golden Age. The modern history or geography of the Arab world was not discussed, and the Israeli-Arab conflict was barely mentioned. And do you think we learned anything about Arabic literature or Arabic poetry? Almost nothing. The Koran, and that's about it. Instead, it was Jewish poetry and literature that were taught—Shalom Aleichem, Bialik, Tchernichovsky. I'm not saying these people shouldn't have been taught. They're excellent writers and worth studying. Yet it was very unfair, and even unwise, to give us so little about our own culture.

"A lot of that has changed now, I'm glad to say. Not so much because the Jews have suddenly become benevolent. They've just become wiser. They've realized that it's better to let us learn in school about our own culture, and better to let us talk about politics in the classroom. Otherwise frustration builds up too much and some youths turn to radical solutions. The government doesn't want that, so they've eased up. Everything's much freer now."

Ghanem glanced at his daughters as they returned, each with a hot dog and bun in one hand, and a soda in the other. They draped themselves over him, with Latifa sitting off to the side. "I'll tell you," he continued, "it's a lot better this way. Much less hypocrisy. It may be hard to imagine—the kids in high school today can hardly believe it—but in my day we used to celebrate Israel's Independence Day just as if we were Jewish kids. The whole school would be decked out in blue and white, and we'd sing these Israeli patriotic songs about *our* country—"

Latifa laughed and said, "Not just in high school. Grade school too. At the top of our voices, we'd sing. I remember the lyrics to this day." She began singing in mock seriousness as her daughters laughed.

"The principal," continued Ghanem, "would give a patriotic speech. And in the end we'd stand and salute the flag. Really, we did." He grabbed a bite of his older daughter's hot dog. "But today, *il hamdu lillah*, there's no more of that. Today we don't celebrate Independence Day, and the kids are free to acknowledge openly that it's not *their* day of independence, and that they're Palestinians. Now kids know what's going on here and they're much freer to say what's on their minds. Look. My daughter, she's only six and already she knows a thing or two. Rigia—" Ghanem turned to

his daughter and asked in his schoolteacher's voice, "—over
in the occupied territories, what's going on these days?"

Rigia took a gulp of soda and answered, "The people
who live there are throwing stones at the Jews."

"Why are they doing that?"

"Because the Jews want to take the people's lands, so
they have to defend themselves."

"And what do the Jews do when stones are thrown at
them?"

"They shoot their guns and try to kill the people. That's
what they do, right?"

Eyebrows raised, Ghanem looked at me and said, "A
different generation. And Rigia, she's only in the first grade!"

Not more than a five-minute walk from Ghanem's house
was the junior high–high school complex. Once an olive
grove, it was now a ten-acre dirt and asphalt tract with a
basketball court and a crude soccer field at the entrance,
and beyond that a hodgepodge of buildings—wooden shacks
and an assortment of concrete, motel-like structures—that
reflected the school's growth over the past twenty years.
Altogether, it was an austere-looking place; not a flower or
a bush or a patch of lawn graced the premises. Had it not
been for the hundreds of students clustered here and there
that morning in the courtyard, it could have passed for an
army barracks.

On the third floor of the newest of these buildings, the
high school principal, Hamza L——, had his office. Hamza—
as he introduced himself—was a friend of Ghanem's, and a
few days earlier it had been informally arranged that I pay
a visit to the school. "According to the law," Hamza had
explained, "we need formal permission from the Ministry of
Education for you to come. But that'll take months, if they
agree at all. So let's just do it spontaneously. Why not? We'll
take a chance."

That morning when I showed up at the office, Hamza
was rather busy. He offered to have someone give me a tour
of the complex, but when I reminded him that I wanted to

meet with a small group of high school students, he quickly dispatched an administrative assistant to "round up a half dozen or so kids—some bright ones preferably." His assistant later explained to me, after my meeting with the students, that about two thirds of the six hundred students in Kufr Qara's high school, grades ten through twelve, were taking college-preparatory courses. Of the two hundred students in the graduating class, about fifty (boys and girls about equally) would go on to Israeli colleges and universities; and an additional twenty-five students, almost all boys, would go study abroad, principally in Western Europe.

Within minutes from the time that Hamza issued his informal command, eight bright faces, three girls and five boys, greeted me at the office and we headed off to an empty classroom. They were eleventh graders (the twelfth graders were busy taking exams that week), and from the initial looks on their faces they were still wondering why they had been summoned. As it turned out, they had been told only that "a guy writing about the village" wanted to talk with them, but since three of the eight knew vaguely about me, they had guessed that it was part of some research project. In any case, we all quickly introduced ourselves, I explained to them about the book, and then I told them that I would like to ask some questions which I hoped they would feel free to answer. They all nodded compliantly but rather uncertainly. For a moment, frankly, I found myself wondering whether I had been wise to follow Ghanem's advice to "go to the high school and talk to kids you don't know—you'll see how open they are these days."

I decided to begin with some relatively unthreatening questions: How many of them were intending to go on to university? (All said they were.) And what would they study? (Two students were unsure. The rest had decided: journalism, law, nursing, veterinary medicine, psychology, and computer technology.) Did they put in much time doing homework? (A couple of hours a day, they agreed.) And what else did they do after school? (The girls stayed at home helping their mothers, while the boys worked in the fields, or played sports, or went off with friends.)

The ice had been broken, but the students now sat there

looking puzzled and even bored. Evidently they had expected something more challenging. "Let me ask you this," I said, "How many of you have contacts with Jews? And do any of you have Jewish friends?" Several looked at me with sheepish grins. There was a brief silence. Then two students began talking about how their fathers worked with Jews in Hadera and Tel Aviv, and two others added that in junior high school there had been exchange visits with some Jewish schools, and that they had made friends. "Are you still friends?" I asked. Both hesitated to answer, and the group again fell silent.

"It's very hard to be friends now with Jews," one boy finally answered. He, Mahmoud, was the one who planned to study journalism, and he gauged my reaction with suspicious, beady eyes. "The situation doesn't really allow it."

"That's not true," countered Hatem, the boy next to him. Turning to me, Hatem added, "I play basketball on the school team and we train sometimes with Jewish teams. No problem. We get along fine."

"But are you friends after the game?" challenged Adeleh. (She had identified herself earlier as coming from Abu Ahmad's clan.) "That's the real question, no?"

"Afterwards, not really. Though once or twice back in junior high I used to visit this Jewish kid from Netanya in his house, and he came to visit me."

"But it broke off, right?" Adeleh persisted, as Hatem quietly retied his basketball sneakers. And then she continued, "That's the problem, the Jewish kids don't really want friendships with us. They're embarrassed to introduce us to their friends. I had this Jewish friend once, too. A girl from Hadera. But when I went to visit her at her home once, she pretended in front of her friends like she didn't know me. It hurt, really it did. Since then, I'm a lot more cautious."

"They go their way and we go ours," offered Riad, a curly-haired boy wearing a hot-pink tee shirt emblazoned with the word *Atlanta*. "We go to the Jewish towns, Hadera and Netanya, and we go to the beaches. But we don't mix with them. It's better that way. I'm not saying it's good, but for now it's better that way."

The students sat there looking back and forth at each

other. We were in a semicircle, the girls on one side and the boys on the other. I found it odd that I hadn't noticed this earlier, almost as if I'd expected it. "Tell me," I said, "you've been to Hadera and Netanya and the beaches. The Jewish kids, boys and girls, behave differently than you do. How do you feel when you see them walking hand in hand?"

"It's immoral what they do," said a pale, stern-faced girl, Lyla, who until then hadn't spoken.

"Wait a minute—" Hatem began.

"I agree with Lyla," interrupted the smallish, sad-eyed girl, Maysoon, who was sitting next to her. "The Jewish kids go much too far. Kissing in public, and you know what else."

"Just wait a minute." Hatem held up his hands like a traffic cop. "So they go too far. But tell the truth, don't we in the village go too far in the opposite direction? Be honest now!"

"No, we don't go too far," insisted Maysoon. "What are you saying? We should be like them? Kiss in public?" She looked around at the others. "Maybe we should open a disco here in Kufr Qara, too?"

Everyone burst into laughter—except for Lyla, who sat there with her arms crossed, her dark eyes glaring.

"Well, why not?" said Hatem, taking up Maysoon's challenge. "Seriously, it might be a good thing. Be honest, there are families here who go on vacation to Tiberias and Eilat, and when they're over there, the kids are allowed to go to the discos. So why not here?"

"Come on, Hatem," said Adeleh. "You know it would never work. Nobody would go. Nobody would be allowed to go."

"I'd go!" Hatem exclaimed loudly.

"Nobody would!" Lyla responded, even louder.

Aziz, a tall and solemn boy (he was the one planning to be a veterinarian), broke in gently. "The Jews go too far, true. Nobody here—" He glanced at Hatem. "Nobody believes in kissing in public or having sex in high school like the Jews do. But most of us—at least I think so—would not be against boys and girls talking together alone and being boyfriend and girlfriend without all the sex."

Several of the students chorused their agreement, and

then Lyla, apparently unable to contain herself any longer, erupted. "Not me!" She looked accusingly at Aziz. "It's against God and the Koran. What are you advocating? Sexual relations between unmarried people?"

"Not sexual relations. Not at all." Aziz spoke softly, attempting to appease her. "Friendship, that's all. Friendship isn't against God or the Koran. Not as far as I know, it's not."

With that, a debate on religion began, as Lyla and Maysoon took on the rest of the students. It soon became apparent that they were sympathizers of the Muslim fundamentalist movement, and in their view Kufr Qara would be a better place if it "returned to Islam." They even went so far as to say that they personally were considering a change in the way they dressed—from the casual slacks and blouses they now wore to the long dresses and scarves advocated by the fundamentalists (a fair sprinkling of high school girls were already so dressing). Hatem exploded when he heard this, announcing that he was "against turning the clock back twelve hundred years" and that he wanted no part of "living in a Khomeini-style country, or village." Several others voiced similar opinions, though in a cooler way. Unlike Hatem, they viewed themselves as religious—they fasted during Ramadan, for example—but they drew a line between religious observance on the one hand and Muslim fundamentalism on the other. The fundamentalists, they argued (with Lyla disagreeing), wanted to "take over the country politically," and they were against that.

After twenty minutes or so of this cross-fire, the group, at my prompting, agreed to take a break. Most stayed in their chairs, as if glued there by the heat of the previous exchange. Hatem and a couple of others went outside for a while, and I walked over to the window to see the view. It was a serene view: hillocks of olive groves and vegetable fields sloping to the southeast, and the steeper hills of the West Bank looming not more than two miles away. Over there, I found myself thinking, kids the same age as these had taken their politics out of the classroom and into the streets. They were running the show over there, some of them leaders of the *intifada*. It must have been strange for these kids, the ones in Israel, to contemplate that. I wondered if they envied the others, or if they were just as glad *their* lives were not on the line. And would they acknowledge any of this?

When we sat down again, I decided to broach the subject in a roundabout way. Turning to the group, I asked them how they identified themselves. "Asked by a stranger," I said, "what would you call yourselves—Israelis, Arabs, Israeli Arabs, Palestinians? What exactly?"

"Palestinian Arabs from Israel," answered Adeleh, as several nodded in agreement.

"It depends who's doing the asking," said Hatem. "If I were in Europe or America, I'd say I'm an Israeli. But here in Israel, I'd say I'm a Palestinian Arab living in Israel."

"I agree with Hatem that it depends where you are," said Abdullah, a pensive boy who, like Hatem, was on the school basketball team. "But I'd put it this way—in the eyes of others, the Jews, we are simply Arabs. And over in the territories, most of them look at us as Israelis, like we're too close to the Jews."

"That's true," agreed Hatem, "you go over there with your yellow Israeli license plates and you'll get stones through your windows just like you're a Jew."

"Not if you're wearing a *gallabiyeh* or *keffiyeh*," said Lyla. "They don't throw stones at Arabs—at fellow Palestinians. Not at all."

The group fell silent for a moment and then I asked them, "How do you regard those throwing the stones—the 'children of the stones,' as they're called?"

"I admire them," responded Riad without hesitation.

"Me too," seconded Maysoon.

"We all admire them," Aziz announced, looking around at the others. There was no dissent.

"I'll even go further," added Riad, fingering his Atlanta tee shirt. "I *envy* them. They're doing what we don't dare do, what we can't do. Because of them, we're able to lift our heads higher."

"We in Israel couldn't put up with what they're putting up with—" began Hatem.

"They're suffering for us," said Lyla, agreeing with Hatem for the first time. "We have to have our comforts, our bellies full. They know how to go on nothing."

"But you know, it's really a strange thing," continued Hatem. "A few years back, before the *intifada*, these West Bank kids were people we looked down on. They dressed in old-fashioned raggedy clothes, and had old-fashioned manners and ideas, and weren't like us. They weren't modern. We laughed at them. We really did. Now they're our heroes. *We* look up to *them*. And *they* look down on *us*. It's like that, really."

"That's true," agreed Riad. "I tell you, I envy them. They've done the job. Because of them, one of these days there's going to be a Palestinian state. That's for sure."

Everyone nodded, and for a brief time there was absolute agreement in the room. Everyone concurred that a Palestinian state in the territories was inevitable, although they personally "would not move" to that state; they would stay in Kufr Qara. A couple of students, Riad and Abdullah, then added that they were hopeful that in the future such a Palestinian state would encompass the entire area and the Jews would become a minority within it; in their view, that would be "the best solution."

"But wait a minute," said Aziz, upon hearing this. "We criticize the Jews for opposing a Palestinian state. Are we going to turn around and deny them a state? Both sides, ours too, have to compromise—"

"Besides that," Hatem interrupted, "I want to see what the Palestinian state is going to be like. We need a state in the territories, yes. But let's face it, it's not necessarily going to be a democratic state, is it? We know what's going on over there—the killings of collaborators, the fighting between the Muslim fundamentalists and the PLO groups, and the fighting within the PLO itself. It's not so pretty, let's admit it."

And again polemical sparks began to fly. At one point it got so loud that a teacher opened the door to see what was happening. I explained what we were doing there, and he smiled diplomatically, although not, I thought, entirely convinced. In any case, the students seemed to get the message, and they piped down. I then turned to them and asked whether this debate they were having was also something that happened in their classes. Were they free to state their views so openly?

"It depends on the class and the teacher," answered Hatem.

"In civics and history classes," Adeleh added, "we have real debates sometimes. Just like now."

"It depends on the teacher," agreed Riad. "Some are more willing to let things go than others. I know a little about this because my father is a teacher here."

Hatem, again playing the traffic cop, held up his hand and said, "Let me explain. I know a little about this too. I've got cousins who told me how things used to be here. We're much better off, much freer. Mind you, the textbooks don't go into things much—"

"The government censors the texts," interrupted Riad.

"They give the government version, put it that way," continued Hatem. "In the textbooks, there's almost nothing about the Israeli-Arab conflict. You'd never know from the books about the tremendous struggle going on here before 1948—"

"And after 1948, forget it," chimed in Abdullah. "There's almost nothing written about what's happened here. Just a little factual information about the Arab countries—Egypt, Syria, Jordan. Nothing about the Palestinian nationalist struggle. The only way we learn about what's happened here and the Palestinian struggle is from the outside. From books, newspapers, and talking to people. In school, we get almost nothing."

"Wait a minute," I said, "I thought you were saying that the teachers discuss this material with you?"

"They do," answered Hatem. "Some of them, anyway."

Mahmoud, the boy with the beady eyes, who had remained conspicuously quiet through most of the morning, said, "They let us talk. But they themselves don't express their opinions. They're not allowed to. Only once in awhile will one of them dare open his mouth and say what he really believes."

"They're afraid of losing their jobs," added Riad. "I know from my father about this. A lot of them don't demonstrate on Land Day because they're afraid of being seen and maybe reported. My father won't go for that reason. And in the school . . . well, they know there are stinkers here—people working for the Shabbak."

"That's right, you've got it," echoed Mahmoud self-righteously.

Everyone fell silent and began fidgeting. We were running out of time, but with the mention of the Shabbak I was reluctant to break off our meeting right there. From past experience, I knew that whenever mention of the Shabbak came up in my presence—particularly when I was meeting with strangers—it was certain that some, or most, were wondering about my connections: Was I a Shabbaknik? I also had learned that sometimes it was better to deal with the suspicion openly and directly; this, I felt, was one of those times.

"How many of you have had the thought that perhaps I am working with the Shabbak?" I asked.

The students chuckled self-consciously and began looking at each other.

"I'll admit it," said Riad, "it crossed my mind when we first started."

"Mine too," said Maysoon.

"I would have thought so," said Hatem, "but I knew about you from Samir." Hatem had mentioned earlier that he was the cousin of Samir, Hassan's close friend. "So really, I didn't think about it."

Mahmoud, looking at me with a thin smile, said, "I heard that on Land Day you were here." I nodded, and he continued, "I wasn't at the demonstration, but someone told me you attended. I was just wondering why?"

"He's writing a book," answered Hatem, as if coming to my defense. "So he was reporting on it, no?" He looked at me and I acknowledged that that was indeed the reason. And then Hatem added, "Anyway, nothing we're saying here today is any different than what Darawsha and Miari [two of the six Arab members of the Knesset] are saying all the time. So if they're free to talk, why aren't we?"

There was a quick exchange, with a few students affirming that what they had said was well within their rights as citizens. Hatem added that he hoped it would all be written down, because he was convinced that people in America didn't know what was happening here.

"Besides, I'll say this—" continued Riad, "going back to the Shabbak question. Once we got going I could tell you weren't a Shabbaknik. So I wasn't worried at all."

A few students nodded in agreement, as if eager to end on an upbeat note. Then there was a knock at the door, and the teacher who had appeared before apologized that he had to disturb us because he needed the classroom. We rose to leave, and as we were walking out I turned to Mahmoud and said, "I guess you still have a question mark in your mind, don't you?"

"That's right," he answered, looking off to the side. "You never know here in the village. Anyone can be working for the Shabbak. Teacher, visitor—anyone."

"I'm not," I blurted out.

"I'm sorry to be so blunt," he responded, "but that's the way it is." He held out his hand and said brightly, "Good luck."

He headed down the corridor to join the others, and as he did so I found myself wondering whether he felt as awkward and foolish in wishing me good luck as I had just felt in telling him that I was not a Shabbaknik.

17

A MIXED MARRIAGE

ON A HILLOCK OVERLOOKING HASSAN'S FIELDS lived an un-usual couple, Aziz and Irena. He was a Muslim and a native son, and she was—or had been—a Jew from Argentina. Their marriage was one of a handful of mixed marriages in the village; the other four or five were pairings of Muslim men and Christian women, the women having come from Europe or South America. Aziz and Irena were the only Muslim-Jewish pair in all of Kufr Qara.

While living only a hundred meters away, not one of Abu Ahmad's sons had more than a "hello" relationship with Aziz, and for that matter the hello was a rather cool one. The brothers did not approve of mixed marriages. Like Abu Ahmad, they believed that the preferred marriage was be-tween sons and daughters of the same village, if not the same clan, and all hoped—indeed, were determined—that their own children would not go astray. Aziz, as far as they were concerned, had taken a foolhardy path; besides that, they didn't much like him.

Aziz's father was a close friend of Abu Ahmad. They had known each other from boyhood, and liked and respected one another. Aziz's father was also a frequent visitor at Abu Ahmad's *diwan*. And thus it was not surprising that ten years before, when he had first become aware of his son's rela-tionship with Irena, he had brought his concerns to Abu

Ahmad. What should he do? What could he do? Abu Ahmad had told him, "With sons it is not wise to use force. Reason with him. Show him other possibilities. But try not to use force. If anything goes wrong, he'll blame it on you." Abu Ahmad was not sure whether his friend had taken his advice, but whatever he had done, obviously it had not worked. Aziz had married Irena, and according to Abu Ahmad, "His father had to make the best of it, which he did. To his credit, he has learned to live with it."

For my part, I was intrigued by this couple, and on occasion, when they would pass Hassan's fields or visit a neighbor, I went to chat with them. With me they were quite friendly. They invited me to visit them at home, and eventually I came to know them.

Both in their mid-thirties, Aziz and Irena had been married for seven years. Aziz was a physician in Kufr Qara and Irena had a master's degree in biology, though at the time she was staying at home—as was expected in the village—to raise their three small children. He was dark, with large inquisitive eyes, and still had the lean look of a college undergraduate. She, blond and green-eyed and pretty, had begun to muffin over in the way of most village women her age.

After living a year and a half in the home of Aziz's parents, they had eventually moved into their own place— a place that was as unusual as they were. It was large, though not larger than many homes, and in its landscaping and interior design it had a singular elegance. This above all was Aziz's doing. He had dreamed for years of how he would build his home, and how he would blend Arab and Western design. He had used fine Jerusalem stone for the outer walls of the house and a lot of pine-wood paneling on the inside. All the downstairs floors were marble, and the windows and doorways were softly arched. On the walls were reproductions of paintings by Spanish artists; oriental ceramic works decorated the living room tables. Most impressive and striking, however, was the dunam-sized garden outside, which Aziz himself had designed and planted. There was not another like it in Kufr Qara. The flower beds were neat and carefully planted with a wide variety of flowers, and stone walkways wound between and around them. A grassy play area on the side was for the children's use, and off in the corner stood an elaborate fountain and some sculpted figures from Denmark and Italy.

It had taken Aziz three years to complete his garden. Now that he had, he and Irena liked to spend the warm summer evenings sitting out there, sometimes having a late supper. One evening after I had known them for more than a year, they invited me to join them. It was then that they told me, for the first time, their uncommon story—how they met, married, and have managed in Kufr Qara. Aziz, as was his way, took the lead; Irena, as was her way, jumped in freely with additions and subtractions.

"I met Irena through a friend at Hebrew University," Aziz began. "She was new in the country and studying biology, and I was a second-year medical student. I had seen her around the campus and she immediately caught my eye. I was trying to figure a way to meet her, when one day there she was with a friend of mine. He was helping her with Hebrew in some reading or other—"

Irena interrupted, "I didn't know Hebrew well, and had turned to some Jewish classmates for help. But they all found one reason or other not to help me. The only one willing to do so was this Arab fellow. He may have had an interest in me. I don't know—"

"She never found out," Aziz cut in, "because as soon as I saw them together, I came over and introduced myself, and then began to chase after her. My friend didn't seem to mind. And so Irena and I started to go out. For me, it wasn't something new to go out with a non-Muslim. A year or so before, I had been serious about a Christian girl—an Arab girl—from the Galilee. But her parents had forced her to back out. I also had been in a number of relationships with Jewish girls, too, though nothing serious. At the time I met Irena, I was sort of involved with this Muslim girl. Once I got involved with Irena, that relationship busted up."

"Not so easily," added Irena. "Remember the party, the dancing?"

"Oh yes," said Aziz. He winked at Irena. "I had brought Irena to one of our parties at the university. Arab students have their own parties, naturally. While we were at this party, my Muslim girlfriend came over to where we were sitting, and right in front of me she started dancing a little provocatively—"

"A little?" Irena laughed mockingly. "She was sticking it right in your face. In mine, too!"

Aziz chuckled without embarrassment. "What could I do? Anyway, she left after a while, and there wasn't any ugliness. Only later a few friends came over and told me I had been wrong to bring Irena to the party. I was driving this Muslim girl crazy, they said. But they had their own reasons for saying this. Political reasons, if you can believe it. It's a complicated story, but the point is that I was involved at the time with Arab student politics. I was part of the communist-led coalition. There was another group further to our left, the Sons of the Village, and they accused us of being too close to the Jews. Our two groups were in competition. My friends, who were also in politics with me, said that by being involved with Irena I was giving ammunition to this other group. Ridiculous, no? Yet, that's what they thought. I just ignored them and continued to go out with Irena."

I asked Irena, "And what about your friends? How did they react?"

"There were some who opposed my being with Aziz," she answered. "I just stopped having anything to do with them. With other friends, those I met after Aziz and I started going together, they all accepted our relationship—or if not, they kept it to themselves."

"And what about your families?" I asked both of them. "What was their reaction?"

Aziz and Irena grinned at each other, and then Aziz said, "That was a little more complicated. My father found it hard to accept. Even though he is a liberal kind of father—he's a schoolteacher, one of the first in the village—when it came to his own son being serious about a Jewish girl, he was against it. I had brought Irena home a number of times. I saw no reason to hide things. So he could see this wasn't just a passing affair. What he did was pretty wise. One day he just showed up at my dorm room in Jerusalem and said he wanted to walk and go visit some friends. On the way he began talking about my relationship with Irena. He didn't raise his voice or start threatening like a lot of fathers from the village would have done—you know, saying he'd disown me, or that what I was doing was giving him heart pains, killing him. Believe me, other fathers have reacted like that. I wasn't the first in the village that was serious about a non-Muslim girl. My father seemed to understand that there was no point in threatening me. What he did was bring me to the house of a friend in Wadi Joz, near the university. This friend had a couple of daughters of marriageable age, and they were sitting there in the salon, all dressed up, when I arrived—"

"The meat was hung out for display," quipped Irena, "though not for immediate tasting!"

Aziz smiled sheepishly. "Really, they were nice girls. Beautiful and smart. Very fine. In fact, sometimes if I'm in a bad mood and get fed up with problems that Irena and I are having in the village, I yell at her that I should have taken one of those Wadi Joz girls—"

"And lived happily ever after, right?"

"But I wasn't buying," resumed Aziz, sidestepping Irena's jab. "I even got annoyed at my father. I told him the girls weren't for me and to stop pressuring me. And you know, he did. I knew he wasn't happy about what I was doing, but he—and my mother too—said nothing more about it."

Irena rose, saying, "My turn next, right? First some coffee, okay?" She went inside the house, and Aziz began telling me about his garden, which he was still shaping in his mind. He wanted to add some fruit trees, papaya and banana, and build a wall around the entire yard. The neighbors opposed this wall, he said, feeling it to be antisocial on his part. But he was determined to go ahead with it because he felt he needed more privacy.

"A real good Arab housewife, aren't I?" teased Irena, as

she returned with the coffee. "Proud of me, aren't you Aziz?" She turned to me and added, "Sometimes Aziz and I have battles about these things. I don't treat him like an Arab wife would. Don't fix all the buttons on his shirt and all that." Aziz shrugged and held his hands over his head as if protecting himself from the bombardment. Irena, laughing, continued, "Well, we were about to get into my family's reaction, right? Actually, it wasn't much different from Aziz's family's. They didn't like the idea of our being together, but what could they do? Except for my brother in Haifa, the rest live outside of Israel. My parents are in Argentina, along with my sister. I have another brother in New York. When they all got word of what was going on, they tried to convince me to take a vacation and go live for a while in New York. I liked the idea of a vacation, but I wasn't about to leave Aziz. So I refused. And my family accepted my refusal. What else could they do?"

Irena sipped her coffee and then began talking about her family and the circumstances that brought her to Israel. In Argentina, she said, she had gone to Jewish schools and Jewish summer camps in keeping with her parents' wishes. Most of her friends had been Jewish. Her decision to come to Israel, however, had been "a turn of fate that had nothing to do with Zionism." She came, quite simply, because in Argentina she feared for her life. The Argentinian *junta* had arrested a number of her Jewish friends, people who were active in politics; they were never seen again. She too— perhaps because her name was in someone's address book— was arrested, threatened with death, and then suddenly released after a few days. That had been enough to convince her to leave. She had one brother in America and another in Israel. She preferred to try Israel, which was easier to enter and which she knew more about. "My parents didn't oppose my leaving," she said. "They were worried about what might happen if I stayed in Argentina."

"The irony, of course," she continued, "is that I fled a situation where I was oppressed partly because I was a Jew, and then I came here and experienced discrimination *from* the Jews because Aziz is an Arab. Strange, no?" She poured more coffee for all of us, and said to Aziz, "Tell him about

what happened in Jerusalem when we moved in together—
in that religious woman's apartment."
   Aziz sighed, but in a bemused way. "Oh, yes. This was
after my father had visited me, and after Irena and I decided
to move out of the university dorms. We wanted a place of
our own. But unfortunately, for an Arab it is not easy to find
a place in Jerusalem. In Arab Jerusalem, they don't like to
rent to unmarried people, and in Jewish Jerusalem they
don't like to rent to Arabs at all. But anyway, we finally
found a place. Both Irena and I signed the contract. The
owner was a religious Jewish woman, actually a returnee to
religion. You could see by the books she had left in the
bookcases that she was once a secular person. So what happened? A few days after the contract was signed she came
and said we'd have to leave. Why? Because she had second
thoughts about our being an unmarried couple—and yes, a
Jew and an Arab together. She had gone to her rabbi—all
these returnees to religion have their own rabbis—and he
told her to make us leave immediately. I wasn't about to
take that crap, though. I told her I would like to speak to
the rabbi. And you know what? She brought him. And the
rabbi and I had a long talk, just me and him alone in a half-
darkened room one evening. I answered his questions, but I
didn't let him turn it into an inquisition. I asked questions
too. We had a real dialogue. I told him that I believed in
God, in a higher power, and that I respected the Jewish
religion's prophets, Moses and Abraham, for they are prophets in the Muslim religion, too. What was most important
to me, I said, was not formal religion or ritual, but the belief
in the value of man which both our religions support. We
talked about these things at great length and there was a
good feeling between us. In the end he rose, shook my hand,
and made a statement that I am more Jewish in soul than
a lot of Jews and that he would tell the woman to let us
stay. Frankly, I was amazed that it turned out that way, but
very glad. And so we stayed.
   "Even though that turned out all right," Aziz continued,
"I knew that if Irena and I were to get married there was no
future for us in Jerusalem or any other city. Our children
would never be accepted, nor would we. The only life I could

see us living together was either outside Israel or in Kufr Qara. And I didn't want to leave. I wanted to live in the village, which I love and where I am loved, and I told her that I thought we could make it here."

"I wasn't convinced," said Irena. "Not at first. By then I knew the village pretty well. I wanted no part of being a village woman. Who would I talk to? At that time hardly any women here had gone to university. It's only in the last ten years that they've started going in large numbers. What was I going to talk to them about—potatoes and diapers? I was really hesitant. I didn't want to lose Aziz, but I sure wasn't crazy about coming here. That's the truth."

"We had a real crisis then," continued Aziz. "We almost split up. And then what happened is that Irena got pregnant. We didn't know what to do. We were both just finishing our studies. We had no house or money. We thought it over and then decided, when Irena was in her fourth month, to have an abortion. It was very hard. Irena and I were both sad. She suffered terribly during this period. When the abortion was over, my father—who knew everything—came to me and said, 'Your Irena is a girl of gold. You can't do better than her.' He had been impressed by how she handled herself and didn't make a problem for the family, and did it all with a quiet dignity. This convinced him. He let us know that he had accepted the idea that I would marry her. For Irena and I, too, the abortion brought us together, rather than pull us apart like it might have done. We realized that we wanted to have children as soon as possible and that we wanted to get married. We began talking about the details. And this was not easy, because the more we thought about it, the more we realized that to raise children here in Israel and in Kufr Qara, they would have to be Muslim—which meant Irena would have to convert. Otherwise the children would be strangers here, born of a Jewish mother and therefore Jewish by the law of the state. If we had a daughter, she couldn't marry in the village. And if we had a son, he conceivably could be drafted into the army. So . . ."

"So," repeated Irena, picking up the sentence, "it was up to me. The whole idea, frankly, was repugnant to me. I am not a believer. Not in Islam, not in Judaism. To convert meant to do something foreign to my nature. But I realized that logically it was the wisest thing to do, and so I decided to go ahead with it. A real joke it turned out to be!"

Irena and Aziz then began to recount the bureaucratic pilgrimage that led to her conversion. They had not known where to turn for such a conversion, so Aziz decided to start at the top: the *qadi* (religious head) at Jerusalem's al-Aqsa mosque. The *qadi* threw up his hands, saying, 'This is not for me,' and sent them off to another *qadi*. And so it went, until three *qadis* later they finally found one in Taibeh who would perform the conversion—*if* he received permission from the Israeli Ministry of the Interior. This permission was also not easy to get, Aziz and Irena explained, because the Jewish authorities tried to discourage conversions from Judaism. But, after long arguments with the appropriate authorities (and with some help from an official who was a friend of Aziz's family), they got permission for the conversion. And thus they returned to the Taibeh *qadi*.

"He brought us into his study," said Irena, "and he asked me to say the *la ilaha illa Allah* thing. I had already told him that the reason I wanted to be a Muslim was so I could marry Aziz. That was good enough for him, apparently. I said the words—that sentence which to this day I don't exactly remember—and I became a Muslim. Or at least enough of a Muslim so we could get married."

"In the end we never had a real wedding party though," said Aziz. "And to this day I regret it."

"Not me," said Irena boldly, and then she added teasingly, "Though I never got to wear my white dress and all the gold jewelry."

"Actually, we had a big party scheduled," said Aziz. "We sent out the invitations, and an orchestra was coming, and Irena *did* buy a white dress—the whole thing. But at the last moment an aunt of mine died. We would have had to wait forty days to reschedule it, and already we had our plans to honeymoon in Argentina and visit Irena's parents. We didn't want to cancel or postpone that, too. My family, really, was just as glad we didn't have the party. Not just because of Irena's background, but because it was well known that we had been living together, and people were saying, 'Why the wedding party, since they are already living like man and wife?' Yet for me it was a real letdown. I wanted to have a wedding party, you see, just like everyone else."

"At least we had a honeymoon like everyone else," said Irena. "It was wonderful. My parents really liked Aziz and we had a great two months there. It was such a relief to be in a place where we were just newlyweds, not an Arab and a Jew. We even thought of staying. The political situation in Argentina was no longer dangerous for me. Yet we both realized that sooner or later the honeymoon would be over, so to speak. And Aziz felt that Kufr Qara was where he could make a living best, and where we could live. So we came back and . . ." Irena smirked at Aziz, ". . . we've been living happily ever after, haven't we?"

Irena rushed inside the house, where one of the children had begun crying. Aziz and I continued to sit silently, gazing out at the balmy moonless night and at the houses and fields below. Aziz seemed calm, as if the recollection of his life with Irena had soothed him. He got up, strolled over to a bed of roses, bent down to smell one, and then came back. "Things have worked out better for us than I expected," he said, almost to himself. "Irena's adjusted better than I thought she would. And the kids are doing fine, too. They're still too young for school, but with their cousins they blend in just like any other kids. They speak Arabic, of course. And they understand Hebrew because, as you can see, Irena and I still speak Hebrew together. They even follow Spanish, because Irena speaks with them in Spanish."

"Not in Arabic?" I asked.

"Not much," Aziz answered. "She's been a little slow picking up Arabic. Hasn't made much of an effort really—"

"There you go, badmouthing me again," said Irena as she approached from the house. And turning to me, she went on, "I can speak a little, but I feel like an idiot mumbling in Arabic with people who can speak Hebrew. I understand everything, though." She ran her pale hand through her blondish hair. "But really, the problem as I see it—Aziz and I don't see eye to eye on this—is not *what* I speak, but to *whom* I speak. I mean, *who* is there for me to talk to here? Really talk to, I mean."

"You look down your nose at the women here," said Aziz. "Admit it, you don't see them as your equal."

"Not true!" Irena, for the first time that evening, seemed unsettled. "They're my equal, whatever that means. We're different, that's all. They are girls from the village. I grew up in a big city. I'm used to talking with women about other things—ideas, politics, books. Who can I talk to about that here? Only the men. Some men. And it's not easy—you know that, Aziz—for me to sit and talk with men. Not in the village." And to me Irena added, "I've gotten used to playing the role of the Arab housewife. In Argentina my family had servants. Now I'm the . . . the one who does the serving. Coffee, drinks, fruit—every time a guest comes. I've gotten used to it. I manage. Maybe not like Aziz expects, but all right."

"You're fine. No complaints." Aziz was attempting to calm her.

"But what is hard here," continued Irena, "is the lack of friends. And we never get out of the village. Or hardly ever."

"Irena's right about this," acknowledged Aziz. "I haven't been so good about that. We need to get out more. Like when we were students in Jerusalem. I keep telling her that as soon as my practice is a little more secure we'll start going to the city more. Tel Aviv, Jerusalem. And we'll visit friends."

"The way it is now," said Irena, "I've just about lost contact with my old friends. Hardly anyone visits. Only my brother and his family once in a while . . ." She paused, and there was a long silence as she and Aziz looked off into the night in opposite directions.

"But I will say this," she finally said, "Aziz's family has been wonderful to me. I'm comfortable with his brothers and sisters, and his parents too. And the kids, bless them, they are managing just fine. They fit in. No problems. It's only me that's a problem, I guess."

"Oh, come on, you've done great," Aziz said reassuringly. "Really you have." He rose and began taking the dishes into the house as Irena and I followed him.

"Sometimes, just sometimes," Irena said to me, "I get down about the friends business. But Aziz is right. We've managed better than I would have thought." She slapped at a mosquito that landed on her cheek. "I've made my peace with the idea of living here. Most of the time I like it. And most of the time I feel quite all right thinking this is the place I'm going to live in the rest of my life." She looked heavenward, and in a slightly sarcastic tone added, "*Fi idayn Allah*—it's in the hands of God. That's what they say—*Fi idayn Allah.*"

18

AN ILLNESS

FOR A MAN WHO HAD BEEN HEALTHY all his life (apart from the gunshot wound suffered when he was nineteen years old), the past year had been an annoying exception. A string of illnesses suddenly beset Abu Ahmad. First was a nasty flu which came on just days before Hassan's wedding; then, only a month later, a strange blood infection in his right leg, just above the old gunshot wound, brought on a week or so of high fever; and when that passed and the winter rains came, Abu Ahmad again found himself struggling with the flu and the reappearance of the blood infection, this time in his kidneys.

While all this caused him a good deal of discomfort, Abu Ahmad gave no outward impression of being worried. It would have been beneath his dignity to do so: a sign of weakness and beyond that—or what amounted to the same thing—a certain lack of faith in God's intentions. Like almost everyone else in Kufr Qara of his age, he believed that God had written each person's fate, and that it was incumbent upon the individual to accept this fate as part of the divine plan. To fret and worry was, ultimately, to second-guess God.

For this reason also, Abu Ahmad had little trust in doctors. Or, to put it more exactly, he had a *limited* trust in them. Who could deny that Kufr Qara today, with its twenty or so physicians, was indeed a healthier place to live in? In his youth, children often died before they were old enough to talk. Malaria, diphtheria, and a number of nameless infections claimed them. And perhaps if the right medications had been available back then, his oldest brother, who had been cut down so suddenly by a blood infection as a young man, well, perhaps he might still be alive today. But then again—Abu Ahmad reasoned—maybe something else would have befallen him. Everything was in the hands of Allah, and doctors with all their medications were powerless before the will of Allah. *Allahu akbar*, God is greater. God alone knew what lay ahead for any man.

It was with this understanding and sense of resignation that Abu Ahmad faced his most recent illness, the one that had come upon him as all of Kufr Qara baked in an early summer *hamsin*. This illness had begun one warm night as he lay on his floor mattress attempting to sleep. His smoker's cough had bothered him throughout the day, and as usual he attempted to stifle it by smoking one Marlboro after another. That night he found himself short of breath. By the time dawn came he was gasping for air. Frightened by the eerie bluish cast of his face, Umm Ahmad rushed for the telephone (she herself did not feel comfortable using it), and Abu Ahmad managed to call the doctor, who also happened to be his nephew. Mussa was there in minutes. He knew his uncle well, and he knew that if Abu Ahmad was calling this early in the morning, something must be deathly wrong. And it was. Abu Ahmad was close to passing out.

They rushed him to the hospital in Hadera, and in the emergency room he was immediately hooked up to an oxygen tank. They made it just in time, apparently. Mussa, who days later was still shaken by the episode, claimed, "Another few minutes or so, and he was gone. Asphyxiated. No oxygen tank, and it would have been all over. Modern medicine, thank God for it!"

For the next week, Abu Ahmad remained hooked up to the oxygen tank, and with each day he showed a gradual improvement. He was placed in a semi-private room on the internal medicine ward (Ahmad's ties to one of the ward's doctors helped there), and the family took turns staying with him day and night. Hospital regulations allowed for this, not least of all because the place was understaffed and it was recognized that families could provide better care than the nursing staff itself. Umm Ahmad, for example, did all the cooking for her husband. He detested the "cardboard taste" of the hospital food, and so each morning when she came to spend the day with Abu Ahmad she brought him the delicacies he liked best: wheat and bean soup, stuffed vegetables, lamb and potatoes, as well as thermoses of that thick cardamom-laced coffee which Abu Ahmad required not only for himself but also for the purpose of receiving his many daily visitors. At night, too, he was never left alone. One of his three sons slept by his side on an aluminum lounge chair, checking periodically that the oxygen tank and hookup were working properly and that Abu Ahmad was resting comfortably.

By the end of that first week, he was able to breathe without the oxygen tank, and a chest X-ray revealed that his lungs, though damaged from all those years of smoking, were nonetheless working reasonably well. The doctors even went so far as to reassure him that if he would stop smoking, his lungs might not cause him any further trouble. But there was another problem—one that nobody expected. The doctors had discovered upon examining Abu Ahmad that his prostate gland was suspiciously enlarged, and when they biopsied the growth it was found to be cancerous. This they did not tell him. Instead, they told his oldest son, Ahmad, and left it for him to decide how to handle it. In the meantime, the doctors were planning to X-ray further to see if, and how far, the cancer had spread; it was *not* in his lungs. In another few days they would make their recommendations.

I was aware of all this because, as it so happened, I went with Ahmad to visit his father on the day he received the news from the doctors. Ahmad had not yet had a chance to speak to his brothers, and he seemed shaken by the burden of it all. As we drove to the hospital, he mused openly about what had to be done:

"Do we tell him he has cancer? Maybe there's nothing to be done at all. Maybe it's spread all over and he's finished.

And if it's just in the prostate, they can operate but he's finished as a man. His manhood is gone. Will he let them do it? Maybe if he knows what the operation will do to him, he'll refuse. And then he's finished for sure, the cancer will spread all over . . ." He fumbled for a cigarette, his hand shaking noticeably. "I just don't know. Ghanem and Hassan will have to decide this with me. It's not up to me alone. In a few days, we'll have to figure it out. I just don't know."

We pulled into the hospital parking lot and Ahmad chatted breezily with the attendant, as if rehearsing a new mood, a more upbeat one, which in a few minutes he would present to his father. He adjusted his shirt and tie—as always, he was elegantly dressed—and we headed for the internal medicine ward. When we arrived Abu Ahmad was sitting up in bed listening to the news in Hebrew on the radio. It was the first I had seen him since the illness began, and I was struck by how calm and rested he looked—better than he had in months. On the other hand, Umm Ahmad, who was sitting next to him along with two of her neighbors, appeared worn and tense. Perhaps, I thought, she had surmised the doctors' true evaluation of her husband's illness, even without understanding their words? She voiced none of this, of course, but instead amiably set about serving Ahmad and me coffee and some homemade cake. She evidently had been busy in this way all afternoon. Dozens of visitors had come by, including several neighbors who were about to go on the *hajj* to Mecca. Most surprising, however, had been the visit by Ibrahim; it was the first time he had consented to see Abu Ahmad in almost a year. (Later Abu Ahmad would say, "My brother's a fool. Imagine carrying on like that for so long. Just ridiculous!")

With her oldest son having arrived for night duty, as it were, Umm Ahmad felt free to return home with the neighbors. She and Abu Ahmad took a short stroll through the crowded corridor—about twenty patients were in beds out there—and then Abu Ahmad returned alone. He plunked himself back in bed and began thumbing through the Hebrew newspaper at his side, while at the same time turning to Ahmad and me and saying, "Looks bad, doesn't it? Shamir is going to form a new government for sure. The Labor party is out."

Ahmad answered coolly, "What difference does it make? You think Peres and the Labor party would have been able to make peace?"

"They had a chance," Abu Ahmad said matter-of-factly.

"No way!" Ahmad took out a pack of cigarettes and moved to light one, but then, remembering that his father was unable to smoke, he snuffed out the match. "The Labor party will never allow a Palestinian state, so how could they make peace?"

"You never know, right?" Abu Ahmad turned to me, as if he knew I agreed with him. "Once you begin negotiations, once you agree in principle to give back land for peace, then—maybe five years, maybe ten years later—you arrive at a solution that works. Some kind of state."

"No way," repeated Ahmad emphatically. "The Jews will never allow it. They know very well that a Palestinian state next to them will be the first nail in their coffin."

"Nonsense!" Abu Ahmad threw his hands up in the air. "Nails? Coffins? How do you know? Nothing is so clear."

"To me it's clear. And to the Jews it's clear. So forget about a negotiated settlement. It's not going to happen, not now—" Ahmad paused as he noticed a white-robed physician walking in the corridor. "And not ever. No solutions. It's finished." He got up and went after the doctor, who apparently was one of those involved in his father's treatment. Abu Ahmad shrugged and shook his head slowly, as if to suggest that there was no point in arguing with his son; they would never see eye to eye on this, and for that matter not on much else either. "My son, he has no faith," he finally said. "How can you live without faith, without hope?"

Abu Ahmad fell silent for a while. I decided to make no comment about his illness, and indeed I felt strange to have knowledge about it that he did not have. We talked briefly about other things—the farm, the price of tomatoes—and then he mentioned that he was hoping to get out of the hospital in time to see off his friends who were going on the *hajj*. Really, he wished he were going with them, that he had the strength to make the pilgrimage to Mecca. How he longed to do it once again! Who knows, maybe he would. *Fi idayn Allah*, everything was in the hands of God.

He then began talking about his pilgrimage to Mecca in 1980. I had not heard about it before, though I was aware that he had been there since quite often he was addressed by others as *Hajj* (and Umm Ahmad as *Hajja*), the honorific title given to those who have made the pilgrimage.

"I was sixty-two years old when I finally got to make the *hajj*," he said while slowly fondling his blue worry beads. He seldom used these beads at home, but had brought them to the hospital with him. "Actually, I had wanted to go for many years. Yet it wasn't until 1978 that the Israeli government allowed Arabs from here to go to Saudi Arabia by way of Jordan. I got on the list as soon as I could along with my wife and about a hundred and twenty others from Kufr Qara. The *hajj* fell in October that year, a good time. When it falls in the summer months, like this year, the pilgrims have to endure the forty-five-degree temperature [110 degrees Fahrenheit] of the Saudi Arabian desert. We had none of that. So in a way, our trip was easy.

"We went in buses all the way from Kufr Qara to Mecca, and that too was fairly easy. In my grandfather's and father's time, the few that went used to travel by donkey or camel. *That* was difficult. They couldn't be sure of getting there in one piece and with their money still on them. Bedouins would sometimes attack and rob them along the way. But today it's safe and organized. Modern, more or less. An Israeli bus takes you to the Jordanian border, and at the Allenby Bridge you switch to the Jordanian buses. Our bus served both as a means of transportation and as our hotel. We slept in it most of the time during those three weeks. And since we had brought most of our food with us, we managed fine. No problems. Besides, in Saudi Arabia there are many vendors selling food—cucumbers, tomatoes, grapes, watermelons, meat, anything you want. It's all there if you can afford it."

Abu Ahmad, who was now running his fingers rapidly over the worry beads, glanced at his oldest son as he reentered the room. Ahmad caught the gist of the conversation and grinned a bit condescendingly, but said nothing; it was one thing to challenge his father on politics—that might be overlooked—but to poke fun at religion was not something Abu Ahmad would tolerate. So, politely making some excuse, Ahmad again left the room.

At that point Abu Ahmad went on to describe in detail some of the standard rituals associated with the *hajj:* the opening cry of the pilgrim as he approaches Mecca, *"Labbaika"* ("here am I, Lord, here am I"); the seven circumambulations of the cube-shaped *Ka'ba* and the kissing of the holy stone; the running back and forth seven times through one of Mecca's streets—a total distance of some two miles—which symbolizes Hagar's frantic search for water for her son, Ishmael; then several days later, the "standing" from noon to dusk at the plain of Arafat, fourteen miles from Mecca, recalling Abraham's standing up to idolatry; followed by the journey back to Mina, nine miles away, for the stoning of the devil (pilgrims each cast seven stones at a low pillar in the main square), just as Abraham cast out Satan; and finally, on the tenth and last day of the *hajj* proper, the sacrifice of animals at Mina in remembrance of Abraham's willingness to sacrifice (according to the Koran) his son Ishmael.

"Throughout this period," Abu Ahmad explained, "the pilgrims must be dressed in a special way. Unsewn garments, all white, with one shoulder exposed—for the men only—and a special type of sandal that leaves the instep bare. Women wear head shawls, of course, but men must go bareheaded. This is the same for everyone, and throughout those ten days you do not change your clothes. All these details must be followed exactly if you want your pilgrimage to be acceptable to God. No exceptions. I can tell you it's a spectacular thing to see, hundreds of thousands of people of different shapes and colors, and from every place in the world, yet all dressed the same, all saying the same prayers, and all worshipping the same God.

"I cannot describe really how it all feels. It's the fulfillment of something very deep in a person. All my life I had read and recited passages about these places. To see them with my own eyes was for me—well, a feeling of being very close to God. In Ramadan one is very close, too, but it's a closeness that is filled with suffering because of the fast. On the *hajj* there is not this suffering, and there is also a feeling of being with so many others in this one place, for one purpose. It is not really possible to describe.

"*Inshallah*, God willing, I will have the chance to go once more. Not for myself, for my mother. She died in 1973, before it was possible to go through Jordan. Always she wanted to go. How I would like to do it for her, to dedicate the *hajj* in her name . . ." He glanced around the room and sighed deeply, as if weighing his current fate. "But what can you do? I must wait and see how all of this turns out. Maybe I'll have the strength and maybe not. Only God knows. The doctors will tell me in a few days where things stand. Maybe I have to have some kind of operation. I'm not sure. We'll see. Maybe it'll be nothing. God alone knows. *Fi idayn Allah, fi idayn Allah.*"

The results of the tests were good. So far, the cancer had not spread, at least not according to the X-rays. The doctors recommended that Abu Ahmad have an operation to remove the malignant tissue, reiterating—again, only to Ahmad— that such an operation would render Abu Ahmad impotent. Without the operation, they said, the cancer was certain to spread elsewhere in his body.

Having heard the initial assessment some days earlier, the three brothers had already arrived at a decision. Actually, there had been some disagreement between them at first. Ahmad had argued that it would be foolish to tell their father that he had cancer and also that the operation would render him impotent; he then might refuse to go through with it. Not so, countered Ghanem. Perhaps they should delay telling him about the cancer, but they absolutely must tell him about the effects of the operation; he, Ghanem, felt confident that their father would do what had to be done. Hassan concurred with Ghanem, and so that was how they handled it. In addition, all three agreed not to tell Umm Ahmad or their sisters about any of this. (In the end they did tell Maysa—*after* they had made the decision—because, as Ghanem put it, "She knows how to keep things to herself, like a man.")

When the brothers went to tell Abu Ahmad, they were somewhat surprised to find how calmly he accepted the recommendation. "If this must be done," he said stoically, "then so shall it be." To their relief, he did not probe further about the whys and wherefores of the operation: he did not ask whether he had cancer. Perhaps he knew but chose to keep this awareness to himself. In any event, he said nothing more; not then, not three days later when the operation was over, and not two weeks later when he was finally released from the hospital.

At home again, Abu Ahmad resumed his place in the *diwan*, slimmer and paler from the ordeal, but back at the center of things, with friends and family stopping by regularly to visit him. He did not talk further about his illness, about the pain he must be experiencing during the recovery period, or about what he thought lay ahead. The only hint he gave at all of what he might be thinking (at least the only hint that I heard in those first weeks) was on one occasion, as he lay there in the *diwan* with a couple of his chain-smoking cronies, he let fall from his lips the comment, "It's hard to go on day after day without a cigarette, without a Marlboro," adding with a sad smile, "A man my age should not have to go without such pleasures. Life is too short for that, much too short. Don't you think so?"

19

A Time to Sow, A Time to Reap

EVERY NEWLY MARRIED COUPLE in the village knew that the next thing expected of them, once the wedding was over, was to bring forth a child—and the sooner the better. A marriage that did not bear fruit or show signs of bearing fruit within the first year was a marriage regarded with suspicion. Village gossips began to talk. Perhaps the couple did not have God's blessing? Perhaps there was a curse upon the marriage?

Well aware of these suspicions and expectations, Hassan and Zaynab were relieved when she became pregnant five months after the wedding. They told almost nobody, however, lest their pride and happiness arouse the envy of others, and with it the evil eye. Instead, on the cold wintry nights they warmed themselves in the private knowledge that their marriage had been blessed. *Inshallah*, God willing, by summer's end they would be parents of their first child.

But alas, it was not to be. As the winter rains slackened and the first flowers of spring shot up across the hills, Zaynab knew that something was wrong with the new life she was carrying. The blood stains on the sheet, the sharp cramps in her belly, made her tremble with foreboding. When she finally told Hassan, he attempted to humor her, to reassure her. Yet just to be sure, they decided to go to the hospital in Hadera. With Umm Ahmad accompanying them, they headed straight to the emergency room. And there they heard: according to the stoney pronouncement of the physician who read the sonogram, their baby was dead, in fact had been dead for two or three weeks.

After her two-day recuperation in the hospital, Zaynab returned home numb and despondent. The house that she had spent so much time cleaning and decorating the past few weeks—with new paintings on the walls, ceramic ware on the tables, and a flower-print rug in the salon—suddenly seemed bare and empty.

"What am I going to do now without my baby?" she wept aloud one morning to Umm Ahmad. Umm Ahmad, who had miscarried three times herself, wept with her. But she told Zaynab tenderly, "You are so young, my daughter. You are just beginning and there will be more, many more. If you wish, I will help you. Everything will be just as you want, I promise."

Umm Ahmad's words were comforting to Zaynab, but they did not dispel the doubts that flooded her whenever she was alone. Actually, these doubts were nothing new; they had been with her before the pregnancy, and for that matter, even before she married. She feared there was a genetic problem that would prevent her from bearing children. Prior to their marriage she had discussed it with Hassan. In her clan—as the whole village knew—there was a congenital blood disorder that affected a number of the children, causing them to die at an early age. Hassan had been concerned about it, and the two of them had visited a physician who specialized in genetic diseases. He had reassured them, after testing their blood, that they personally had nothing to worry about; Zaynab would be able to conceive normally and none of their children would be affected. Zaynab had believed the doctor. But now that she had miscarried, these fears came back to her.

Zaynab chose, however, to keep this self-doubt to herself and not disturb Hassan, who at the time was coping with his own private worries—worries that had nothing to do with her or the miscarriage. Only days after Zaynab returned from the hospital, Hassan had received notice from his lawyer that in two weeks time he was to appear in court. He was finally going on trial for the accident in which he had run over the youth near the school. He was being charged with negligent homicide, a crime that carried a maximum penalty of three years imprisonment.

In the past year he had managed to put the accident out of his mind—particularly since he had married Zaynab. But now, suddenly, here he was going to court and everything was on the line. "What if I get a nasty judge?" he asked Ahmad, who accompanied him to court that gray morning in March.

"Don't worry, we've got a good lawyer," Ahmad said to him soothingly. "The prosecutor will accept the plea bargain and you'll get off lightly."

"And the judge?"

"He'll go along, you'll see. Trust me. I know how these things work."

And sure enough, Ahmad was right. In less than an hour, Hassan was whisked through the conveyor belt of justice and came out with a verdict that was the best he could expect: revocation of his driver's license for three years and a fifteen hundred shekel fine. Hassan was overjoyed. He rushed home, embraced Zaynab, and for the first time in weeks they laughed again. It was only later that evening, after the party in which they had celebrated the outcome, that it finally hit him that what had happened in court might not have been pure chance, but rather the result of a divine reckoning. Yes, he had been lucky to get off so easily. But could it be that the real penalty had been assessed earlier by a higher judge? For the life of the boy, he had paid with a life—that of his first child. And as that thought coursed through him he turned to gaze at Zaynab's gentle face asleep on his shoulder, and he found himself overcome by a river of remorse.

The spring is a time of choice and chance for the farmer. It is then that he decides what seeds and seedlings to sow, gambling with fate on the price of vegetables in the summer market. The previous year Hassan had played it safe with tomatoes and peppers and eggplants—the old standbys. He had made only a small profit. So this year he decided it was worth sowing something different. He had just hit it lucky with the carrots and the winter cabbage, and so perhaps if he went with some winter vegetables he might catch a price. After talking it over with Ghanem, who, surprisingly, told him to take the risk, he decided to plant cabbage and cauliflower. He knew he would be busy spraying against bacteria and funghi every other day, and even so he could not be sure. Yet if the gamble worked, by July he might reap a profit of five thousand shekels—enough for him and Zaynab to go on that long-awaited honeymoon.

That April morning as Hassan and I sat at the edge of the fields, having just finished planting the last of the cauliflower seedlings, Samir came by in a rush to talk to Hassan. He took one look out at the fields, and then with a smirk on his face said to Hassan, "I guess you're feeling lucky these days, aren't you?" Hassan shrugged, and Samir immediately went on, "Not me, I'm playing it safe. Squash and some tomatoes. Can't take any chances this year. Not with my engagement party coming up."

Samir sat down and began talking with Hassan about the party, asking a few questions about an orchestra and video crew. It seemed that despite his former opposition to throwing parties with the *intifada* going on, he was now planning a huge affair. It also seemed that he was quite nervous, and not his usual boisterous self.

"Tell me, Samir," Hassan interrupted at one point, "You been drinking again? You look like you had one too many last night."

Samir chortled. "You can tell? I had *ten* too many— beers. Me and Mustafa last night." He massaged his furrowed forehead. "I've got problems, brother. Problems you wouldn't believe. I don't know what I've done to deserve this."

"Speak up, my friend," Hassan encouraged him.

"Well, it sounds crazy, I know. But last night while I was sleeping, I suddenly woke up struggling for breath. It's weird, but there was this guy sitting right there on my chest." Samir stared at Hassan, his dark eyes frightened. "He was huge, powerful, with a big head, and dark as a Negro. He didn't say a word. Just sat there crushing the air right out of me."

"Wait a minute," Hassan said slowly and skeptically. "You saw him there or you were just dreaming?"

Samir sighed deeply. "I saw him and I felt him, so help me God."

"You were just dreaming, my friend. Too many beers, and you were dreaming crazy—" Hassan stopped short as Zaynab yelled to him from the house that there was a telephone call. "Stay put, I'll be back in a minute with some coffee," he shouted as he ran off.

Samir and I sat quietly for a while and then he pulled a newspaper from his back pocket. He searched through it and pointed to an item. "You catch this? On Iraq's leader, Saddam Hussein. He says he's got the chemical weapons now to scorch half of Israel if he wants."

"And you think he's going to do it?" I said.

"He used them in Iran, right? So he's not afraid to do it. Personally, I think there's going to be a war here. Soon. Israel's going to reap what it deserves. Nobody else may think so, but I tell you in another year or so—" He paused and looked at Hassan, who was approaching with a tray in his hand. "The party here is going to be over—a real catastrophe is coming, if you ask me."

"What party over? What catastrophe?" asked Hassan, laughing. "You're only getting engaged. Stop worrying about it."

"I'm not talking about my engagement party, idiot," Samir sneered. "I'm talking about Iraq and Saddam Hussein." He thrust the newspaper at Hassan. "There's going to be a war here, I'm telling you. In another year, maybe less. Chemical weapons, everything."

Hassan tossed the paper back. "You *are* nuts," he said, patting Samir gently on the back. "That black guy who was sitting on your chest is now sitting on your head."

"You don't believe me, do you? He was really there last night."

"Here, drink some coffee. It's good for the brain. In

another couple of months, after the engagement party, you'll be normal again."

Samir shook his head peevishly, as if misunderstood. "I'm telling you, he was really there."

"*Sure* he was," said Hassan mockingly. "And Saddam Hussein is going to attack this year. *Sure* he is. Drink the coffee Samir, and you'll feel better and stop all this dreaming."

Zaynab liked sleeping late in the mornings. It was a habit from her old life which she had transplanted into her new one, and which Hassan was still trying to weed out. He wanted her to rise early with him, be with him in the mornings, and then make his breakfast of toast, eggs, and minted tea. Yet despite his importunings and insults ("You're the laziest two-legged creature I've ever seen," he once told her), she continued to rise late, and only then to go out to greet him with some mid-morning coffee.

One morning late that spring, however, she did wake up early, even before Hassan. She seemed to have had a bad dream, though she couldn't remember it. Lying in bed, she listened to the cackle of the neighbor's hen, and old man Abdullah's horse-drawn cart clomping toward the village center. These sounds, penetrating the stillness, disturbed her. She rose unsteadily from bed, and as she did so she could feel that once again it had happened. In the middle of the night, just as she feared, she had begun to menstruate; once again, for the third time since her miscarriage she had failed to conceive.

She put on her slippers (actually Hassan's slippers, which she liked wearing) and headed to the bathroom, and then downstairs to make herself some tea. She was weeping softly and bitter thoughts flitted across her mind. Why was it that she, who had the best marriage of all her friends, could not conceive? Everyone she knew—Zahra and Rafiq's wife, and even her own sister—was either pregnant or had just given birth. Why not her? She felt sure that some of the women she knew had already begun talking about it. She could just tell from the way they looked at her and the way they asked those pointed questions about her health. It made her so angry she wanted to scream or do something outrageous.

While she sat there lost in this bitter brooding, Hassan suddenly appeared in front of her with a broad, clown-like smile on his face. She looked down at his feet, and he was wearing *her* slippers, the pink ones with the puff on the instep. She burst into laughter, and then into tears. He came over and held her tight.

"What's wrong?" he asked, and before she could answer he said, "Your period again?"

She nodded and they sat together silently, as if in mourning. Finally she said, "I want to go see a doctor. I want to know now if something is wrong."

"We'll go, I promise," he answered.

"*Now*, this week," she insisted.

Hassan kissed the top of her head. "Next month, I promise. Once the cauliflower and cabbage are finished. We don't have any money now. And you know as well as I do that it's going to cost a lot of money—particularly if there is something wrong. So let's wait. I promise you, next month." He rose to put on his work pants. "But look, until then let's do something else."

"What else?" she asked, miffed.

"My mother. You know she wants to help. You may not believe in all that Koran-reading stuff—I'm not sure I do either—but let's try. There's no harm in trying, right?"

Later that morning, as she lay in bed unable to do any housework or even make Hassan his mid-morning coffee, Zaynab decided she would ask for Umm Ahmad's help. It was true that she didn't have much faith in such old-fashioned things, but she *was* fond of Umm Ahmad and she knew how much her mother-in-law wanted to help her. Besides, Umm Ahmad had a good reputation as a faith healer who helped women become pregnant. She knew from Hassan that Umm Ahmad had been doing this kind of work for the past ten years; it was something she had learned from one of her neighbors. According to Hassan, she had helped at least half a dozen women to conceive, including two of her own daughters, Nihal and Rana. So why not? If it didn't work, she would go next month to a doctor in Hadera and get the medical help she needed. Meanwhile, as Hassan said, what harm was there in turning to Umm Ahmad?

Two days later, with Zaynab in the middle of her period, Umm Ahmad came by to start the massages. It was shortly after dawn, and Umm Ahmad went up to the bedroom where Zaynab was still asleep. She woke her gently and the two of them talked briefly. Umm Ahmad asked several questions, "almost like a doctor," Zaynab felt. She wanted to know if Zaynab was feeling nervous or angry: For example, if there was a knock at the door, did Zaynab feel startled? Or maybe there had been a fight recently with Hassan or someone else? Zaynab smiled and told Umm Ahmad that, yes, all this was so. "In that case," explained Umm Ahmad, "the massages should help. They will help bring down your uterus. Anger, nerves—they make the uterus shrink upwards. Massage brings it down. Massage, and the will of God. If it is God's will, you will conceive."

So saying, Umm Ahmad removed a small glass of olive oil from her dress. "Olive oil is blessed because it is so written in the Koran," she explained. With strong, sure fingers she began kneading Zaynab's belly from bottom to top while reciting sayings of the prophet Muhammad. The whole procedure lasted not more than five minutes, and when it was over Zaynab felt strangely soothed. She was not sorry when Umm Ahmad told her that in another two or three days, on the last day of her period, the massage treatment would need to be repeated.

And so it was, at the same hour and in the same way. Except the second time Zaynab found herself less skeptical and more relaxed. Indeed, when Umm Ahmad told her at the end, as the two of them sat at the edge of the bed holding hands, that she believed the treatment would work—with God's help—Zaynab felt for the first time in months that maybe it was so; yes, maybe there was nothing wrong with her after all.

It was a hot, hazy morning in late June and Hassan was dancing right there at the edge of the fields. A transistor radio on the ground was playing a number by the Egyptian torch singer, Umm Kulthoum, and Hassan sang and danced along with her as if he were at a wedding. Umm Ahmad laughed, knowing full well why her son was so gay that morning: he was about to catch a great price on these, the first cabbage and cauliflower of the season. Forty crates, twenty of each, were stacked off to the side. According to the Tel Aviv wholesaler to whom he had spoken that morning, they were worth twelve shekels a crate for the cabbage, and eighteen shekels for the cauliflower. And in the next week or two, as the rest of the crop matured, there was a good chance the price would be even higher.

"Guessed right, didn't I?" Hassan said pridefully. "As they say, there's a time to sow and a time to reap. And this year, I got it right. *Il hamdu lillah.*"

"*Il hamdu lillah,*" repeated Umm Ahmad, heading toward Hassan's house. "All praise to God."

Hassan and I moved off to the shade of the fig tree. He picked a handful of the plump green figs that were just coming into season, and we sat there quietly devouring them. "A Garden of Eden, this place could be," he said at one point. "If only I had the money, I could turn these twenty-nine dunams into a paradise. I swear I could." He leaned back on the ground, and with his eyes closed began musing about what he would do if only he had fifty thousand shekels.

He had already started mapping it out in his mind, he said. He would deep-plow the whole area and remove all the remaining rocks. Then in the far fields he would put in fruit trees, peaches or plums or apples—ten dunams in all. And maybe in another area, nearer to his house, he would install those plastic hothouses like some of his neighbors had; in these he could grow cucumbers in the summer and tomatoes in the winter, and thus he'd always be sure of catching a price.

"But all this takes money," he finally said. "And right now I'm still paying off debts. And let's face it, being married has a lot of expenses too. So who knows? Anyway, at least this season I've got myself back on track—" He turned abruptly as he heard footsteps nearby, and looked up to see Zaynab's face beaming above him. She was wearing her white summer dress, the one he liked. She sat down, placing the tray of coffee next to him.

"Guessed right this time," he told her, nodding toward the crates. "Six hundred shekels, and it's just the beginning."

"Really? *Il hamdu lillah.*" Zaynab stroked his shoulder affectionately.

"Maybe we'll take a couple of days vacation in Tel Aviv now, just like we said."

"Yes? You think we can afford it?"

"When all the cabbage and cauliflower are in, sure. We've got our anniversary coming up, no?" He poured a cup of coffee for himself, and this time also for Zaynab. They chatted briefly about what they would do for their anniversary the next week. And then, as if to reassure her, he said, "And, of course, I haven't forgotten my other promise either. About the doctor. I haven't—"

"I have a doctor already," Zaynab interrupted, her voice playful and knowing.

"You already have a *what?*"

"Your mother—Umm Ahmad. She's my doctor now."

Hassan gazed at her, not comprehending at first, and then he burst into a grin. "*An jad?* [Seriously?]"

"I think so."

Hassan leaped to his feet, whirling about. His eyes were turned heavenward, and so he did not see his mother who right then was seated barefoot at the side of his house, a cabbage and a cauliflower in a sack on her lap, her face a lantern of laughter glowing in his and Zaynab's direction. "You're really serious, aren't you?" he repeated, still not quite believing it.

"*An jad,*" she answered. "We'll know for sure in a few days. But yes, I really think so."

20

FEDAYEE— BY CHOICE OR BY CHANCE

ONE SUMMER EVENING as Hassan, Samir, and I were sitting on the wrap-around porch of Hassan's house, a fellow stopped by whom until then I had never met. He did not stay long, half an hour or so, but he was there long enough to leave a distinct impression; a certain sense that he was a person who had been through something, knew something, that others did not know. Even so—that is, despite this aura he seemed to exude—I must say that I was surprised when Samir joked, as this fellow was about to leave, that "Toufiq here is a *fedayee*, a PLO fighter—or was, anyway. Isn't that right, Toufiq?" And Toufiq smiled, but it was the smile of one who was not about to answer, certainly not in front of a stranger.

It was not until the following day, as we were working in the fields, that I had a chance to ask Hassan whether there was any truth in what Samir had said about Toufiq. "One hundred percent true," Hassan answered. "And not just Toufiq. Several of his family are with the PLO. They're well-known throughout the area. Especially his brother, Walid. He's a PLO leader in Saudi Arabia. Everyone knows about him, he's a real hero. Quite a family, really!" And then Hassan added, seemingly with a sense of pride, that in a way he too was related to this family—for a year now. Toufiq, whom he had not known before, was now his brother-in-law. Toufiq's wife was Zaynab's older sister. However, since Toufiq and his family lived in the next village, Ara, he seldom saw him. "A good guy, really," said Hassan. "He's no hero like his brother, but he's someone who means well. . . . You'd like to meet him?"

A week later, on a muggy evening, we sat in the salon of Toufiq's hillside house in Ara. A warm breeze laden with earth-smell wafted through the huge open window that faced out toward the main Wadi Ara road below. The twin village of Ar'ara (the place where Abu Ahmad and his young family had stayed during the war in 1948–49) rose on the hillside just across the road, lit up in the night. Just beyond its summit was the northern border of the West Bank.

Toufiq, who had seemed somewhat guarded when I first met him, was smiling graciously. He was a tall man in his mid-thirties, and had the rugged look of one who made his living with his hands; in fact, he would later mention, he worked as a welder for a Jewish contractor who had no idea of his *fedayee* background. Speaking in a fervent voice, he immediately said that he had been looking forward to my visit ever since Hassan had phoned him. "There are some things I'm sure you haven't heard over in Kufr Qara. And here in Ara is a good place to hear them. We're known as a village that the Jews hate—" He peered at Hassan and me as he stroked his bushy moustache. "And let's face it, we hate them, too!"

Having bluntly prefaced the evening, Toufiq rose to go get some coffee. As he did so, another man, whom Toufiq quickly introduced as his cousin, Adel, entered the salon and sat down. Apparently Adel had been told that we were coming this evening and he wanted to be part of it. Adel's older brother, it turned out, was also a *fedayee*—or rather, he had been one until he was killed in a skirmish on the Lebanese border in 1974. "I'm one of the black sheep of the family," Adel said softly, his light blue eyes radiating a wry humor.

"I've never been a *fedayee*, and for better or worse I'm not intending to be one in the future either."

Returning with the coffee, and having passed out some expensive cigarettes, Toufiq continued where he had left off. The village of Ara, he said, was known as a village of patriots. And his clan in particular had a number of men who had gone off to join the PLO. Some were dead or in jail now, and others were still operating in various Arab countries. "My own opinion," he stated with gruff assurance, "is that most Israeli Arabs would join the PLO if they had a chance. It's just that they can't join easily, that's why there are so few. Israeli Arabs have no strength, no father, and everyone wants to feel strong. The PLO gives us that. In my opinion, if they knew how, eighty or ninety percent of the young people would join—"

Adel, who had been listening quietly to Toufiq's remarks, jumped in suddenly. "Strength, yes, we want strength. But tell me, where do you get those numbers from? Ninety percent? You're off the mark. Kids hear about the PLO and admire it. But join it? No, not even if it were easy. Only a few would join. How many are willing to risk their lives? And let's be honest, Toufiq, how many join for nationalist reasons, and how many just fall into it?"

Adel paused and slurped down his coffee. We all sat there silently, and I found myself looking back and forth between Toufiq and Adel. After Toufiq's opening remarks, I had braced myself for an evening of propaganda. Now, quite frankly, I couldn't believe what I was hearing.

Breaking the silence, Adel finally turned to me and added, "My brother was one who *did* join for patriotic reasons. He knew what he was doing. He went to Russia in 1967, got training as an expert in placing and removing mines, and then went to Lebanon to fight with the PLO. Four years he was there, and then he was killed. If you ask me, what he did was honorable. Personally, I wouldn't do it. I work as a male nurse, and I'm against killing in any form. By anyone. It's not my way. But I respect my brother. He knew what he was doing, took the risks, and paid with his life. Not everyone who joins the PLO is like this." And then, looking back at Toufiq, he said, "Let's be fair about it,

Toufiq. What you did wasn't really the same, was it? You fell into it, didn't you?"

Toufiq, who seemed a little taken aback by his cousin's sharp remarks, nonetheless acknowledged that there was some truth in what Adel was saying. Yes, it was so that he personally had fallen into it. Unlike Adel's brother or his own brother, he hadn't set out to join the *fedayeen*. It had happened more or less by accident, though it was also true that for many years he had been wishing he could join. "My brother, Walid," he said, "went off to join the *fedayeen* in 1964. I was only ten years old at the time. Over the years we heard about what he was doing, and naturally I admired him. We all did—or almost all of us. My oldest brother, who is head of the family, was against it. But for the rest of us, Walid was a hero. We looked up to him and wanted to be like him.

"My chance came back in 1980," continued Toufiq. "I had gone on a trip to Italy with friends. Just a vacation, that's all. We were sitting in a restaurant in Rome one night, and with us were some Palestinians we had met there. We were talking, and when I told them that I was from Ara, and who I was, their ears perked up. We talked a long while and finally one of them said to me privately that perhaps I should call such-and-such a phone number. He didn't say so directly, but I understood it to be an invitation to contact the PLO. So I did. And that was the beginning of my involvement with them.

"I was sort of naive, I'll admit it. I didn't really know at the time who and what I was joining. I thought it was the main PLO faction, Fatah, run by Yasir Arafat. But it turned out to be another *fedayee* group, Abu Nidal's faction. I didn't realize this—they hadn't made it clear—until I got to Iraq for training. When they finally did make it clear, I told them honestly that I supported Arafat. 'Never mind,' they told me. 'We used to believe in Arafat, too. But he's lost the way. You'll understand in time, too.' You see, Arafat was too moderate for them. The Abu Nidal group are extremists, they don't believe in any negotiated settlement at all, only war. They were against the PLO altogether. They were even murdering some top PLO moderates. That made no sense to me. But what was the point in arguing further with them, I figured. So I went through their basic training in Iraq, three months of it. And then I went back to Israel, not planning to work with them—though I didn't tell them that. They, in any case, sent me back to Israel with a set of instructions. What instructions? Simple. I was given a number. I was told to listen to Radio Baghdad every night at 8:00 P.M. If my number was mentioned, I was to go the next morning to a particular restaurant in Israel, dressed in a white tee shirt, jeans, sneakers, and carrying a pack of Marlboros in my hand. Someone would meet me there and give me further instructions. Well, I never went. My number was called five times that first half year, but I decided that I didn't want to work with the Abu Nidal group. I dropped out. I did nothing for them, and nothing against them, and after a while they left me alone.

"But then three years later, in 1983, there's a knock on my door and it's the Shabbak—" Toufiq paused as a heavyset man with grayish hair entered the room. It was his older brother, Muhammad, who lived next door and had come to get a kilo of sugar. Seemingly surprised to see such a group gathered there—me especially—and perhaps even more surprised at the subject of conversation, he slowly but definitively took a seat on the sofa and poured himself a cup of coffee. Toufiq looked at him without smiling, and then in a more subdued voice he resumed.

"What happened is that a large arms cache was discovered in the territories, and the guys they brought in talked. My name came up. That's why the Shabbak arrested me. They told me that they knew all about me but they wanted to hear more—every detail from beginning to end—how I was recruited and what I had done with the Abu Nidal people. Everything. I said I didn't want to talk, and wouldn't talk. But they have their ways. Eventually, when you're in jail, you hear about all their methods. They're not stupid, they're very clever. You see, they prefer not to beat you, that only leaves marks and then they get criticized around the world or in Israel itself for using torture. They don't want that. So they use ways that don't leave marks. They tie your hands up on a pole above your head and let you hang there for days with your feet barely touching the ground. And if that doesn't work, they have you bend one of your knees and then they attach a thin nylon cord between the foot that is bent at the knee and your testicles—you're standing there on one leg, but if you try to lower your bent leg, you yank your own testicles. No marks, you see, but you can't stand it. Clever, no? And they have other ways, like what they did to me.

"They put me outside half-naked in the middle of winter with the rains coming down and with a sack over my head. Just sat me there day and night for a week. In the end I couldn't even feel my body anymore, couldn't even grasp a breakfast roll in my own hand. I saw I had no chance. It was talk then or talk later. So I told them what I knew, about myself and the eleven others who went with me to Iraq. After that, they put me on trial and I got three years. They told me that I didn't have to serve another day if I was willing to help them. They wanted to send me back to Italy, back to Iraq, and see what I could find out. I said no, I preferred to stay in jail. I wasn't going to be a collaborator. So I sat for three years. Until I got out in 1986."

Toufiq glanced around the room as we all sat there silently, each absorbed in his own thoughts. I looked at Muhammad, wondering what he was thinking, and he apparently was sizing me up, too. In colloquial Arabic—until then, we had been speaking Hebrew—he asked Hassan who I was. Hassan explained, and I also joined in with a few words. Muhammad nodded slowly and mumbled "*Ahlan wa sahlan.*" Then, as if for my ears, though obviously he meant it for Toufiq and the others as well, Muhammad said somberly, "Three years in jail, for nothing. Pointless. The whole thing, pointless." He shook his head in quiet exasperation, and looked over at Toufiq.

"I don't regret it at all." Toufiq's tone was not so much challenging as matter-of-fact. He evidently had been through this before. "I'd do it all again if I had the chance."

"I don't get you," said Muhammad, his voice rising. "What did you accomplish? What point was there in joining the *fedayeen*? What—"

"It was an adventure," interrupted Adel, as if trying to

head off a confrontation between the brothers. "Isn't that part of it, Toufiq? Admit it. Suddenly you were given a free ticket to Iraq, a chance to see something new, do something exciting, and so on the spur of the moment you went."

"Sure it was an adventure. I won't deny it. I had never been to an Arab country before and I wanted to go. But that wasn't all of it. I wanted to take part, to join Walid's people in Fatah. Where I made a mistake was getting hooked up with Abu Nidal's group, who were against Fatah's stand. That's all—"

"That's all?" repeated Muhammad sarcastically. "You're even more foolish than I give you credit for. Your life's half ruined. You've got the Shabbak watching over you. You can't even get a license to open a business like you want. And you sit there saying your one regret is that you weren't with Fatah? I don't figure you." Then, turning to the rest of us like a lawyer addressing the jury, Muhammad added, "At least one can make a case for Walid. At least one can understand him. I'm not saying I agree with what he did, but I understand it. He had some real reasons for joining Fatah."

"Reasons, yes," agreed Adel. "And I respect him for what he's done—"

"He's a hero, a real hero," said Toufiq emphatically, looking at Hassan who was nodding his head in quiet agreement.

"I don't think so," said Muhammad solemnly.

"All right, he's a hero," said Adel. "But Toufiq, you know as well as the rest of us that he didn't start out with the idea of being a *fedayee*. It was something that happened by chance."

"I know, I know," said Toufiq. "But he wound up with them, right, because he was a patriot who had taken too much crap from the Jews and he wasn't about to take any more. He stood up to them, right? And he became a hero. Why question it?"

Again a heavy silence hung over the room, as muggy and burdensome as the night air outside. Finally I broke it by saying that I was unfamiliar with Walid's background, and that if anyone were willing, I would like to hear about him. Nobody responded at first, and then Muhammad, assuming the role of elder spokesman, opened with a phrase that seemed—bizarrely—to be out of Hemingway's *The Sun Also Rises:* "My brother Walid was once lightweight boxing champion of Israel, and that title meant a great deal to him." Then, veering from the Hemingway script, he went on, "It actually meant a great deal to all of us. We were all proud of him. The problem was the Jews were not so happy to have an Arab as lightweight boxing champ and therefore representing them at international tournaments. They came to Walid and told him to change his name to Yitzhak. He refused. Of course they couldn't stop him from representing Israel at these tournaments. But very often when the Jewish newspapers reported the results, all names would appear in the sports column except his. It would be mentioned that the lightweight division was won, but not by whom. Walid had a lot of pride, and this really hurt him badly."

Moreover, said Muhammad, this instance of discrimination was only one of several bitter things that happened to Walid. One time, for example, he was nearly murdered by "Jewish racists." This was in 1963, when Walid was working as a lifeguard for the city of Netanya; he was the only Arab. His fellow lifeguards were against his working with them, and they went on strike. The city council of Netanya, however, insisted that Walid stay, and after a long legal battle the city council won. Walid kept his job. But one day he was given a tip-off by one of the Jewish lifeguards. He was warned that there was a plan to murder him. Someone was going to pretend that he was drowning, and when Walid swam out to save him along with another lifeguard, Walid himself would be drowned. Walid didn't really believe it, but sure enough, that's exactly what they tried. Walid managed to break free, however, and he made it back to shore. He thought about reporting the incident, but decided not to bother; nobody would believe him, he figured.

"After that incident," continued Muhammad, "he was through with the Jews. He was still only a twenty-one-year-old kid, but he'd had it. He was completely disillusioned. And then something happened that was the final straw. It happened one night in a gas station. He was buying gas and some Jewish guy insulted him. Walid was not the kind to take insults lightly—never—and so he let the guy have it. Hit him right in the face. And the guy fell backwards hard, real hard, and hit his head on the pavement. Walid thought he had killed him. He feared what might happen to him for killing a Jew, so he took off. To Gaza. He got hold of an Israeli map—he didn't even know exactly where Gaza was— and went south and then managed to sneak across the border. But what happened? The Egyptians sent him back. Why? Because they figured he was some kind of Israeli agent. And of course the Israelis then arrested him. They put him in jail in Ashqelon. But we didn't even get a chance to see him because a few days later he busted out along with some other prisoners. And again he went right back to the Gaza border and snuck across. This time the Egyptians let him stay. The escape had been written up big in the Israeli newspapers, and Walid's being the Israeli lightweight boxing champ was also played up. The Egyptians saw that, so they knew he was no agent. They gave him no more problems. And that was that. From there, Walid joined up with other Palestinians and became a *fedayee*. This was in 1964. From then on we didn't hear from him or about him. Not until he got caught by the Israelis in Nahariya in 1973—"

"Wait a minute," interrupted Toufiq. "You're forgetting something."

"Forgetting what?" asked Muhammad impatiently.

"The Radio Cairo broadcasts."

"Oh, right."

And to me Toufiq said, "Walid didn't forget us. Several times on Radio Cairo, which we listened to all the time, Walid sent us greetings—'Greetings to all the family in Ara from Walid.' I remember hearing it for the first time myself. We knew then that he was alive and well, right?" Toufiq glanced at Muhammad who nodded slowly, but appeared put off by Toufiq's evident enthusiasm. Muhammad made no move to continue the story about Walid, and so Toufiq picked up the thread.

"Walid was in dozens of military attacks on Israel. He was one of the first people who fought with Fatah. First out of Egypt and then out of Lebanon. Eventually though, in 1973, he got caught in a raid that Fatah made on Nahariya.

He was captured and they locked him up in Ramla, in a maximum security prison. He got sentenced to triple life imprisonment plus twenty years. They never intended for him to get out. But I knew he'd get out, break out. I visited him in jail then—that was the first time I'd seen him since I was ten years old—and we talked about where he'd been and what he'd done. It was great seeing him again—"

"Great? What are you talking about?" Muhammad broke in forcefully. "He was a half-broken man then. They had tortured the hell out of him. With electrical prods. He had scars all over his body. He was a mess, a real mess."

"But he wasn't broken, not at all," insisted Toufiq. "I know what it is to see a man broken—at least as well as anyone sitting here—and I'm telling you he wasn't broken. He was full of spirit, full of fight. He told me he was going to escape somehow, and I knew he would. And he did, didn't he? A year and a half later he made it. He and a couple of others. They cut the bars, went over the wall, and took off. One of the guys was captured, but Walid and another guy made it to Lebanon. And then he was at it again."

From that time on, Toufiq said, he had not seen his brother. But he knew about him from people who had been on the *hajj* to Saudi Arabia. Walid was living there now. After his escape from prison, he had returned to Lebanon and continued with Fatah as a military trainer of new recruits. His particular speciality was the use of RPGs (recoilless projectile guns). He had stayed in Lebanon until 1982, when the Israelis invaded, and then he had gone to live in Saudi Arabia, where he was still involved "in some capacity" with Fatah. He was a man in his late forties now, and according to those who had met him there, he was the father of six children, two boys and four girls. He had married a Palestinian refugee back in 1976, after he had broken out of prison.

"I wish I could see him," said Toufiq, and then added with a laugh, "He's living the bourgeois life now. Hard to imagine. But he deserves it. He's put in his time. I really admire him."

"Not me," said Muhammad, stroking his unshaven face, which now seemed tired and drawn. "Look at what he's been through. He would have been much better off if he had stayed with us in Israel and the only fighting he did was in the ring. Lightweight champ of Israel, that was plenty."

"He did what he had to do," concluded Toufiq, and then, appealing to the others, he added, "Everyone knows about Walid now. He's a national hero, everyone knows that. No?"

Adel and Hassan nodded their heads in affirmation, but Muhammad, rising from the sofa and throwing his hands in the air, said, "He's a brave man, maybe, but no hero. Not to me, anyway." And without another word, Muhammad went off to the kitchen, apparently to get the kilo of sugar he had come for.

A few minutes later, Hassan and I also left, returning to Kufr Qara in Ghanem's Subaru, which we had borrowed for the evening. It was late, almost midnight, and a full moon spotlighted the Wadi Ara road as we drove along. Hassan and I were both silent for a while, and then Hassan asked, "You found tonight interesting?"

"Interesting, yes," I answered. "But, tell me . . ." I hesitated, debating just how to phrase it. "Was all that business between Muhammad and Toufiq for real, or was Muhammad just talking for my benefit? You know, pretending that he opposed the *fedayeen* because he was suspicious of me."

Hassan smiled knowingly and blew some cigarette smoke out the window. "For real," he said. "I've heard him before. He's still sore at his brothers. You see, he got stuck supporting the family alone. And legal bills? He's laid out a fortune for both of them. He thinks they were fools. Particularly Toufiq."

"And what's your thought?"

"Me? Well, I like Toufiq. The way I see it, he was trying to follow in Walid's footsteps, that's all. He just didn't succeed. Though to tell you the truth, I wouldn't be surprised if he was a little more involved than he told you. I mean, he got called by Radio Baghdad—what did he say?—five or six times. It's hard for me to imagine that he did nothing. But look, that's what he says, so—" Hassan yawned, flicked his cigarette butt out the window, and yawned again. Then he peered over at the clock on the dashboard. "My God, it's midnight already. Oh, hell!"

"Something wrong?"

"I told Zaynab I'd be back by ten o'clock." He craned his neck to look down the road leading into Kufr Qara's main square. "All the stores are closed now. Shit!"

"What do you need?"

"Mango juice."

"Mango juice?"

"Yes, mango juice." He tugged at his chin and sighed. "That's what she wants these days. She's got these whims since she's pregnant. She has to have mango juice."

"What do you want to do?"

"Head home. What else is there to do? Sounds stupid, doesn't it. But there's probably going to be a battle now. If only we had left an hour earlier, right? Then we'd have the mango juice. Shit!" He lit up another cigarette and inhaled deeply. "It's going to be a war now. We'll be at it half the night, you'll see. A *real* war!"

21

ABU AHMAD: A LAST WORD

BY MID-SUMMER Abu Ahmad had begun to seem like his old self again. His hospital pallor was gone, he put on weight, and his eyes, which had been dulled with pain for months, regained their luminosity. He was no longer sleeping away most of the day, and at mealtime he ate with more gusto than ever. "Only my stomach is still working right," he said with a wry laugh one day, after downing a roast chicken which Umm Ahmad had prepared for his lunch. "All the rest of my body—lungs, back, you name it—are *khallas*, finished. But, *il hamdu lillah*, at least I can still eat."

Another sure sign that Abu Ahmad was feeling better was that Umm Ahmad, who had stayed by his side every day for two months, returned to the fields. For this, Hassan was grateful and relieved. She rejoined him just in time to harvest his bumper crop of cabbage and cauliflower, and then she helped him plant ten thousand seedlings—onion and again cabbage and cauliflower. All this work under the sweltering summer sun was good for Umm Ahmad too. It soothed her and relaxed her mind, she said. At least in the mornings, she was able to get away from her worries about her husband.

As for Abu Ahmad, these hot summer mornings were

spent as they had been for the last seventeen years—in his *diwan* with friends. And this summer, more than any other in recent memory, there was something crucial to talk about: Saddam Hussein's invasion of Kuwait. "Since the invasion, my father's come back to life," Hassan claimed. "Before that, he was feeling down. Now look at him. He's back in command again, full of opinions and enthusiasm. Just like always."

Indeed, from August 2 on, with the news of Iraq's conquest of Kuwait, Abu Ahmad was once again eager to rise in the mornings, eager to hear the news on the radio and read the morning paper, and to join his cronies for their daily discussion. The men all came now, even those who had left him alone while he was recuperating, and again they sat for hours drinking endless cups of coffee and smoking cigarettes (Abu Ahmad too) as they weighed what had happened, and what could and should happen in the Persian Gulf and Palestine. Abu Ahmad was their leader, now as before, and it was his opinion that seemed to linger in the air and focus the discussions.

One morning—it must have been about a month after the invasion—I dropped by the *diwan* as about a dozen men sat together with Abu Ahmad. They were all laughing uproariously, apparently at some news item that someone had just read from the local Arabic paper. The item was about a man from a nearby village, who had suddenly called the police in the middle of the night the previous week, claiming wildly, "Saddam Hussein is attacking! The chemical bombs are falling! The noise and odor are everywhere!" According to the news item, the man kept ranting into the telephone until his wife woke up and made him put down the receiver. "Forget about Saddam Hussein and go back to sleep!" she shouted at him. "It's only the municipal trucks. Don't you remember? Tonight they're spraying against mosquitoes."

The men all laughed again as Abu Ahmad repeated the story, this time in Hebrew for my benefit. Then, on a more somber note, they began talking about the Gulf crisis and the possibility of war. Like everyone else in Kufr Qara, they supported Saddam Hussein and were angry at America for having intervened. An "Arab solution" was needed, they said; by which they meant a face-saving arrangement whereby Saddam Hussein would wind up with control over Kuwait and its oil, though the Iraqi army would withdraw to Iraq's former borders. Apart from these specifics, it was clear that they admired Saddam Hussein—"today's Nasser," one of them called him—and they saw him as the only one on the current scene willing "to stand up for the Palestinians against Israel and America."

On that summer day the consensus among the men in the *diwan* was that there would be no war. They did not believe Saddam Hussein would fire the first shot, and the Americans—they estimated—had too much to lose by going to war with Iraq.

"Bush knows Iraq is no pushover like Panama," announced one of the men sitting to Abu Ahmad's side. "Thousands of Americans would die if there was a war."

"And the oil. All of it would go up in smoke," added another.

"And Bush himself would be out of office, just like Carter after Iran," chimed in a third man.

"*Inshallah,* there will be no war," stated Abu Ahmad and then, with a sweep of his hand around the room, he added, "We old men here have seen too much war. So let us hope that reason will prevail this time and there will be a peaceful solution. Me, I think there will be a solution, with God's help."

"With God's help," the men around him chorused.

"And then," continued Abu Ahmad, "the world can focus again on the Palestinian problem. *That,* they seem to have forgotten, is the real problem and real reason we have no peace in this area. No?"

The men nodded their heads in agreement, and Abu Ahmad refilled the enameled coffee cups, which again were passed around. The men sat for a while, fiddling with their worry beads, and then the silence was broken by the muezzin's call to the noonday prayer. Several rose to leave, including one gaunt man whom I vaguely knew. (He was Samir's father.) He came toward me, seized my elbow, and said in a low, almost ghostly voice, "Abu Ahmad speaks well and true about the Palestinian problem. But I'm sorry to say, about

Iraq he is wrong. War is coming—" He glanced over at Abu Ahmad, who was chatting with two other men. "Saddam Hussein must not give in. And he *won't.* He's coming this way, you'll see." Samir's father released my elbow, began walking toward the mosque, and then turned back and said, "God knows what it will mean for us, the Palestinians— maybe good, maybe bad—but war is coming. Soon. I am sure of it."

After the noonday meal and a long nap, Abu Ahmad generally preferred to remain in his *diwan* and again visit with friends and family. At least this had been his pattern since he retired from farming in 1973. However, this summer— the summer of 1990—he suddenly insisted on breaking the routine: in the afternoons he wanted to be out by the fields, out at his sons' houses, and to spend the time there with them. "It's much cooler out by the fields," he explained simply. "My *diwan* is too hot in the afternoons. I want to be where there's a breeze and a nice view."

So each afternoon Ghanem would go fetch his father and bring him out to Ahmad's place (he had the most comfortable patio). And there Abu Ahmad would stay until the evening, playing cards and dominoes with the men of the family or, more often, just lying around on a wide red and black Turkish carpet that was dragged out especially for him and placed facing toward the fields.

Quite often these days, Abu Ahmad seemed to be in a contemplative mood. Resting on a set of pillows, he would gaze out at the fields and the rolling hills, and beyond them to the silver sliver of the Mediterranean Sea. Sometimes his lips would move slightly, as if he were talking to himself, and at other times his eyes would slowly close and he would drift off into the most peaceful of naps as flies camped out on his nose and ears.

On one occasion—during the last week of my visits to the village—he called me over to join him on the Turkish carpet. During the two years that I had known him, he had seldom shown open curiosity about the book I was writing, but now he wanted to know how it all was going. "You've gathered all the research you need?" he asked with concern.

"Yes, just about," I answered.

"That's good," he said. "And what are you going to call the book?"

"I don't know yet. Do you have any ideas?"

"Me? No, no. That's your job. I don't know what sounds good to American readers. You'll think of something, right?"

"Eventually, yes."

He smiled and peered out at the fields where Hassan was working alone. Pointing to a hill some three hundred meters away, he said, "That slope over there, just beyond our fields, I don't think I ever mentioned it to you. Well, that's where I met with the Jews at their army encampment, back in 1949. Remember—after the war? That night when I came out here walking through the thick, wet grass, I thought I was a dead man. I thought the Jews were going to kill me when I came to ask them to stop shooting at us when we went down to the well to get water. But God spared me. Me and Hammad. And we were able to help save the village. Remember? You've written about all that?"

"Yes, I have," I answered. "But tell me, what ever happened to Moti? You never told me that."

"Moti? Yes, God bless him. I don't want you to write his real name—he might object—but yes, we've stayed in contact all these years. Until three years ago, anyway, when he went on a sabbatical to America. Since then I haven't heard from him, and he doesn't even know that I've been ill. But God bless him. Without him back then, I don't know what would have happened to my family and to Kufr Qara. It's just a pity that there aren't any like him around nowadays. All those in the government today—just scoundrels. Nothing for the Jews to be proud about. They're going to lead their people to ruin, that's what I think. . . ."

Abu Ahmad's voice trailed off as he turned to watch Hassan coming over to us. Hassan's mud-caked hands were cupped together; he was carrying some purple figs, which he placed in front of his father. He sat down and the two of them talked briefly: first about the cauliflower seedlings which were gleaming just in front of us, and then about the price of onions—the expected price, that is—in the early winter market. "*Inshallah*, I'll catch a price again," Hassan said to Abu Ahmad, who nodded slowly and answered, "*Inshallah*. In any case, you've made a good choice—cauliflower, cabbage, and onion. The rest is in God's hands."

Later, when Hassan had returned to the fields, Abu Ahmad said to me, "He's done a fine job, Hassan has. Kept the farm together, and that is good. As a boy, he didn't seem like he could do it. Of course the work was a lot harder in those days. No tractor, just a wooden plow. I told you about that, didn't I? We all had to work together as a family in those days. The boys, my wife, and the girls too. It was harder than you can imagine, especially because this land which the Jews gave us in 1954 was full of stones. But I tell you, hard as it's been, it's also been a good life. Some years and seasons were better than others, of course. *Yom asal, yom basal*, as we say in Arabic—days of honey, days of onion. Overall, though, I'm not complaining. We've managed to survive and to live off this land. And for this I am grateful."

Abu Ahmad reached into his cloak and pulled out a pack of Marlboros. He hesitated a moment and then lit one. "The doctor tells me I shouldn't, but I'm too old for such advice." He shrugged his shoulders fatalistically and continued. "All this land that you see out here, it used to be just fields. Now look! A housing boom! Twenty, twenty-five years from now, no more farming, *khallas*. My grandchildren will probably put up houses here—where else do they have to go?—and that will be it. Hopefully, Hassan will keep the farm going for a while longer, but after that, who knows? Anyway, I did what I had to do. Now it's their turn."

Abu Ahmad paused and finished his cigarette slowly, pensively. He then went on to say—in answer to a question from me—that, yes, he had formally made out a will. About a year before, when he began feeling ill, he and Ghanem had gone to a lawyer in Hadera to draw up the two-page document. A lot of men his age, probably most, didn't bother to make out a will, but he wanted to put it all down in black-and-white even though the provisions of the will were the customary ones: all his property would be divided by his three sons; his daughters would not receive a share, inasmuch as they all had husbands to provide for them; and Umm Ahmad would receive no property either, since his sons would take care of her. (According to Hassan, Umm Ahmad would live with him: "Traditionally, the mother usually goes to the oldest son's house. But I'm the one who has the most room for her, and besides, once Zaynab has children, my mother will want to be with us, I'm sure.")

Abu Ahmad continued. "In addition to the formal will, I've also written them all a letter. I did this when I was in the hospital, before the operation. I told them in this letter that my deepest wish is that no matter what happens in life, they always remember they are one family, and they never let anger or spite come between them. When I am gone, I told them, I want them to continue to watch over and care for each other. Just as we always have done."

Abu Ahmad stubbed out his cigarette and leaned back on the pillows. His eyes looked weary, but he indicated that he wanted to go on talking. "I don't know how much more time I have," he said finally. "Yesterday, you were here in the afternoon? You heard the announcement over the mosque loudspeaker about Abu Mahmoud R——? He was in the hospital with me, the same ward. Now he's gone, dead. Cancer of the brain. He had no chance. Me, I don't know what I've got, and really it doesn't matter. When your time comes, that's it. From Allah we come, and to Allah we return."

Abu Ahmad gazed out at the fields and then up at the poignantly blue evening sky, where a formation of white birds—egrets, it seemed—were cutting a high path to the south. He followed them with his eyes and when they were gone he said, "Fall's coming soon. You can tell by the birds. A fine season. As a boy I used to look forward to it. The summer harvest—all that reaping and threshing—was over and you had a few weeks rest. Then the winter rains came and you were back at it again, plowing and sowing for the next year." He turned to watch Hassan rumble by on his tractor. Then, calling over to Ghanem, Abu Ahmad announced that he was ready to be driven home. And to me he added, while slowly rising on his stiff legs, "You can feel it coming, can't you? The evening air is just a little damper now. And cleaner. A short season, but a good one. I'm looking forward to it."

AFTERWORD

THE editors at the University of California Press, to whom I am very grateful for publishing this paperback edition, have asked me if I would add a few remarks regarding the circumstances of my field work for *Days of Honey, Days of Onion.* Specifically, they wondered what impact my person (as an American, Jewish male) might have had on my informants; and also, what impact spending some two years with the Family Abu Ahmad might have had on me. These are certainly important questions; I must admit, though, that the editors at Beacon Press had asked me to address similar issues in the original hardback edition. I refused because of my conviction at the time that the entire focus of the book ought to be on the family itself and not at all on my interaction with them. In retrospect, I believe I may have overdone it. In any case, it now seems worthwhile to take up these matters, particularly with the advantage that two years' hindsight and additional contact with the family have afforded me.

Before doing so, however, I cannot resist the temptation to mention some of what has happened with the family and the village since September 1990. When I completed the manuscript, I went to the United States for a half year. I returned in May 1991, two months after the Gulf War was over. Since then, I have been in regular contact with the family. Once every three or four weeks I go to Kufr Qara, usually for some family event or holiday, or on occasion to work with Hassan in the fields. These contacts are deeply satisfying to me, especially so since I no longer feel the constant obligation to record what is happening. Our relationship now is simply—or really, not so simply—one of friendship.

All in all, these past two years have been difficult ones for the family. Abu Ahmad's health continues to deteriorate and at this point he, Umm Ahmad, and everyone else in the family are aware that he is dying from cancer. Several times he has been rushed in an emergency to the hospital. Yet, sturdy ship that he is, somehow he has managed to fight off each storm and again sail along stoically. On his good days, he still shows up at his favorite place, his *diwan*, and whiles away the morning with his lifelong friends. The person on whose face one sees the true measure of this ordeal is Umm Ahmad. Her lantern-like smile is gone. For a period, before she was aware of her husband's cancer, she returned to the fields to work with Hassan. But now she no longer leaves Abu Ahmad's side, even on his good days. "My mother is bearing the real burden of all this," Hassan told me. "Working in the fields would be good for her, but she refuses. What can you do? *Fi idayn Allah*, it's in the hands of God. The rest of us must go on somehow, that's all."

Even in the shadow of Abu Ahmad's illness, life has gone on for the family. In the spring of this year, Maysa finally got married. The backyard of her parents' home was cleared of two years' accumulated rubble, and the *lelat il henna* party was celebrated in front of hundreds of guests. The next evening, the wedding itself was held in a fancy, rented hall twenty kilometers from the village (such modern venues are now preferred by some of Kufr Qara's new couples, who eschew the generally more informal setting of the groom's family's backyard). Maysa, at long last, seems content. And just recently, she let it be known that she is pregnant.

Maysa is not the only one to have good fortune. In the past two years, Ahmad's wife, Nufissa, has given birth to a son; Ghanem's wife, Latifa, has had a daughter; and Hassan and Zaynab—after the massage-and-Koran-reading ministrations of Umm Ahmad—have had two children, a boy and a girl. Abu Ahmad and Umm Ahmad now have thirty-one grandchildren.

Hassan continues to operate the family farm, and in the lean winter season he helps Ahmad sell books. With his growing family, Hassan remains as worried as ever about slumping prices for his vegetables. He has even begun to ruminate about giving up the farm altogether and starting up some kind of business, as Ahmad has done. "But if I do that," he said, "I'll wait at least until the Jewish *shemitta* in 1993–94 is over. There's a bundle of money to be made then selling vegetables to the religious Jews. Though, God knows, I'm going to watch my step this time. I want no more troubles with the 'evil eye'!"

Some of these happenings (for example, Abu Ahmad's fading health and Hassan and Zaynab's growing family) would have been foci in the book had I arrived at the village a year or so later. And there are other family matters too (Ahmad's troubles with the income tax authorities and Hassan's nasty falling-out with his friend, Samir) that I would have included. Yet, as I look back on it, none of this material is likely to have altered the sense of the family as I presented it: I would have entered the river at a different place, so to speak, but it would still be the same river.

There are, in addition, a couple of developments affecting the village at large that I would have covered had I been writing the book today. One of these is the phenomenon of Muslim fundamentalism, which continues to gather steam in Kufr Qara, just as it does elsewhere in the region. Actually, I did attempt to include something more on this subject when writing the original manuscript. I wrote half a chapter on a friend of Hassan who is a leader in the local fundamentalist movement, but it didn't come off (I didn't much like this fellow) and I tossed it out. Today, I'd find some other way of covering this phenomenon. For it is now clear to me that, like it or not, the fundamentalists are here for the foreseeable future. In Kufr Qara, their numbers are still small, maybe ten or fifteen percent of the population, but they are more active than ever. Last summer, for instance, they organized a sizeable group of volunteers to repair some of Kufr Qara's roads and sidewalks. They followed this up by painting religious murals on walls in the center of the village. And now, every week or so, several of the white-frocked brethren tour the village with a loudspeaker, inviting the villagers to attend some lecture or prayer meeting at their new mosque. The word in the village these days is that in the 1993 elections to Kufr Qara's local council, the fundamentalists may take two of the eleven seats. Where all this political-religious activity is leading, in Kufr Qara and throughout the area, is not clear. But, in my view, the prospects for peace in the region will be affected—and likely in a negative way—if the fundamentalists continue to win over the hearts and minds of people in Israel/Palestine and elsewhere.

A second event of political importance that I would have included had I been writing the book today is the Persian Gulf War and its aftermath. As already mentioned, I left the village several months before the war broke out. The general view in Kufr Qara at the time, one held by Abu Ahmad and his three sons, was that the United States would avoid a military showdown with Saddam Hussein; but if it did foolishly go to war with him, it would pay a heavy price. It was very evident whose side Abu Ahmad and his sons were on, and despite misgivings about Saddam's motivations and goodwill toward themselves, the Palestinians, they nonetheless saw him in a positive light. I openly disagreed with them. I couldn't see anything worthwhile in the Iraqi leader, and instead found myself in support of Bush's determination to oust him from Kuwait. As might be imagined, this difference of opinions—our first major disagreement—caused some awkward moments between me and others. And frankly, I am not sure how all this would have played itself out, or become part of the book, had I been in Israel during the war. My hunch, though, is that we would have maintained close ties even during the war period, and moreover that the book would have benefited from inclusion of this material. As it was, I sat out the war in the United States and knew nothing of what happened in the village until I returned in the spring of 1991.

According to Abu Ahmad and Hassan, who subsequently filled me in on some of the details, the war itself and the Scud missile attacks on Israel did not cause them, personally, much hardship. In the first days of the war they, like all other Israelis, rushed to their sealed rooms and put on gas masks whenever there was a Scud attack. But when they realized the missiles were honed in on Tel Aviv, fifty kilometers away, they stopped donning the masks and went to their roofs or stood outdoors to watch the spectacle of red, flaming Scuds streaking overhead. "It was an amazing sight," Hassan told me, "and the truth is, even then I was still with Saddam." Yet when the war was over and the enormity of the Iraqi defeat became clear, a familiar sense of disappointment set in: Saddam had brought them nothing, and furthermore, they figured that Bush's "new world order" would bring them nothing either. This skepticism—or to put it more exactly, reluctance to believe that American policy will ever bring any benefit to Palestinians—is still the predominant mood and perception of those in Kufr Qara, as well as among many Palestinians in the area. Even the open political pressure which the United States has exerted on Israel and the downfall of Yitzhak Shamir's right-wing government have so far not done much to change their views. "I don't trust Yitzhak Rabin any more than I trusted Yitzhak Shamir," Abu Ahmad recently said to me. "Right now, it's up to the Americans, and they say a Palestinian state is out of the question. So what good can they bring? But, one day, after I am gone, we will have a Palestinian state, with or without American help. Don't you think so?"

The reader may be wondering what impact such statements had on me; and further, what role I played as an American Jew in inviting or influencing these remarks from Abu Ahmad, Hassan, and others. This is a question, obviously, that can be raised with regard to much of the book's content, and since I made no attempt to address it before, I would like to do so now.

Throughout the period when I was gathering material for the book, I was aware that my identity as a Jew, an American, and a male was in the minds of those around me—generally, I think, in a subconscious way—and as such my identity might be influencing what I was told and what I saw. But how and to what extent? I cannot answer this question with any certainty, but I'll try to sketch in here a few of the assumptions, or speculations, that I have arrived at. First, I believe that there is one broad category of events where my presence made little or no impact. These are the various events or occasions at which I was only one of a large group (Hassan's wedding, or the family's Ramadan observance, for example). To be sure, my perspective influenced what I chose to write about, but my presence did *not* alter, as far as I can see, the unfolding of the event itself.

I contrast this with a second category of events in which my identity did, at times, substantially influence the unfolding of material: namely, one-to-one and small-group conversations. It is only natural that I, as a member of the dominant society, would at least initially arouse suspicion and ambivalence in some quarters. Abu Ahmad's readiness to talk with me, as I stated in the book's introduction, caught me somewhat by surprise. I later understood that this openness on his part issued from his own broad life experience, in which there had been some positive relationships with Jews. His children, in turn, had adopted his outlook. Even so, I was not completely accepted or trusted right away, and the process of gaining their confidence was one that took many months—perhaps the better part of my first year with them. The fact that I spoke Hebrew with them, and not Arabic, also contributed to an initial sense of distance between us, though I am inclined to believe that in time this factor, too, did not significantly impede our communication.

In looking back, I think that what was essential in winning their trust, especially that of Hassan and Umm Ahmad, was my working with them in the fields. This "fieldwork" removed an element of formality and helped establish an easy kind of relatedness between us. It also enabled me to listen to (I understand far more Arabic than I speak) all sorts of conversations between Hassan, Umm Ahmad, and a variety of friends who often stopped by to visit in the fields. These friends were puzzled at first to see me there, and even more so when they were told that I was a "doctor from America," the phrase typically used to introduce me. Only afterwards was it added that yes, I was *yahudi*, Jewish. Frequently, I was then subjected to a political litmus test, with Hassan usually indicating to the inquisitor that I was *b'seder*, okay. In time, a number of these casual meetings in Hassan's fields led to contacts and friendships which provided me with a broader perspective than I might otherwise have gained just by talking to the members of Abu Ahmad's family.

While it was possible over time to surmount the obstacle of my Jewish-American background, there is one aspect of my identity which interfered persistently with my presenting a full view of the family: to wit, my being a man. In the patriarchal and highly protective society to which the Family Abu Ahmad belongs, it was difficult, and in some ways impossible, to spend sufficient time with the women. By custom, I could not sit in their company and spend hours listening to them talk. Nor was I allowed to be alone with any one of them. The only exceptions were the times when I was working next to Umm Ahmad in the fields, or when Maysa invited me to visit her at her office *outside* the village. A female anthropologist would not have had this obstacle. As a result, she would have been able to present a more complete picture of Umm Ahmad, her daughters, and her daughters-in-law. I found this restriction quite frustrating, and while I did what I could to gather material, I was well aware that my account was somewhat limited in this area.

At this point, having briefly commented on some of the ways in which my person and presence influenced the family and the shaping of the book, I would like to conclude with a short note on how the family has influenced me. I hope the book has conveyed something of the vitality and variety of this experience which was, as it turned out, a good deal richer than I anticipated. My contact with the family and the village remains to this day an important part of my life in Israel. As one might surmise, I am no longer the same Zionist who came to Israel in the early 1980s and went to Kufr Qara in 1989. I still believe in the need for a Jewish state, but as a result of my experience in the village, I have come to believe just as strongly in the right of a Palestinian Arab state to exist. I am also more aware than ever of the discrimination against Arabs in Israel, and feel more fervently than before the need to eradicate it. All of this represents for me not only a shift in political opinion but also a major change in feeling. As a consequence my life here as a Jew has become more complicated than it was before. But, I by no means wish to complain. Today, in Israel/Palestine *any* political position is difficult to bear. Besides, if I had it to choose again, I am sure I would again risk going to the village to meet the Family Abu Ahmad. And let the chips fall where they may. *Yom asal, yom basal.*

Fall 1992
Jerusalem